THE SEARCHER

MARTY RIDER

THE SEARCHER

First published in Australia by Marty Rider 2020

Copyright © Marty Rider 2020
All Rights Reserved

 A catalogue record for this book is available from the National Library of Australia

ISBN: 978-0-6489765-0-9 (pbk)
ISBN: 978-0-6489765-1-6 (ebk)

Typesetting and design by Publicious Book Publishing
Published in collaboration with Publicious Book Publishing
www.publicious.com.au

No part of this book may be reproduced in any form, by photocopying or by any electronic or mechanical means, including information storage or retrieval systems, without permission in writing from both the copyright owner and the publisher of this book.

For Tippy and Flossie

Contents

Chapter 1 — 1
    Introducing Coppertop — 1
    School days — 2
    Rock n Roll — 9
    Flossie-Mum — 11
    First cut — 15

Chapter 2 — 17
    Save yourself! — 17
    Out-of-the-body — 19
    Ambos — 24
    Healing — 26
    Reading the vibrations — 27
    Reincarnation — 29
    Instant love — 30

Chapter 3 — 33
    Camping with Tippy-Toes — 33
    The river crossing — 34
    Learning by osmosis — 36
    Toddler meditation — 38
    Wakey, wakey, Glapiac — 40
    Boys don't cry — 41
    Kiki-dolphin — 43
    Scary girls — 46
    The joy of soccer — 47

Chapter 4 — 49
    The wounded healer — 49
    Bio-energy healing — 50
    Tragic loss — 52
    Devil-rash — 53
    A daunting haunting — 56

Chapter 5 — 63
    Rebel with a cause — 63
    The big shit weekend — 66
    Ole Hobie — 69

Chapter 6 — 73
    Mischievous Andrew-Poo — 73
    Astro boy — 78
    Falling on his sword — 81
    A stranger — 83

Chapter 7 — 86
    Coconuts and clashes — 86
    Ole-Lillah — 89
    Dream drifter — 90
    Odd Street — 94

Chapter 8 — 97
    The perplexed Searcher — 97
    A black-belt tribulation — 101

Chapter 9 — 110
    Dismal waxheads — 110
    The Thinker — 115
    Pet hates — 118

Chapter 10 — 125
- Hollow men — 125
- Saviour Brian — 126
- The trouser leg — 127
- Grace and the race — 131
- Weary Seeker — 132
- Chopping off the head or polishing the diamond — 135

Chapter 11 — 138
- A ghost with attitude — 138
- Viper — 140
- Wizard — 142
- Bluebottles — 148
- Daydreamer — 149
- The orb incident — 150
- Man sparks water search — 151

Chapter 12 — 154
- A phantasmagorical encounter — 154
- Dark night — 156
- A place of awe and mystery — 161
- Cause of dis-ease — 162

Chapter 13 — 167
- Have we gone too far? — 167
- Ernie — 168
- The paradox of animals — 172
- Beautiful loser — 174

Chapter 14 — 180
- Expectancy — 180

Lay down your sword! 184
  Explorer without a compass 185
  Only humans 188
  Tails and scales 189
  Curious Andro 191
  Are you serious? 194
Chapter 15 **195**
  The many and the one 195
  Preparing the way 197
  Sitting on the fence 198
  Seeking on Seek 203
  True friends 204
Chapter 16 **206**
  Flossie at peace 206
Chapter 17 **210**
  A dream revelation 210
  What next? 212
  A book 213
Addendum **216**
  An alternative ending 216
  Parting words 219
Endnotes **221**

Chapter 1

Introducing Coppertop

His hero-dad Tippy called him *Coppertop*. He was a mop-redhead, a little tiger. Three years before Tippy abruptly left this world to fly to that great-beyond-of-no-time-and-place, he wrote an entry in Coppertop's autograph book. Flossie, Coppertop's beautiful mother, had purchased the little blue book for him earlier that day. It read: *Love many, trust few, always paddle your own canoe!*

Strange? Coppertop didn't understand it. Not for years. He guessed it was something about paddling canoes and being nice, but … he couldn't figure it out. Nor did he ask his hero-dad Tippy what it meant or where the quote had come from. Coppertop would grow up one day and learn that the first part comes from Shakespeare and the 'paddle your own canoe' part was an add-on American saying that originally meant *you're on your own, mate*. Not very encouraging—but that's not how it's meant these days and that's not what hero-dad would have meant. He meant *be true to yourself, son*.

That old quote in his little blue autograph book would prove prophetic. It became a prescription for living; a way of living kindly in the world without being anyone's fool; a way of acting independently and deciding one's own fate, you might say.

Quite a normal childhood it was, growing up in a small mining town where men worked hard, drank even harder, and women looked after everything else. Boys were always up to mischief. Coppertop was no different. He and his brother, one year older, would build cubby houses and, thanks to a massive mandarin tree in the backyard, had a never-ending supply of mandarins to hoick at the passer-by neighbourhood kids. Bikes, skateboards, cricket bats, soccer balls—well, you know, they were just elementary.

Television was tempting in the afternoon, especially with shows like *Happy Days* and *The Brady Bunch*, but playing outside was where it was really at. There was way too much fun out there! How could you possibly beat kicking a soccer ball around for hours, or bouncing a yoyo up and down, or having a ding on a dingbat?

Who would not want to ride their bike across town to see their mates and enemies? And to ride that skateboard where they just weren't designed to go? 'How many steps can you jump, mate?' They had so little, but felt they had everything. What could be better than shooting firecrackers at your cousins at night and receiving holes in your pyjamas?

'I've got a ten-shooter.'

'Well, I've got a fifteen shooter. Cop that. Pow!'

There were still problems, though. Like, for Coppertop, how would he ever get the guts to ask out that bombshell girl with the blonde hair, cute dimples, and braces? 'I think I might die on the spot if she talks back. Maybe I'll just faint,' he deliberated. Perhaps he could ask his friends; they seemed cooler than he was when it came to chicks. And being a Catholic boy ... hmm.

'Those Catholic boys think they're better than us. Arseholes.'

Male aggression starts early. Yes, they were always in danger of being beaten up by a group of public schoolboys when walking home by themselves. But there was no greater danger than that of the other species—the opposite sex. Yes, they were the scariest thing of all!

School days

Time rolled on. Like most kids, Coppertop didn't notice it, other than growing a little and changing grades each year. Some cared about school results and some didn't. He didn't see any value in school. It was just what every kid was forced to do, but it would all be over one day.

Coppertop was a daydreamer from a young age. He started kindergarten at four. As a pupil, he was pleasant enough, although even from such a young age he wouldn't just blindly accept the teachers were perfect and had all the answers. He was shy but questioning.

His mother, Flossie, thought he was a *little angel* and recalled how, as a baby, he had the most beautiful lilac eyes you'd ever see, or so she believed. Flossie was so proud when he won that baby contest, as proud as Punch. But he would clash with teachers over the coming years. Not all! Not if they were decent. Just the fake ones—well, fake in his eyes, at least.

Later, he attended high school. It was a *special* school because it was a Catholic school, and the students were supposedly superior to the public kids. Here he would witness the true colours of many teachers. It was open slather. The teachers would get away with anything they liked because parents were so unquestioning back then, especially when the priests and brothers were involved. After all, they had a telephone line straight to God-the-Father.

In high school, Coppertop didn't understand how some of those sadistic holy brothers and the ordained teachers would simply love punishing students like himself. He rebelled against them and would pay the price. Oh, how he paid the price! You see, he could smell the scent of bullshit from miles away, like a bloodhound. He had an inbuilt bullshit-detector, probably inherited from his aunty, his mum's sister. She had a bullshit-meter as well.

The brothers thoroughly enjoyed inflicting physical pain on the poor little lads, especially by dishing out the cane, which was a stick made out of bamboo or some such. They just loved whipping a kid's hands with the cane. How civilised! 'Give him four, no, six of the best, little bastard.' For the student, the natural impulse was to pull the hand away, and the brothers just loved that response for they always doubled the punishment for pulling away.

And in winter, oh cripes. It was better in winter, because the pain was so much worse. The students would get welts and blisters on their hands, and it really did make Coppertop-Tiger question whether he should go on being a smartarse or just comply and shrink smaller and smaller into oblivion.

Tiny little squeaky Brother-Mousey knew how to land it. Jesus, that little fellow could hurt, and he always followed it with a wry smile. You just knew holy Brother-Mousey thoroughly enjoyed the mighty power that God had bestowed on him, in hurting those young smartarse boys.

They should have called him *Mighty-Mouse* actually. That scrawny little, moustache-wearing, sardonic, persecution-expert must have practised his penance-giving skills every night—more times than his holy prayers and even more times than teenage Coppertop-now-Red had thrown his Coca-Cola yoyo up and down. How else could he be so damn good at it? Nonetheless, he wasn't always cruel. In the playground he could be quite affectionate when he'd approach from behind, gently rubbing himself against the body whilst whispering in the ear …

Brother Wodger was worse, though. One day he beat the crap out of grade-A-student Tobias, punching him all around the head at the sports park. He actually knocked the bandages off his head. Grade-A-student Tobias had just had brain surgery. Evidently, Brother Wodger thought he could do a better job on young grade-A-student Tobias's brain tumours than the medical-gods could.

On Coppertop-come-Red's first day of high school, Mr Greedy, a soon-to-be-consecrated brother who was on his first day of teaching, decided to cane Coppertop-Red for being a smartarse. Red enjoyed the fact that he was Mr Greedy's first-ever victim; however, Greedy couldn't cane for shit. He really needed to up his game like the more experienced terrorist-brothers, who could make those little bastards' hands bleed.

Perhaps he would require lessons from holy Brother Mousey, and fast. Sadly, it turned out Red-once-Coppertop wasn't Mr Greedy's first victim. Evidently, some smartarse boy upstairs in a higher grade, who would later become a Callithumpian and create his own philosophy, so to speak, had been caned by Mr-soon-to be-Brother before Red was. Damn!

The Searcher

A certain Mr Broadway hated young Red and never once addressed him by his first name in four years. Four years! So, Coppertop-now-Red spent every moment possible of those years trying his darndest to make it hell on earth for that aloof young smartarse teacher. To his credit, at least Mr Broadway never caned the students. He was a man of science and not cruelty it seemed.

Unfortunately, high school wasn't Red's first exposure to cane punishment, for even in primary school it would be utilised on occasion. One penguin (holy nun) used to cane his hand in rapid-fire motion, in perfect unison with every syllable she would shout. She had quite a vocabulary, it seemed, so he would sustain untold whips.

Fortunately, she executed too much quantity and not enough quality, in his young opinion. Holy sister never hurt; hence, it was hilarious to see her frothing at the mouth, red in the face, and yelling what sounded like expletives to no effect. But he never laughed in her face, for somewhere deep inside he was concerned she might have a heart attack right before his eyes.

In high school, however, things suddenly shifted up a gear—and fast. There is nothing quite like pain to welcome a child to a new reality. Mr Bart was a cross-eyed teacher and Coppertop-now-Red never knew if he was screaming at him, or his smartarse mate beside him. It was genuinely hard to tell.

He caned a poor sucker hard one day, but instead of hitting the poor sucker's hand, he hit his upper arm in the bicep region. The welt was terrible to look at, although the other boys found it so hilarious their bellies ached just thinking about how far Mr Bart had missed the poor sucker's hand.

And Gidgee, oh boy! When Mr Arm's ball bearings started falling out of his artificial leg, student Gidgee couldn't stop laughing. He truly lost his shit, bursting at the seams. Unfortunately for Gidgee, however, he wasn't the only one to lose it. To this day, Redmond has never seen anyone blow a whistle such as Mr *Arm* did when his *leg* started coming apart.

He grabbed that young Gidgee, who was always immaculately attired, and tore him to shreds, even attempting to throw him out of the second-storey classroom window. Literally! Those boys were horrified! Gidgee fought for his life and damn well nearly lost the battle.

One teacher, a brother, well, he just seemed to love that young Red-Tiger, and not in an unhealthy way like *that*. It all started on the first day of Year 8 when Neville-nice-Brother asked young Red what colour house he was in. Now, back then, you were either in red, blue, green or gold. They represented one's sports house colours—separate divisions, which made it possible to compete against each other.

Red-Tiger answered Neville-nice-Brother literally, because the colour of his real house at home was pink; or at least the weatherboards were a light pink. The whole class exploded in laughter but thought young Red-the-smartarse might not survive the day. Neville-nice-Brother pressed and pressed but young-smartarse-Red would not budge. He was in a pink house! Eventually, Neville-nice-Brother gave up and let him have his way, 'Okay, your house is pink.' Red was a stubborn kid!

The next day at the swimming carnival as young Red was about to jump in and race against his competitors in their various allotted sports colours, Neville-nice-Brother approached him and said, 'Hey, where's your pink swimmers?' That was it. From that day forward they got on fabulously. Red performed well too in his studies that year—funny that!

Sadly, poor Neville-nice-Brother cracked one day. He slammed his fist through a student's wooden table, which literally exploded into countless pieces. So had his patience for smartarse schoolboys it seemed. He disappeared and the boys never saw him again. Damn! Young Red really did love that Neville-nice-Brother. Incidentally, he was replaced by a nun-teacher of God. 'Strange that she is a female in an all-boys' school,' pondered Red.

One day she caught young smartarse Wal-then-Christo in the act. Some boy had handed him a porn magazine in class. Well, you know what teenage boys are like. His inquisitive face and moans must have given it all away. She demanded to see what the fuss was all about. Sitting up in the back of the room, red-faced, he was caught in the act.

'Give it to me now!' demanded the Sister. His life was over. (Don't you just hate it when you cop the blame for things, while the ones who instigated them come out smelling of roses?) Christo-Wal carefully wrapped the porn magazine in paper and walked it up to holy-Sister and awaited his fate. His parents would kill him, no doubt about it.

It seemed it was all over for young-Wal-come-rock-drummer-one-day. The funny thing about that incident, however, was that it was never mentioned again. Hmm? Holy-Sister-of-Mercy-and-Light took that disgusting filthy porn magazine from disgusting filthy little Christo-Wal and that was the last of it. Guess she enjoyed it just as much as disgusting filthy little Christo-Wal and his disgusting filthy little mates did.

Incidentally, as an adult, Christo-Wal reminded Searcher-Red how their friendship first engaged. According to Wal, their Year 7 classroom teacher was conducting what seemed like his own little social experiment on his despicable students. He asked over half of the class—those who he believed had committed various wrongdoings—to choose their own punishment. Students would concoct punishments like 'I will write three pages of lines' or 'I will take *four of the best*' (cane brutality) or, 'I will stay in detention during my lunch,' and so forth.

When Mr Merry came to the young and defiant Red, he demanded he select his punishment for his crimes. Red said, 'None, sir. I haven't done anything wrong; therefore I will not be accepting any punishment.'

Mr Merry, assumingly satisfied with the answer, in the interests of his curious social experiment, simply said, 'Okay'.

Now young Christo-Wal immediately saw something in young Red and decided there and then, he would like to be mates with him. In fact, they sparked up a friendship and would later go on to play in several bands together: Christo-Wal on drums and Red on guitar. And as they grew up, they would share many worldview ideologies. Searcher found it intriguing how seemingly small moments in one's early life can have such far-ranging effects.

Pretty soon Red spent his time on motorbikes riding in the bush each afternoon, after those dreaded school days under the tutelage of the holy-close-to-God-brothers. Loud, noisy, dusty machines were they. He didn't care about that. The young are often narcissistic and don't give a stuff. And rightly so. Like, life is just about having fun, isn't it?

Who cares about all the poor neighbours hearing that *screaming* motocross bike fish-tailing up the lane and bringing up a world of dust and rocks in its wake? Who cares? If only he knew. You have to wonder just how relaxing it could have been screaming through those dusty, bumpy, God-forsaken hills without a care in the world each day.

Red knew what wasn't relaxing, however: being chased head-on by police highway patrol cars! Those guys were NUTS! Young Red-once-Coppertop thought at times they were trying to kill him. The cops were fast. Really fast. Red was fast too, or at least nimble in the *bush*, slipping through the cracks.

Out on the *roadway*, however, with their unregistered bikes, the brazen boys barely stood a chance. Red's heart quite nearly jumped straight through his chest and bounced away towards kingdom-come, such was his fear of those crazy cops.

As he grew older, he would think back to those incidents and laugh at just how much those coppers must have enjoyed getting paid for terrorising teenage hoods on bikes. Red's passion for tearing up the bush on motorbikes would come to an abrupt end, however.

It was on a long bush ride with an apprentice friend. On the way back they parted ways. Red was close to home and only had to spin anti-clockwise through a dirt-bike circuit, down a gravel road, up a few tarred streets, fish-tail it up *annoy-neighbours-lane* and, Bob's your uncle, home. He wonders now, looking back, why we didn't slow down when riding alone? Red was absolutely hammering around the dirt-bike circuit and only faintly saw a grey flash ...

Someone was waking him up. It was Ronny, another apprentice he worked with. Ronny told Red-now-white-apprentice that they'd had a head-on collision and he needed to go get help. He must have seen what Redmond hadn't. After Ronny left, somewhat dazed, Red-once-Coppertop decided to stand up. He looked at his left forearm and it was bent at a right angle, bone protruding through the skin. His bike was in pieces, forks snapped. Blast!

The trees decided to dance around and around his head for some peculiar reason and that was the last he knew for some time. He was out cold. Unbeknownst to Red, his dear mother-Flossie had that gut-feeling that only mothers get. 'Something's wrong, something's very wrong with my boy,' Flossie thought. She rang the hospital, the same one where her soulmate had left for the great-beyond-of-no-time-and-place.

'No – no kid from any motorbike accident,' she was told.

So she jumped into her car and went looking for him. Panicked-Flossie would have found him, you know, if not for the ambulance having already been and gone. She intuitively went to the exact area where they had already carted off the unconscious young man to the hospital of births, deaths, sickness and 'accidents'.

In this instance, he was lucky. At the same time, several other local motorbike incidents happened where young men he knew were hit by cars and never lived to tell the tale. To this day he still can't bear to think of their parents' anguish. So that was the end of that.

Rock n Roll

Then there was Chisel. Cold Chisel! The Aussie band rocked and rocked hard. The guitar playing was intricate, intelligent and melodic. Red had already been playing guitar for a few years. Bert, his teacher, may as well have been *Santana*. Everything he said was cool, and he addressed other musos as those *cats*. Whatever he played, well, just talked to young Red. The weed didn't agree with him, but he tried to fit in. They jammed and jammed.

Bert was classically trained and taught in that arena, as well as rock and roll. However, young Red was just not a polished kid and still is not. Polished, that is. He especially loved Bach, Mozart and

Vivaldi; particularly the Baroque-era pieces. But then there was Chisel, and The Angels, and Midnight Oil, and Jon English, and The Radiators and ACDC, and Choirboys and, and ...

Red-now-Redmond performed in his first band at seventeen years of age. They played good, honest rock music from the above-mentioned bands. A passion had been ignited. He just couldn't get enough of the guitar. Every weekend he would play live in one line up or another. Early on, he played at a rough pub called the *Pit*. The locals liked it loud and honest, so the boys cranked those Marshall amps up.

One night, after the gig was over and all were pleased and pissed, a chair was suddenly thrown. Then another. Then without warning, the whole pub erupted in a brawl. It was an *all-in* and those guys were nuts. Red had not seen anything like it since watching John Wayne the Indian killer on television. Punches and air swings and blood and beer were the order of the night.

It was quite a shock for the scrawny Coppertop-now-Red seeing objects fly past him. Adrenaline was pouring through his terrified young veins whilst he wondered if he'd ever get out of the place alive. Gradually things settled down among those crazy bastards. With blood all over his face and hands, the publican nonchalantly walked up to Red and said, 'You went well tonight, young fella, you really laid it down. Did you enjoy yourself?'

Stunned, Red thanked him and asked what the horrifying brawl was all about. The publican replied, 'Oh that, don't worry about it. The boys really love letting it all out on a Friday night. It's just a discharge, it's all good.'

Redmond was an apprentice at a local aluminium smelter for four years, so he gigged around his availabilities. 'There is just something about the guitar. You can express yourself, vent your emotions and yeah, there's girls too,' he mused. You can tell a lot about a guitarist. Red's favourites were honest and original. They didn't follow anyone else or give a damn how others played or how fast.

Often when you become obsessed with the guitar, you tend to end up learning jazz. Everything else just feels too easy or scripted.

Jazz is free-flowing, spontaneous and complex. It's not for the faint-hearted, nor for the egomaniac. Ultimately, however, music is music, and in his view, heaven-sent.

A front-man must have ego, and lots of it. Pizzazz! A guitarist needs a balance of many things: restraint, control, yet unbridled expression. They must be indulgent. The bass player lays that groove down and *sits on it*, which can penetrate your bones. But the drummer? Red just couldn't define drummers. It was like they were from another planet, creating such climactic energy and seemingly willing to live or die for the *moment*. He never saw a musician as honest and committed as a good drummer.

One night, Redmondo actually thought a drummer had possessed him. He awoke to loud sounds in his right ear, the loudest sounds he had ever heard. Bang, bang, bang, bang. 'Ah, it's so loud, what the hell?' It sounded just like a drummer. No, no, it wasn't a miniaturised drummer. It was, it was … a moth in his ear.

Moth-man decided to enter Redmondo's ear to play him a beat or two but then couldn't reverse out. Red could not get him out either. So, the now crazed Redmond with the would-be drum-buddy-moth in his ear drove himself up to the hospital in torment. The nurses somehow found it all hilarious; Red found it maddening. They flushed it out and sent him on his was—Red, that is.

Flossie-Mum

Redmond's mother was a treasure. Oh, there was self-doubt and what she perceived as her faults and failings, but others saw her in a better light. She never put herself first and may have paid the price for that. She needed to be free!

Flossie was a genuinely happy soul and lived for her family. She wasn't complex and didn't waste time, as Redmond later did, pondering the depths of creation and what God is and isn't, where we're from and why we are here and so forth. Those questions were of no use. She just wanted family closeness. It was a simple life, or at least until her husband, her soulmate, her dear Tippy-Toes was taken away from her. Life just lost its shine after that tragic and cruel day when Tippy died …

They'd been on a holiday. A big holiday. Tippy had previously asked Flossie and the children, should they have to make a choice, what would they prefer—to have the house all done up and renovated or buy a caravan and a patrol and go heading up the highway, northward bound towards the sun and surf and way yonder?

Silly question that one! It was a great time. Just perfect. There seemed nothing better than burying one's siblings in sand on that Island of Fraser. They were blessed. Life was wonderful! Tippy had some issues though. He was suffering from high blood pressure and was medicated, although not always responsibly.

Not long before the big holiday up north, he was unknowingly prescribed the wrong medication. While he was driving the family back from a short trip away he started driving all over the road. To the left, to the right, slow, fast. 'Wazza, what's wrong, darling? You're all over the road.' Turns out that a reckless medical-god had prescribed him sleep medication—sedatives instead of anti-hypertensives!

A day before they arrived home from their last marvellous trip up north, they stayed at Forster. Coppertop had a terrible dream and woke up crying. He had dreamt his beautiful mother had died. He was eleven years old and somewhat clingy; it was shocking. Flossie also had a terrible dream but probably not on the same night. Unfortunately, hers was more prescient. She dreamt that her soulmate, her *one and only* had died. She saw him being carried out of the church in a rosewood coffin.

Years and years later she would become upset when Coppertop-come-Searcher bought her a lovely big rosewood piano, because the rosewood reminded her of her dearest's coffin. However, she did come to love that piano, and my, how she played merrily on that thing. But that would come later; for now, joy was far away for Flossie.

They returned home. Tippy and Flossie, soulmates were they, had spent all of their last pennies on the best holiday ever. Coppertop went back to school the next day, as did his siblings. Unbeknown to all, a day of horror awaited poor Flossie. Tippy felt sick, just strange. She talked him into going up to the hospital. A young inexperienced medical-god was on duty who kept telling Flossie it would all be okay; it was just indigestion.

Mind you, it really wasn't his fault. In context, they didn't quite have the modern medical knowledge, equipment and interventions back then, especially in a regional hospital. It was a big heart attack and it was not good. Tippy was monitored somewhat but left alone, except for Flossie's constant presence by his side. He kept saying cryptic things like, 'Keep the caravan, love, you're going to be fine.'

Flossie looked down at his hands. He was a hard worker at the aluminium smelter, but his hands had turned young, opaque, almost angelic. She didn't understand. Then there was the second heart attack. It was massive! He wouldn't be coming back from that one. Poor Flossie was running down the hospital corridor screaming for the young inexperienced medical-god to help her. Tippy was not breathing!

Fortunately, or heaven sent, a young man-of-God happened to be there and helped her find the medical-god and stayed with her. Later that day, the young man-of-the-cloth had to come and advise young Coppertop and his siblings that their hero-dad would not be home for dinner.

Coppertop was removed from the primary classroom, taken into a small orange mini-minor that the man-of-God drove, and was told the fateful news. Coppertop looked up at the sky from the mini-minor and saw how dark and grey the clouds were. 'The clouds are so grey today.'

As he grew older, he would love nature, being a hippy of sorts, but for some reason he would never like grey clouds. They were ominous to him. Oddly, he always imagined the grey clouds he saw from the little orange mini-minor were the same as the clouds on the day the Immaculate One was beaten up, tied and nailed to a cross for no good reason.

Flossie loved painting landscapes and almost always painted large grey clouds in her works. Son-Red never liked those clouds. He wasn't sure if it was because his mother was perhaps expressing inner feelings of grief, or it was simply how he had felt the day he was told his hero-dad was gone. Perhaps there was a shade of truth in both.

Man-of-God was a fun-loving guy. Popular in the community, he was vibrant and musically gifted. He became good friends with Flossie over the years after that fateful day; and a kind of bond developed. It was his first family death of this kind in his new parish and it connected them because it was also Flossie's first death of a soulmate.

Following their loss, he would visit and have dinner with the family every week. Unfortunately, the man-of-God who had such musical talent would later be accused and charged with certain crimes involving children. Rumours around town suggested the man-of-God had strong feelings for Flossie. Others, however, suggested he had far more sinister interests ...

Aunty was horrified. She raced up to see Tippy lying there dead on that cold and clinical hospital bed. Right in the next room her soul-sister was lying unconscious on another cold and clinical hospital bed. It had all been too much of a shock for Flossie. Her love was gone. Gone to the great-beyond-of-no-time-and-place.

She was a mother first, however, that Flossie, and so she put her best foot forward, pushing on as well as she could in those impoverished times of little money and three hungry young mouths to feed. Thank God for the help from her close brother, sister and parents.

Decades and decades later ... that old emotion. Ah! It can sit inside you like a hibernating python. Searcher-son-of-Flossie-once-Coppertop had a passion for healing. He believed unreleased emotion caused us to get sick. Flossie agreed. And boy did she get sick. First leukemia, then breast cancer, bone cancer, metastatic cancer and finally end stage! She didn't go without a fight, though.

Seventeen years of illness, in fact! Even after been sent home to die and abandoning all modern medical treatment, she fought on for years. She was a warrior! Second-son-Coppertop-come-Searcher would do energy healing on her, or some such. She especially like those tuning forks—nice frequencies!

But we must be free. Flossie no doubt buried the pain and anguish of her love being torn away from her all too soon, and later made choices that didn't always support her freedom. 'Who's to say? We all have our crutches, our cross to bear, one way or the other,' Searcher-Red mused.

First cut

They say the first cut is the deepest. It hurt, oh it hurt. Red was in love and things were good. Young was he and didn't think too far ahead. He just wanted to rock it out on the guitar and get away from that stinking smelter. A bit shy and introverted, it was good to have someone who accepted him, warts and all. After all, the *singers* mainly got the chicks. Perhaps he was lucky at the time.

Nonetheless, everything comes to an end. She dumped him three and a half years later. And abruptly. 'Ouch, that hurt.' He didn't see it coming. And his response was over the top—embarrassing, actually. He felt like he was drowning. He moped around and felt sorry for himself and well, he thought the world was going to end or at least it should because his first girlfriend had just dumped him. Quite a lesson, and *Cat* sang about it too. In his initial shock and depression an unusual thing happened …

He went to the bathroom and a great big insect was sitting in the bathtub. It was so damn big and ugly; he has never seen anything like it since. Shattered Red-once-Coppertop just turned the tap on full tilt and tried to wash it away. 'Bloody inconvenience!' It held on to the sink tightly, which pissed him off all the more. So, he tried again and again and again.

'I don't understand,' he thought, 'why won't this frickin stupid big insect just give up? Die, you stupid insect, just piss off!' But no, it would not die. At least not on his demand. So, he tried to drown it with lots of water. Almost half a bathtub full in fact. It just continued to lie there on the sink drain with legs spread and wouldn't let go for minutes on end. Impossible? It was the strangest feeling for Red.

It clearly felt like the insect was saying to him, 'Fuck you back, you wanker. I'm not giving up on life like you, you fucking big sook loser.' It just made Red madder and madder. It was probably therapeutic in a way. Although he may have been delusional in his clouded sense of depression, he just couldn't seem to kill this inconvenient bug-insect for all the money in the Vatican.

The saga went on and on. Eventually, finally, he broke down. It won. It was over. It was all over. He tenderly grabbed that big-long-legged whatever it was, whilst sobbing like a baby, totally whipped and defeated, and carried it outside and gently placed it under the giant mandarin tree with the most reverence he would ever feel in his life. He thanked the teacher-insect for such a great lesson in courage and acknowledged its victory. He finally understood …

Chapter 2

Save yourself!

They were young. Young boys, Coppertop's brother and he, and the tiny little cute blonde-haired happy sister of theirs. They just idolised her; she was perfect. Beautiful-sister! Their parents had just driven a long way from home to holiday on the Golden Coast, the godly paradise of sun and surf. Straightaway the boys asked if they could go to the beach for a swim.

It looked glorious out there. A perfect day! Sparkling blue waters of paradise, with white frothy chop, just beckoned them in. Straight into the south end near the rocks went they. Yeah, straight into heaven. Life was just so exciting. 'You wouldn't be dead for quids,' Tippy used to say.

The ocean was being so kind and accommodating. So friendly! Unbeknownst to those naïve little fellows, she would take them on a very quick ride *out the back*. Quick. Very quick. 'Wait. Too quick. What?' Yeah, the young suckers had entered straight into a strong rip. It was scary, terrifying.

The waves were crashing over and over and dragging, dragging down, oh that drag! They say, 'Never fight a rip. Just go with it and it will take you out and, eventually, you can swim sideways and find the bank, which will carry you back to the shore.' They were too young and didn't know any of that.

Coppertop-Red's brother was a little older and stronger than he. Older brother fought like a banshee; he wasn't about to die on that perfect day. He was about 10 or 15 metres closer towards the shore than Coppertop, but still was a long, long way from safety. Within those short moments of panic, Coppertop yelled out to his older brother, 'Save me, save me!'

Panicked older brother yelled back, 'Save yourself!'

It was too much. Coppertop started breathing in water and going down, down, down. He felt sleepy.

Poor Flossie was beside herself, screaming for help. 'Help, help, please save my boys!' Then ...

A giant! A Greek god of the pantheon he was. Buffed, strong, chiselled and with a steely gaze that would stare down a hungry lion. He swam out to save them. Coppertop's brother, the courageous one, had tamed the beast; he beat the god-forsaken rip and brought it home. But Tiger was down for the count.

That little Coppertop would not go on to become the thinker, the truth-seeker, the searcher. Or to grow up and even have a couple of crazy kids of his own. No, it was all over. It would end here. Greek god could swim, however, and fear? He ate it for breakfast. Out he swam, pushing through the swell like an ocean-cruise liner. Coppertop doesn't remember much after then; he was out to it. Greek god rescued him and dumped his scrawny little body on the sand.

Coppertop came to, surrounded by a crowd, vomiting and spitting salty water out like he was possessed by demons. Flossie was grateful, bloody grateful and was crying and expressive. When she calmed down, she searched for the seven-foot chiselled giant who'd saved her little treasure, but she could not find him. Lo, he was standing right there all along.

He was a little knee-high-to-a-grasshopper fellow with a great big heart. Tiny but solid. Coppertop-now-Searcher wished he could go back in time and thank that little man. He wouldn't be here if not for that random act of bravery, putting young Tiger up on his shoulders in such a strong rip without a surf rescue board or jet ski. No, just raw courage drove him.

The brothers arrived back at the caravan and were wondering what else there was to do. 'Skateboard?' Don't you love that about kids? Like, the near-drowning incident was a distant memory just an hour later because there was so much more to do; they were on holidays, yippee!

Poor-brother-now-Callithumpian still thinks to this day that Coppertop somehow feels he abandoned him in that fateful rip when he yelled out, '*Save yourself.*' He was nine, and Coppertop eight. How could a little boy save a little boy when Mother Ocean wanted to swallow them whole? If only Brave-brother knew that those two words would be the wisest words he would ever say to Coppertop …

Out-of-the-body

A strange opening. Red-once-Coppertop was an apprentice working in big industry with lots of forbidden machinery. He started at fifteen. An aluminium smelter makes aluminium from raw products and it's crude work, hot, and dusty. Oh yeah, it was very dusty. When his father, Tippy, had worked there years before, he complained to Flossie after his very first day, 'That place is the dirtiest, dustiest, noisiest shit-hole I have ever worked at, love.' Tippy persisted.

Red was a daydreamer. During some of those moments at work, he would go into a reverie and would be imagining what would happen if that heavy motor simply fell without warning, or the tagged-out crusher abruptly turned on, and so forth. And suddenly they did just that. It truly freaked him out and not just because it was a close call from real and imminent danger, but because it was like he somehow knew or sensed something was about to happen; and it did.

It was the true start of an odd life for him. At about the same time, he started having what some people call *out-of-body* experiences, which were bizarre to say the least. Imagine feeling like you are totally awake and fully conscious, yet you're as free as a bird because you happen to be flying along the main street of your town, at about the height of the telegraph poles.

Or flying around an old hospital with a strange voice saying, 'Why do you always hang around these old buildings when you're out?' And you're answering, 'Because I like the vibrations. What? What vibrations? What the hell am I talking about and who belongs to the strange voice and how come I can fly, and where is my body?' Yes, it was certainly a strange time for the young man.

Coppertop-now-Redmond never paid much attention in church every Sunday. He would daydream, though. Sometimes Tippy and Tippy's dad Popeye would drop off dear Flossie and the three small children at church, because they thought it was probably good for them. Then they would go and whack a few quick schooners in at the local watering hole until it was time to go back and pick up the now-holy family. As Redmond grew up, he came to appreciate how hilarious that was.

Anyways, in church, somewhere in that boring state of inattentiveness, lack of reverence, and unwillingness to sing hymns with any feeling, Coppertop must have heard Grumpy-old-priest talk about a thing called a *silver cord.* The priest said it was like an invisible umbilical cord which connects you to spirit, but when you die it severs, and off you go back to heaven—or, if you've been a bad boy, down, down, down to the evil fellow who loves fires. Oh, how he loves fires!

Searcher felt a bit sorry for the fellow down there with his eternal damnation fires. The one who sometimes sends emails but probably calls them god-mails, up through the heavenly realm of angels and saints and says, 'God. I'm keeping to myself down here. It's okay, I'm warm. I get to toast marshmallows on my eternal fires any time I want. Life's good.

'One day you'll let me return whence I came. But the problem for me is this: every time one of your sons or daughters does something wrong up there, like have an affair or screw someone over, they blame me! Like, give me a break! Can't they take responsibility for their own actions?'

It was clear, so clear. Redmond was *out of the body* again, and it was amazing. He was flying around watching birds and insects. 'What a beautiful morning, just scintillating with life!' He even sat underwater and watched fish swimming through the reeds. 'But I can't breathe underwater,' he contemplated. Hmm, strange. And to walk right through a brick wall? It just didn't make sense. The freedom was blissful, but oh the clarity!

He wished he felt so clear during his normal waking day. He had a sense of foreboding, though, that Redmond-Tiger. He wasn't quite *Searcher* yet, because it was these very experiences that would turn him into a searcher. It was like he needed to hurry up and get back. Back to the body. Why? He didn't know.

'Just hurry up and get back.'

Flossie had moved out but liked to visit her now grown-up second son each morning before work. He was hopeless. She understood that and didn't know how he survived; he could barely make toast for himself at that time.

'That's it. I've got it. Mum is on her way and if I don't hurry up and get back into my body, she will think I'm dead,' he realised. He turned back from the yard between the big mandarin tree and the outside toilet and oh what?

'That's that, that, that weird *silver cord* Grumpy-old-priest was talking about. Wow!' It was beautiful. It shone and glistened and pulsated. It was alive, it *was* him somehow. It spiralled from him, in rhythmic pulsations of light through the back door of the house towards his body.

'Shit, Mum is on her way. Hurry!'

He thought of the show *I Dream of Jeannie* and sort of adopted a blinking motion, just as Jeannie used to do, and attempted to reappear in his body.

'Hurry! Okay, here we go. Yes, yes. I'm back. Thank God, Mum will be here soon, I can feel it,' he said to himself.

Redmond-soon-to-be-Searcher was looking up enjoying being back and feeling really good and relaxed. He was looking up at the ceiling. 'But wait. What? Shit, you're not back in your body, you idiot, you're in the kitchen lying on the kitchen table.' He could tell by the Fluro lights on the ceiling. There were none in his bedroom. He'd never laughed so hard in all his life. He felt tears running down his face, only he couldn't have because he wasn't back in the body yet.

'Mother! Okay, do the Jeannie blinky thing again and get your travelling spirit-ass back into the body before you freak her out,' he said to himself. Bam, zip, snap. He was back.

It really does suck, you know, returning to your body. We love our bodies and all they offer, but after being *out*, it just feels terribly restrictive. It was like he had a straitjacket placed on him, and each finger and toe had to fit back into lead socks. Heavy and debilitating!

Up he jumped, that Redmond-almost-Searcher, for Mother was walking around to enter via the back door. No-one locked their doors in those days for they didn't have to. As Flossie entered through the door, he emerged from the bedroom. She said, 'You look vibrant this morning, love'... If only she knew!

His silver cord was not *complete*, though. It was incredibly alive and dazzling and glistened like a cocoon rope, but also patchy. Later, when he became Searcher-the-Seeker, he heard that our cords are patchy due to a spiritual evolutionary thing. Like, the better the person you become during your long slow march to your own awakening in consciousness, the more complete the cord is. Maybe?

Either way, it's elastic. When you return to the body, it makes a very strong pingy, snappy, zippy sound. At least that is what Searcher always found. And if you come back at the *wrong* time, somehow you either get a headache or you feel out of sorts. The feeling will persist no matter what you do, until you grab some shut-eye. Even just a ten-minute nap seems to do the trick, and then you feel normal again—grounded, *here-now*.

There was one thing that young Seeker found to be even more bizarre than being out of the body, however. He once became aware in his sleep and watched himself dream. Now that was without doubt the most perplexing experience of his life. It was like he was perceiving just behind his brain and watching holographic images flash in and out at warp speed, with neural firings appearing like little lightning strikes.

It was bizarre and almost inconceivable to witness such a high velocity of kaleidoscopic images. He had never known how intense and intricate a simple dream could be, for he just considered them as *mind junk* release.

Redmond used to worry about not returning to his body. He was somewhat fearful as a teenager for there were so many horror movies to watch. Normally speaking, though, it's much harder to *stay out* than come back in. A single logical thought can ping you back in an instant.

One night, though, he kept waking up out of his body, over and over again and couldn't seem to stay in! He didn't travel far, mainly just out into the loungeroom and so forth. He was aimlessly staring at the stereo and speakers or perhaps better stated, *perceiving*.

This particular night was unusually alarming for he was worried he wouldn't return to his body at all and be pronounced dead! Brave-older-brother was a nurse. He was down to earth and had experienced so much more than Redmond-almost-Searcher, as he had travelled around the world for a year on a shoestring budget and at a young age had seen many things.

Yes, he had seen some things. And tripped too! Brother-later-Callithumpian returned to Australia with bucketloads of songs and poems that he had written overseas; even to this day, Seeker-Searcher cannot fathom their profundity and brilliance. Songs of true spirituality and nature—insightful, witty, moving and emotive. The words sounded like they were channelled from a *being* that was Confucius, Yeshua, Lao Tzu, a Greek philosopher, and Bob all mixed together.

And yet, he was somehow sceptical. Seeker used to wonder if brother-of-his actually had any idea about his own genius or what his own words meant. How could he be a sceptic when he seemed so wise in his words? Perhaps he wasn't a sceptic deep down and was just humouring Searcher-brother? Searcher would never know. Actually, he went on to create his own philosophy, well, so to speak. He's a Callithumpian floating downstream. Anyways, back to the story.

Brother got home from his afternoon nursing shift just before midnight. Seeker just had to tell him. He needed that scepticism; he was desperate and fearful. Redmond told him he couldn't seem to stay *in* the body and pleaded for his brother to share a cuppa to calm him down. Strangely, Brave-and-wise-sceptic-brother obliged him. It worked. Seeker-Searcher remained in the body that night, and in fact is still in the body to this day.

Brother wasn't always so obliging, however. Seeker-Searcher was quite *out there* after all. One time, at the dinner table, Seeker raised his suspicion that when one eats meat, as in the furry four- and two-legged varieties, one also eats their *fears*. Such as the fear and anxiety the animal feels just before being killed and chopped up. That was it.

'You're a fuck'n idiot,' future-Callithumpian-brother hollered.

Searcher was pissed off at the time but would one day find that very, very funny.

Ambos

Years later, Seeker-Searcher joined the ambulance service. Brave-brother and Brother-in-law-Pearl were joining, so it seemed like a good idea at the time. In fact, the honour of helping others sounded like a mighty fine idea. It was intense; lots of *anat-and-phys* and all the jargon, but you get through. He was a paramedic for around fifteen years.

'You see a lot of things. The variety is wonderful; although, after a while, it all becomes the same. People needing help, you providing help, and the wheel just goes round and round,' he asserted long after.

The public often say to a paramedic, 'You must see some terrible things.' Seeker did. Not so much the heart-still-beating-after-being-forcefully-ejected-from-the-body type of terrible, but terrible human behaviour. Seeker recalls going to his first cardiac arrest. It was a big deal and he was both tense and anxious.

However, what he noticed mostly was the other paramedics laughing and joking around on scene. The case was in public view, just outside of a shopping centre. He was mortified. 'Why don't these guys tone it down?' he asked himself. The lady was middle-aged; it could have been his own mother or aunty. 'Can't they pay her some respect and give her some dignity, for God's sake?'

The Searcher

Searcher-Gra[*] was advised it was just *dark humour*, which a paramedic adopts in order to cope—a satirical sort of thing. 'Yeah right!' He worked for long enough in the service to have earned the right to comment. 'Once you do enough traumatic cases, you really don't care in quite the same way. It's not that you don't feel or that you don't have empathy or compassion, not at all. It's just that you repeatedly notice that, while other people are going through trauma and loss, you return home after your shift and haven't—besides, of course, the typical daily accumulative stresses all paramedics endure.'

So, it's a sense of detachment that occurs over time and is both understandable and regretful. Boy Searcher-Gra paid the price for that, though. He bottled up all the emotion. He was too dense to realise it at the time, for he'd always been slow off the mark. Sure, he knew something wasn't right inside but couldn't figure out what it was.

Searcher became angry and intolerant and had no patience for *losers* or *bludgers*. Most of all, he disliked *posh* people. He could handle drunks, druggies and fools but not so much those who had both a plum in their mouth and the sun in their arse. Those who thought they were better than others. Searcher became resentful. He snapped at people (fortunately not the patients) and lost all patience.

He disliked some of the other paramedics for their meanness, lack of empathy, and poor professionalism. Seeker stopped appreciating the blessing he was bestowed in helping others. He was dark, lost and afraid …

Finally, he left the job.

Not once in fifteen years did any supervisor ever ask, 'Are you okay?'—although, to be fair, one time, after he'd attended a young mother who had been shot dead early in the morning, a supervisor said

---

[*]*Gra* was one of Searcher's many nicknames and the most predominant one throughout his life. Curiously, it found such resonance, that he was rarely ever called by his given name as an adult. His ocker mate Pantz; sometimes termed Scooter, started calling him Graham, named after a certain musician. When Pantz was finally satisfied enough that he had successfully annoyed the Searcher with the term Graham, he simplified it to 'Gra'. Searcher liked the name Gra and it just seemed to stick thereafter.

they needed to *debrief* back at the station. Wise-cracking-supervisor bought some biscuits from the service station. They all gathered around, talked some unrelated shit for a while that had nothing to do with the case, and then returned to work.

That was the closest Searcher ever came to receiving any emotional assistance from the ambulance service. Mind you, he never reached out for help either; he was too proud. He just knew he had to escape, and the best way to do that was to run away from it all like a coward. That placed so much financial pressure on his wife and family as a result. It was very irresponsible!

Searcher, who was in a dark place, was sitting over a cliff face by the ocean. *'Jump, you loser. Just jump. You're no good to anybody. You've never done anything worthwhile. Come on, you chicken-shit, put them all out of their misery having to put up with you, ya loser, just jump. Jump. Jump. Jump!'* It was a dark time for Searcher-once-Coppertop. He wanted to jump for sure but how do you do that to your wife and kids, your mother, your family and friends?

Some people think only cowards commit suicide. That may be true. But for Searcher, he just felt like a coward every time he didn't jump and felt all the worse for it. Yeah, it wasn't just once. It was protracted. But he's a fighter. A tiger! He's got some grit. He kept on living with loser-self. The insect had taught him courage, grit and determination, after all. He put up with the darkness, but just couldn't *heal* it.

Healing

He was a tough guy, that Chudley. He loved motorbikes, drugs and guitar. Searcher-once-Glapiac[†] met him through guitar connections. As hard-arse as he was, he was learning classical guitar from Bert. It felt like an oxymoron at the time. A guy who reminded Searcher-Glapiac of Alexander the Great (or at least as he envisioned Alexander the Great to be), learning the sensitivity of the classical guitar.

[†]Glapiac was a strange nickname Searcher's coach and football mates called him when he was young.

They hit it off well and hung around a bit. But Chudley made a blunder. He was working at a different aluminium smelter from Redmond, as an operator. Someone reversed a mobile diesel plant and ran straight over his leg. It was bad. It had to go.

But those damn phantom pains! Chudley hated them. Medicine didn't seem to relieve them, not even the recreational type. Red-then-Glapiac, who was into some kind of energy healing at the time, offered to have a go on his missing leg. Chudley-Alexander-the-Great just loved it. Red didn't actually touch him but worked around the site of his lower-leg-now-removed, in the *energy field*. Chudley gained some real benefit and said it was the only thing that gave him relief. Guess it's hard to relieve pain from an area that no longer exists.

Red-Glapiac must have worked intuitively because he didn't know jack shit; he was nineteen. But it slowly sparked a desire in him towards healing. When Chudley-Alexander had healed enough, Redmond jumped on the back of his Harley Davidson to accompany him on his first ride since becoming an amputee. It probably helped Chudley's confidence to ride again, although Red was no doubt the fool.

Nothing phased Chudley, however. A local guy called Big-Bird used to terrorise everyone in the town and loved giving anyone a hiding to nowhere. Big-Bird was extremely tall and solid and just didn't lose fights. Even though Chudley had recently lost his leg, when he saw Big-Bird walk into the local pub, well, you know, he just had to take that fuckin' smartarse down.

Reading the vibrations

Redmond was at that time dabbling not only with energy healing but also with psychic readings. He even attended a weekly group to learn more. Before attending, each participant had to grab a flower from home, breathe on it, put it in a paper bag and place it in a basket at the venue for someone else to *read the vibrations*.

This 'reading the vibrations' was supposed to harness one's psychic skills and develop sensitivity or intuition. The owner of the flower would appraise and give feedback to the reader to see if anything made sense.

A large elderly man with a great big white beard used to come to the group each week and appeared to be somewhat of a drinker, for he left the spiritualist group to go straight to the pub. He was pleasant, but some people shouldn't play with fire. One night he brought his grown-up daughter along and everything seemed quite peaceful.

Suddenly, during a meditation, the elderly man started shouting at the top of his voice in a crude and heavy pirate accent. The group teacher asked all present to make a circle and hold hands. The man swayed and swung screaming at the top of his voice, *'I used to drink rum when I was on your planet. Hardy, Har-Harrrrr. RUMMMM. I JUST LOVE RUM!'*

He most definitely sounded like a depicted pirate of old. His poor daughter was dismayed. 'What on earth has happened to my dad?' Searcher still finds it hilarious, remembering the daughter's reaction. The teacher kept repeating, 'Go you unto the light, entity, go you unto the light.' Eventually, he must have gone somewhere for the old man seemed to come to and was very sombre indeed, although without any recollection of what had just happened. He was never seen at that group again. No doubt his daughter barred him from returning.

With this newfound psychic knack, Redmond decided to try it out on a few people. One night he was with Chudley, who said, 'If you can do so-called psychic readings, why don't you try it out on me?' Chudley was intimidating so Redmond decided to oblige him. He held Chudley's watch to read the vibrations, and went on to tell him many, many things about his life.

Things Red could not have possibly known, including incidents and accidents that had happened during his childhood as well as various family dynamics. When the reading was finally over, Chudley stood there gobsmacked. Redmond was even more surprised than he that it had actually worked.

His confidence was soaring high, and he was now willing to do readings for free and did. However, it all came to an abrupt end. His school and drummer buddy, Christo-Wal, asked him to do a reading for his mother. So, mother of Wal, brother of Wal, sister of Wal and Wal all sat there listening to the so-called reading, which turned out to be the worst, most pathetic, inaccurate psychic reading of all time. It was entirely embarrassing for young Redmond, for he just could not relax into the vibe with all those gawking eyes and attention, and hence became a ship lost at sea. So that was that!

Reincarnation

When you're a bit different, you wonder why, and how it was and when it was you became that way. It's hard to put your finger on it. Coppertop was young, maybe twelve. They were away up north on a short holiday. His mother Flossie was chewing the fat with a friend who was quite zany, uncouth and very bold. They were sitting on the sand when wacky-friend-of-Flossie's said one word that made Coppertop jump.

She said, wait for it ... wait ... *'Reincarnation!'* Well, she probably said it in a sentence like, 'Hey, do you believe in reincarnation?' Something like that, although Coppertop only heard that one word. It was like a bolt of lightning had run through him. It lit up his cells. Reincarnation? What is reincarnation? He had no idea what it meant.

These days it's not such a foreign term. Buddhists teach it and others embrace it, especially Eastern philosophies. But a good little Catholic boy would never hear a strange word like that back then. Coppertop had heard words like *shame* and *guilt* and *punishment* and *temptation* and *vengeance* and *the devil*, but no, not reincarnation. Guess the word just resonated with him.

When he finally understood what it meant much later, it just felt *right*, like common sense, you know. 'Of course we reincarnate, dumbass. How could it be any different? We live forever.' They kind of explain it like you come here to earth to experience and learn stuff, but *you are not the body*; you are living *in* the body and *as* the body, but only for a set time. *Time* being of significance here.

Just as you wear clothes for a certain time until they wear out, you *wear* your body for a certain time until it wears out. And on and on it goes ad infinitum throughout eternity, as you keep on growing and dusting off that ole silver cord and evolving in some spiritual way. Who knows? It sure seems fair and compassionate. Like if you stuff up, you will always get another chance, and another and another, or more precisely, another *opportunity*.

Some contemporary thinkers, however, propose that the concept of reincarnation is a myth because time doesn't actually exist. Hence, if there is no time but the present; *now*, other lifetimes are therefore happening simultaneously and not sequentially. Searcher also liked that concept.

As a youth, Coppertop-later-Searcher always wondered, 'Why the hell is some so-called holy man asking a child in a dingy confessional box what they have done wrong this week?' If the sinful-not-so-sinful children hadn't been naughty enough, then they had to conjure something up, just to satisfy their curiosity.

Searcher later pondered how certain priests did the things they did. 'If any of the priests or brothers who specialised in paedophilia really believed in God, and an angry male Christian one at that, wouldn't they be terrified of molesting young children because of the terrible punishment and vengeance that angry-male-father-God would dish out once they died?'

He hoped for their sake that is was a kind, loving *female* God at least waiting for them beyond those pearly-luminescent gates, who didn't behave like humans and instead granted them compassion, love and forgiveness. Seeker later gained insight into that particular dilemma when he watched a documentary on paedophilia within the Catholic Church.

It seemed at least some of the priests or brothers were not scared of Male-God's vengeance—because, no matter what they did, He would forgive them after all. A get-out-of-jail-free card, you might say. How convenient!

Instant love

The band had set up without a sound-check. 'Should be a good night.' Redmondo was actually on a *set-up* of his own. The singer's girlfriend was bringing her cute younger sister to hook up with him.

The first set is the most important for rockers. It's where you find your groove. They were just entering the *zone* at about mid-set and there she was—not the set-up girl. The love of his life! She smiled. He lit up. He smiled. She lit up. He turned to the drummer, Christo-Wal, and said, 'Mate, I'm in love.'

Turning to the lady she baby-sat for, she said, 'See that guitarist there? I'm going to marry him.'

During the first set break, a few amusing words were exchanged between the two, but that was it. They had finally made contact. They already knew each other to the core but had just met. In fact, unbeknown to them, they had made close proximation many times prior by chance, but she was too young. Seven years younger than he. Redmond-now-Pookie-to-Kiki hadn't noticed her at all back then. 'Sorry, blind date, but this one is the *one*.' There wasn't a choice. She was irresistible. They simply must be.

Thirty years on and still interwoven. Tight, close, whacky and child-like. *Immature* actually.

'I wanna have kids.'

'No, I'm too selfish,' replied Seeker.

'I wanna have kids,' said Kiki.

'No way, I'm too selfish.'

'I need to have kids!'…

She came into this world quickly. They didn't understand she was a cyclone. How could they? Babies are just cute, adorable and lovable. Perfect and innocent! If only they knew who she was back then. This one was different, very different. Step aside, incoming has arrived!

This one wasn't just a wind. She was a cyclone! She came to live. And live is what she does. A free soul doesn't crave for anything but to spread their wings and fly. Security repulses them. Monotony nauseates them. They live and utilise the forces that are at their fingertips. How could he call this one *my* daughter? What an insult! She belongs to the wind. She is not *my* to anyone.

Searcher: 'She needs a play friend, though.'

Kiki: 'Yeah. Maybe a boy, hey?'

'Yeah, a boy would be great.'

'You will have a son who bears my name. He is yours, and yours, but mostly mine!' That was in the *Dome of Light*. Husband-now-father was told boy came to teach him how to live. Searcher-father lived behind his own bars, his own prison cell. Son lived. He was a rascal! Mischievous. Whatever he was told to do, he just did the opposite.

They say you *create* your kids based on how you shape and condition them. Is that so? Parents certainly influence them along their paths but sometimes they just *are who they are*. Searcher expressed it like so, 'Some parents honestly think they *own* their children. "They are *my* children", you hear them say. They think they are theirs to mould and shape from their own clay. Sadly, they will never learn from their children.

'They believe they can teach their children how to live. Foolishness! Children are most times teaching *us* how to live. Wake up! Have you ever really stared into a baby's eyes? What on earth could you teach them? Sacred is that immaculate gaze that spells out eternity.'

A whirlwind. She cried every night for three years. No sleep for young lovers. Then Rascal came. It couldn't possibly be as bad? No. Worse. He cried for three and a half years. No sleep. The soulmates clashed. It was ugly. How did they survive six and a half years on so little sleep? Who knows? Perhaps by grace alone …

Chapter 3

Camping with Tippy-Toes

Coppertop and Brave-brother loved going away camping with Tippy-Dad. It was very exciting and Tippy-Toes would always insist they bring another friend along. He was concerned some kids didn't have fathers to do the same for them. He was like that, Tippy.

They would trudge up towards the mountains passing through river gorges whilst sitting on the bonnet of the great big blue Monaro, hanging on for dear life as Tippy hammered through creating a big wake of water that splashed all over them.

There was simply nothing better for the boys and they couldn't wait for the next river passing. Finally, they would reach the camping area and learn how to set up the tent and make a fire. Impatiently, they would want to jump in the river.

One time they hurriedly jumped in and just as hurriedly jumped back out again, so quickly that Tippy must have near wet himself laughing at the sight of the blood pouring down their scrawny bodies. Leaches! Blood-sucking leaches. It was quite the panic trying to remove them from their bodies with lit matches.

Later, up to the summit Tippy would take the boys, and the views were spectacular. It was good. Really good. No. More than good; it was slippery. There had been lots of rain. The dirt roads winding up the mountains were only just wide enough to pass another car with steep and perilous drop-offs to the side. Tippy was driving back down when he edged to the left to allow another car to pass and, alarmingly, lost control and drove over the edge.

It really was a steep edge and the boys scrambled out of the Monaro like there was no tomorrow (and there damn well nearly wasn't), precariously positioned as they were on that mountain side. Many nice men in 4WDs stopped and tried to winch the Monaro out without success. The rake of the angle over the edge was too much to pull and snapped their straps.

Eventually, Tippy had to concede, 'We're in the shit, boys.' Thus, they had to leave the mountain and seek accommodation. They stayed in an old farm homestead. Country people are always nice and helpful, and kindly invited them to stay. Tippy would sleep inside and the boys would sleep in the hayshed. Unreal! It sounded like fun to the boys. It was not.

It was a long, itchy night. The hay in the hayshed was riddled with fleas. The boys were infested. The following day the ranger helped out and the ole blue Monaro was freed, and the family was homeward bound. During the very next camping trip, the boys were so proud and excited to see a new sign had been installed where they'd nearly lost their lives over the edge of the mountain. It read: SLIPPERY WHEN WET. Small things amuse small minds. The camping trips were many and so were the adventures.

The river crossing

After Tippy had passed to the great beyond, a neighbour decided he was going on a camping trip with his wife and children. Lazarus invited Flossie and her children to go with them. Flossie was good friends with his wife, Dafina, and so off they proceeded. The plan was simple. Flossie and Dafina would drop off Lazarus, his boys, Coppertop and Brave-brother five miles upstream with their inflatable rubber-ducky boat.

A few hours later, they would drive to a designated river crossing and wait for them. But some plans don't always go to plan. The maps that Lazarus possessed looked ancient and sketchy. Nonetheless, it was time to paddle. There was no motorisation for this would be a manual expedition.

The Searcher

At the crack of dawn, off they ventured. They paddled downstream. They paddled some more. And they paddled some more. This was getting somewhat tiring for all the boys, especially Lazarus's, who were younger, but they persisted on and on throughout the day.

Abruptly, the calm river transitioned into nasty rapids and things became altogether faster and bumpier. Coppertop was sincerely worried he might have his head blown off from behind by Lazarus's shotgun accidently going off. At first the rapids were a nice reprieve from the monotony and a welcome change for all. Quickly thereafter, however, the same sentiment was not shared.

Up and down they all bounced, screaming and yelling whilst holding on for their dear lives. Items were falling out, bodies were flying and bumping everywhere, and Lazarus was barking orders to keep steering with their oars. All of a sudden, the inflatable-rubber-ducky catapulted into the air and all and sundry were now in the raging waters, hurtling downstream and smashing into the rocks. Just when they were all thinking they might drown in that very river, on that very day, the rapids swiftly ended. They were back to the calm, false serenity again.

Lazarus, his boys and the brothers gathered the boat and whatever oars and equipment they could find and composed themselves. It was late afternoon. It had been a long day. It's amazing how one can go from being scared to death one moment to bored to tears the next. They set out downstream and progress was slow and laborious indeed. On and on they paddled. Other sets of rapids lay in their way, but none would be as treacherous as the terrifying one in which they were all tossed out.

Darkness came. Lazarus did have some ideas at times and so they carried the boat over several barbed-wire fences to look for other ways out. Finally, he figured they had *missed the pass*. 'No shit!'

Meanwhile, poor Dafina and Flossie and the other children had been trudging up and down those snaking rivers looking for their lost loved ones for hours and hours—all day in fact. They searched every river crossing there was.

Paddle, paddle, paddle. It became hypnotic. To their credit, no-one gave up; all kept trying their best. They were Aussies, and Aussies never throw in the towel. 'Something will work out sooner or later,' a common thought shared. They continued on in darkness until, at last, a farmhouse was stumbled upon.

The warm farmers cared for them and then drove them back up the country road to the campsite. Coppertop-to-be-one-day-Searcher never forgot the drive back along the river. So delusional he'd become that every time they drove around a bend he would flap his arms in a paddling motion, all the way back. The women were beside themselves. The boys were alive! They were beyond exhausted, but they had survived and their families were elated.

But yes, somehow, they had made it. Evidently, the ole map of Lazarus's was just a little too old. The designated river crossing they were supposed to rendezvous at had long since disappeared.

Learning by osmosis

'You've gotta go back in there and sell those potatoes.'

Coppertop's friend's father drove trucks. He was a good man and would throw a few extra pallets of potatoes on his semi-trailer from his return interstate trips and take his sons and friends around the streets with a trailer full of spuds for sale.

It was a sound idea to help the boys earn some pocket money. The spuds were a good price and of good quality, but some people just didn't want them. He insisted they go back and retry the sale. 'Try harder. You have to push. These potatoes are great value. Go on. Push harder, sell, sell.'

Some people felt pity and were polite; others said, 'Fuck off, I told you I didn't want any.' Very few changed their minds. This was the time when Red first developed a bad relationship with money. He felt shame. He felt like money wasn't *flow*; it was something else and just didn't feel right. It didn't suit him to push like that, but his friend's father was just trying to teach them how to sell, after all.

It wasn't all bad, though. His friend's dad took him away on long trips in his *semi*, which was very exciting. Coppertop also loved being involved in *truckie strikes* and would go and learn all about the battle for the little guy.

Coppertop-then-Glapiac just loved that. Loved the little man's fight—the fight of the battler. Glapiac would go on to other jobs as a kid, like washing his uncle's many business cars every Saturday. Money was both necessary and confusing, but he had to save up for those motorbikes and their accessories and fuel.

Some people, as it appeared to him, genuinely felt money was more important than God. Even at Church on Sunday money was really important because you had to give money in order to enter heaven. You know, the place where all those fine priests and brothers went after they died. Oh, and let's not forget those beautiful nuns who loved to beat and torment the boarding schoolgirls. They go to heaven as well.

After Tippy flew the coop, poor Flossie struggled on. With emphasis on *poor* here. She didn't have a cracker and worked various jobs including working for her brother who had a security service. Flossie would work all night and then come home and be Mum during the day, sleeping only sporadically in dribs and drabs. At one time, she sent one of her rug-rats down to the local corner shop, way back before the big shopping centres took over, and asked them to buy just *one* egg. One egg!

Poor thing. That must have embarrassed her, although they bred them tough in her day, much tougher than Glapiac-once-Coppertop's generation. Flossie pushed on, never voicing the fact her soulmate had been stripped away from her in an instant, and at such a young age. She missed the tickles. Missed the giggles. They used to wrestle and tickle each other on the bed every night, laughing hysterically, that perfect Tippy-and-Flossie team.

Tippy-Toes loved his beer too. Flossie was square. Her mother had been assaulted by Flossie's biological father involving alcohol abuse, so it just wasn't for her. But Tippy was a good drunk. She'd let him go for his beers after work with his mates with a limit of seven middies. If he should ever get back after 7 pm (the 'dead'line) well, she'd just wack him over the head with a pot. And did!

However, Tippy was thick-skinned and loved Flossie to the core. Brother-later-Callithumpian nearly fainted whilst anticipating the response from a pot-over-Tippy's-head incident. But after a few seconds' silence, which felt like an eternity, Tippy came to his senses and exploded in laughter. EXPLODED! 'Come on, love, you can hit me harder than that. I deserve it.' My, how he loved his Flossie. She missed him dreadfully, though never bitched or moaned. She had a job to do.

Perhaps we learn by osmosis. Some people believe children learn *not* from what you say, but by what you do. In other words, adults best lead by example. Searcher-father-of-Cyclone-Izzy-and-Rascal-Sam did not find that to be the case at all. Searcher reckoned, 'You can exemplify things to your children, like keeping tidy, 'till the cows come home, but if you honestly believe they will eventually be tidy simply because you are tidy, well, you either have rocks in your head or you have never been a parent.'

Best go study a degree in psychology and release a doctrine on how to parent, even though you've never been one. Searcher believed he learned a kind of *poverty consciousness* whilst growing up, not from what his parents said, but from what they were feeling or fearing.

He was very sensitive, to the extreme. Times were tough back then and he has nothing but respect for their courage and will, through great adversity. Nonetheless, he observed how a child who was brought up in wealth most often continued to be wealthy into adulthood and vice versa for poverty. 'Perhaps because one learns vibrationally throughout childhood,' he pondered in retrospect.

Toddler meditation

'You are a Catholic and always will be a Catholic,' she said to Searcher. She was nice, hot and Catholic. Married with kids, her husband was a lovely man. Searcher noticed how she'd also bonded well with another man, his neighbour. One day she and her pal, Searcher's neighbour, started talking and instructing Searcher on the wonders of being Catholic, for that mattered to God. At least, that is what they advised. Silly-Searcher mentioned to them how he was once brought up as a Catholic. She kindly reassured him that he *still* was a Catholic, as if he had been honoured with the greatest of gifts.

Searcher remarked, 'I was, until I woke up out of my body. That's when I knew the Catholics had either forgotten to tell me something or weren't aware. Once I was out of my body, those chains just broke. I was free!'

She fell silent.

Sometimes things don't compute. Like when your computer freezes for a few seconds, then resynchronisation occurs, and a return to the lie happens. To be fair to the Catholics, though, Grumpy-old-drunk-priest did discuss the silver cord, which Searcher got to witness. It's in the Book of Books somewhere—the old one.

Flossie had a photo of Coppertop as a baby—a small toddler really. He was sitting bolt upright on the beach with a striped yellow, black and white terry towel crossed around him from left to right underneath, then right to left back over. Toddler-Coppertop had his eyes closed. Flossie and her mother, *Nanna*, had often mentioned how cute he was that day when he suddenly just *fell asleep* sitting upright. Much later when he was an adult, she even gave him a photo of the incident. He had no interest in it at the time.

One night, when he and Kiki were asleep in their great big and dangerous wavy waterbed, he began dreaming. A voice was talking to him. It said, 'Wake up now. Go to your bookshelf and find that old photo of you as a toddler and look at it closely. You will understand that you were indeed not asleep at all. You were in deep meditation.'

It was after two in the morning. 'This is crazy!'

Nonetheless, Searcher did as *dream-voice* told him to, and retrieved the photo and yes, it did seem as if the toddler was in meditation. Baby meditation!

At that time in his life he was very much the seeker, the searcher, and as a consequence, was very much the meditator. Even a follower of spiritual teachers, he would have to admit.

Searcher performed yoga and meditation and whatever else he was prescribed to do, in order to find happiness and enlightenment. However, what caught his attention was actually the way Toddler-

Coppertop had wrapped his towel across his body for meditation; left over right, right over left.

It was exactly the same as now-Searcher did when meditating, especially in the chilly winter. Searcher contemplated, 'Who knows where it all starts? It just is. We are who we are and can pretend for a time, but inevitably we just end up being ourselves again. And thank goodness for that, for who else would you want to be?'

Wakey, wakey, Glapiac

To a kid, is there anything better than hitting a ball up against a wall? For hours on end they can just hit the ball as if for the first time. In high school, Red lost half of his free recess and lunch time over four years, waiting in line at the giant outdoor double squash court, to play *hand-ball* on. It was Corky's fault.

They would line up in the forever-line, and Corky would dish up a serve that would hit the side wall and floor simultaneously, offering no possibility of a hit. Impossible! It would mulley-grubber off without a bounce. They would feel short-changed. It really did suck! Corky was always too good and they knew it and he knew it. He was the champ and owned the court. Consequently, on the weekend, Red and his mates would practise up against the primary school wall closer to home, to hone their skills so they could hopefully whip Corky.

One day on the same grounds where the primary school was, just metres away from the great big church where Grumpy-old-priest and the others spread their brand and drank their wine, the boys' beloved ball became stuck high up in the gutter. Glapiac-once-Coppertop-not-yet-Searcher volunteered to climb the heights and retrieve it.

On the way back down, he slipped and fell, catching his foot on a sharp, rusty downpipe. It was alright, but he cut his big toe quite badly causing bleeding from *arsehole to breakfast time*, to use the lingo of the day. His best mate, Geronimo, and others were there. They'd been best mates since they were three.

Geronimo, whilst staring at the profuse bleeding, kept telling Glapiac-once-Coppertop he might have to have his leg amputated so he didn't die from gangrene, like his uncle had. (He was just a kid and so lacked medical knowledge. And death sounded delightfully extreme to him.) 'What?' Glapiac was way too sensitive for this and actually believed Geronimo. The mention of amputation was bad enough, but death?

Yes, Glapiac-Red truly believed he was going to die of gangrene and die very soon. And he'd be placed in a long timber rosewood box like Tippy his hero-dad was, in the big church right next door. Grumpy-old-drunk-priest would burn incense and say incantations and well, warn the Father in Heaven that another lowly soul who'd died too soon was coming back for His judgement …

They were laughing. All laughing. Laughing profusely. Oh my God, it was his best mate's older sister and he was lying there stark naked. Glapiac really did want to die now … of embarrassment that is. She had woken him up. He had fainted from either the sight of blood or the fear of dying from gangrene or both. As she woke him up, for some strange reason, he thought he was lying there as naked as a jaybird. It was funny, really funny—just not for young Glapiac.

Boys don't cry

'Boys don't cry.' That's what he was brought up with. He didn't even cry at his dad Tippy's funeral, nor did his Brave-brother because they were told they had to be *strong*. His grandad Pop (who actually sounded like Popeye when he talked) and his uncles were tough men. They loved a beer, and you've never seen a party like theirs. They consumed a venomous homebrew called, 'Parker's Panther's Piss.'

They had good hearts, but Coppertop kind of always felt sorry for the women—the aunties and so forth. They just seemed to bake cakes and talk politely whilst the men became progressively inebriated throughout the night. Those men turned happier and happier and louder and louder from a consumption of homebrew that would bring a bull down. They liked playing darts. Coppertop was anxious because there were always snotty-nosed children running around everywhere and he worried that one of them would wear a dart between their eyes sooner or later.

One of the pissed uncles missed the dartboard entirely and hit the wall; another hit a kid's arm. Coppertop innocently happened to tell his nana and the other women what had happened. He was just being *chatty*. When he returned to watch pissed uncles and fathers and grandfather playing darts, ole grandfather Popeye said, 'Ah well, *Tell tale tit, your tongue shall be split, and all the little dickie birds will come and have a bit.*'

Coppertop didn't really understand Popeye's poeticism, but he kind of got the impression that he had *dobbed in* the men to the women about the dart incidents, and well, let's face it, he was a lowly snitch. He felt small. It was awful, but you can't argue with the truth. 'Sometimes you just have to suck it up and realise when you're a fool,' he accepted as he grew up.

Uncle-Pirate-Pete was crazy. He was a chippy and those skills came in quite handy when he'd grab his saw, hammer and nails to prepare his ole black guitar for the oncoming family parties. It only ever had one string of fishing line on it, but in all the years Coppertop-later-Searcher would learn every style of music known, he never saw anyone play with such gusto and joy as his Uncle-Pirate-Pete. He would smile and sing and drink like he was the happiest man alive. And he was!

He'd merrily strum away on his one-stringed, patched-up guitar, his pride and joy, the *ole black bastard* he called it, and sing loud like a pirate! He called all of the young boys *champ* or *sport* but mostly *horse*, which somehow made them feel good or important or large. And he was always the last one standing.

Coppertop didn't really learn about *honour* for the longest time. These days, he would die for it, straight up. There is nothing more important to him, except *freedom*. But when you're just a kid, well it's a long road, isn't it?

He loved his little blue dragster bike more than anything in the world, apart from his family. He could *wheelie* it up the whole street because of its unusual centre of gravity and the small crank arms.

Young Coppertop kept leaving it outside, though. He just wouldn't learn. Daz the neighbour must have told Tippy how Coppertop kept leaving his blue bike in his rear-lane drive entry, and he was scared of running it over each afternoon when he returned from work, especially when it was dark.

Coppertop woke up. 'Where's my bike?' He couldn't find it. 'What's this?' He thought it was a bike, but all he really saw was a horrendous bundle of blue strapping, wrapped around and around his little blue. It took an eternity to remove it. It really did. He didn't know who or what did this. 'This is crazy!' he complained in childhood anger.

Lessons were taught differently back then. He never left his bike out again. Well, not for a long, long time. After Tippy had gone. However, he did lie. He kept getting tyre punctures on *little blue*. Tippy-Toes told him not to ride his bike up the other lane because there were nails lying everywhere. Coppertop ignored the advice or, perhaps caught up in child-bike bliss, just forgot. Nonetheless, he denied he rode up the lane. 'No, I didn't ride up that lane, Dad,' said Coppertop. Those would be the last words he'd ever say to his hero-dad. A lie!

Tippy was dead the next day, dying from a heart attack at age forty-two. Coppertop was eleven, and a liar. Flossie was sliced in two. Big twelve-year-old brother was brave; he stood on the veranda and shook the hands of all of the adults who visited that day and thanked them for coming to honour his dad. His sister, the little angel, was six, but she understood. Their hero had left this world and would not be coming back.

Kiki-dolphin

She wakes up every day smiling. Searcher doesn't understand how that's possible, but it's true. She is simple. It sounds derogatory to talk of wifey like that. Far from it. Even the Book of Books, which Grumpy-ole-drunk-priest liked to quote from, said, *'Unless you change and become like little children, you will never enter the kingdom of heaven.'*[1]

Childlike, not childish. She doesn't ask any deep questions or waste energy trying to figure things out. Life's too short. Many women are like that, actually. Wifey and Pookie-the-Searcher laugh at how he is like the whale diving deep, deep, looking for pearls of wisdom. And she is like the dolphin merrily swimming on the surface enjoying the sun and frivolity. It's not wrong to be deep. One is not better than the other, but he and Kiki just seemed to balance each other; together they iron out the creases.

Kiki says she can't be bothered searching for pearls but still wants to admire their beauty as long as *he* dives for them, and not her, and he *must* bring them back for her perusal. (That would come in handy one day in Kiki's future.) He loves her, although sure as hell doesn't deserve her. Far from it. It was a strange twist of fate that they met, and she stayed and hung around with Searcher whilst Searcher was busy searching and looking for *Searcher-the-Searcher*.

He kind of always believed an all-loving-force felt sorry for him and thus granted him the pleasure of spending his life with a real-live dolphin in human form. In the meantime, life happened, and Cyclone-Izzy and Rascal-Sam arrived and completed the package.

Kiki gets on with everyone but she's no shrinking violet. She's a *fire* sign, and yeah, she has fire. Someone needs to keep Searcher in check! Once in school, a bully was bullying another kid and Kiki told him to stop doing that. He said, 'Oh yeah, what are you going to do about it?' Well, little Kiki just whipped that bully's ass right there and then.

Bully's mother knocked on Kiki's door and accused *little* Kiki of being a *big* bully because she beat up her son who was three years older than Kiki and a damn sight bigger. Poor Kiki and her mum had to stand there and not laugh hysterically.

Years later, mother-of-Kiki was living with an alcoholic who was a large, cigar-smoking man with mental health issues. He was rich too, a big-wig manager of an entire shopping centre. One day he was having an episode. He tried to beat little Kiki into submission. She fought back for she was a *westie* chick and had learned from her brother, who took no prisoners back in the day.

Kiki used a steel vacuum cleaner pole to keep him at bay and fought hard and hit him back repeatedly. Fifteen years old and knee-high to a grasshopper. 'That's it,' she grabbed her bag and left. No money, no home, nothing. She jumped on the train and never looked back.

The Searcher

Kiki leaped onto the bed, right on top of Searcher. It was early on a Saturday morning and Ra was already blasting his glorious rays into the bedroom. Wifey wanted him to *Wake up now!* (As did he, during all of his searching.) There was life to live. 'C'mon.' However, Searcher had just had an epiphany.

Just the day before, Seeker had purchased an interface for his laptop that allowed him to record music. Along with it came some free software, and he was able to record orchestral music on his keyboard. Immediately upon commencing recording, he had ideas pouring through him like he was somehow thrown back into a renaissance time-loop. There was no sleep, just melody after melody after melody.

Strange, he was a rocker, or at least for most of his life. He had later gone on to learn the violin, cello, piano and lots of other instruments. He played in a bluegrass band and performed as a soloist and in duos. But this classical orchestral style? He didn't understand, but it just started flowing as soon as he purchased the recording equipment, which would turn it into an album.

Just as Kiki jumped onto him in the bed, the whole tune was there. Right there in his head. It was called *Creation* even then, before he had even uttered a sound. He could hear the lot. It was powerful, he knew it. Sadly, for Searcher-Gra, he also knew that in his lifetime, he would never produce a better piece. Sometimes you just *know* and know that you know.

Always the fool, Searcher would still waste time trying, though. They say the best songs come quickly and without effort. It's true. They come fast. *Creation* was like that. Searcher loved it. He felt humble, like it wasn't his to give, but his to receive. He hurriedly jumped out of bed and recorded a quick snippet of it. You don't want to lose something like that.

It was enough and he had captured it. Phew! Actually, it didn't change much at all from that first recording and was barely even edited. Friends and others loved it, or the album at least. Searcher later moved on and recorded two more albums of instrumental music: *Always and Ever* and *Glow*. He was able to add lead guitar to those. They're nice albums. He's proud of what he achieved. But *Creation*.

Well, there was something *special* about that tune. They even had it played at dear Flossie's funeral. Now that's saying something!

Scary girls

On his first day of kinder, Coppertop shit himself. No, not the fear type, he literally did *shit* himself. He was four, probably a bit freaked out and missing Mummy. He wouldn't have understood the toilet block system, or maybe those free little bottles of milk they dished out in those days, to make your bones strong did it. Yeah, all excuses.

Um, na, he just shit himself, although he didn't know it, he swears. Those older, scary girls on the big red double-decker bus, those five-year-olds, held their noses staring and pointing at the four-year-old stink-pot and said, 'He pooed his pants. Oh yuk! That's disgusting. Poo!' It was totally embarrassing. Girls were always scary to Coppertop-come-Searcher after then.

One day, five-year-old Pauline was sitting next to him in class when she swatted a fly, making quite a racket. Sister Penguin was infuriated. She asked Pauline if she'd made the noise. 'No, he did it, Sister,' pointing to Coppertop. Like what? He hadn't done anything. Coppertop was confused. He felt rage—young rage, but still rage. Sister Penguin blasted him all the way to Brazil and back. She hated little Coppertop from that day on, because he dared to try to defend himself and lie to her.

Now, why do we segregate boys from girls at school? Things were good in primary; Glapiac even had some girls as friends. When he had to go to the pious all-boys' Catholic high school—the one where the brothers got their kicks—well, girls just became alien to Red-Glapiac.

You know the feeling when you're desperately attracted to but also terrified of someone? He lost the ability to talk and communicate with the other sex. It was not healthy. Later, when he became a rocking guitarist, he made up for all that. Chicks were cool then and communicated in *other ways*.

The joy of soccer

Coppertop was a good soccer player, a very good one, although he had no talent. None! He was never blessed with raw talent for anything but tried hard at stuff until he became good at it. He was obsessed with the round ball and lived for that *kick and chase*. It was Grand-Final day, every boy's dream.

First half, he managed to whack one in the nets. We're ahead (1-0). He was Tiger! Tippy had put a sticker on his shirt that said: *I Come on Strong*. He didn't even know what it meant, but it worked like magic. Coppertop felt invincible that day (1-1). The best day of his life. 'We're gonna win, we're gonna win.' They were not particularly good as a team; it was a miracle they had even made it to the Grand Final at all (2-1).

Second half: the ball came screaming towards him. Coppertop was almost back at the halfway line and time was running out for the opposition.

He put his head down and shut his eyes and kicked that round ball like there was no tomorrow. It sailed high, and higher still. It went long. Even unto this day he feels sorry for the poor little goalkeeper. It floated just over his reach and into the back of the net. A freakish shot. It's all over (3-1). They won the GRAND FINAL! His life was forever complete.

Do you know, even the next year at training, Coppertop's coach would rave about his miraculous *goal* that sealed the deal for them, like he was a rare talent. Coppertop, however, never had the guts to be honest. It was a fluke and he knew it.

It *was* miraculous. He didn't even aim the ball. He just kicked it as hard as he could, and fate did the rest. Coppertop-Searcher felt like a fraud after that day and still does sometimes. He should have told the truth to fat-coach and everyone else and owned up to it. It was a simple fluke …

The whole family trudged all the way to Grafton for him to play in the northern NSW under-10s representative side. Sounded fancy—he felt important. They had round-robin games all day for two days. They stood there. It got hotter. They stood there. It got tiring. They stood there. Day one was over.

Young Coppertop-the-Tiger had not had a run yet. Day two. They stood there. It got hotter. They stood there. It got tiring. They stood there. It was getting late in the afternoon; the tournament was nearly over. Tiger felt embarrassed because he *wasn't good* enough to play with all the other boys who had come from all over the state.

Now he was a narcissistic kid and really only cared about himself, but at this particular event, he felt sorry for Tippy, Flossie and his brother and sister, embarrassed in fact. Of course, back then they were *Mum and Dad*. The family were not well off, this he understood. But imagine the money they had sacrificed for Coppertop to have his day in the sun.

Finally, those *men in power* gave young Coppertop a run for about five or ten minutes and then the event was all over. One of the parents had complained how it was cruel for the snotty-nosed mop-head kid to not even get a *run* on the field all weekend. The man told Tippy and Flossie later that it was because they didn't *fit in*. They didn't piss-up with all the rest of the crowd at night, hence they were ostracised. They weren't on the *in*.

Guess the family all learned something about human nature that day. Curiously, Coppertop remembers more of how bad his farts were in the back of the car going home. He thought it might have been due to the shiny new representative tracksuit pants that Mum and Dad had somehow managed to buy for him. Like they somehow trapped in the repulsive gases? Now, they were truly disgusting. Poor family!

Chapter 4

The wounded healer

Perhaps Searcher was drawn to healing because he wanted to heal himself. They call it *the wounded healer* syndrome. It's what motivates a lot of people to want to help others, because subconsciously, they want to be healed themselves.

But Searcher found it hard treating thousands of patients in the ambulance when something inside was coming apart. He'd give compassion and empathy to some who were, frankly, travelling much better than he was.

Seeker dabbled in many different healing modalities. He figured he had accrued about fifteen years of paramedic experience, had some understanding of Eastern and Western philosophies, and had a knack for music, all of which enhanced his sensitivity.

Holistic kinesiology sounded cool. Using muscle monitoring, crystals, essences, counselling, tuning fork therapy and so on was very interesting. It really grabbed him. It appeared to Searcher at least that all we need as people is to be *tuned up* once in a while, in order to maintain health and wellbeing—similar to tuning a piano.

He was never drawn to any *magic wand* type of energy healing where the therapist or healer was going to blast the client with some holy, pure energy and bam, their problems were over. No, healing had to come from *within*. Besides, if there is enough energy inside our single cells to power the whole of New York, why would one need more energy? Emmanuel said, *'The Kingdom of Heaven is within*

You!'[2] Searcher took that statement at face value; hence, at all costs, healing had to come from within.

His work colleagues called him *the witch doctor*. He liked the term, but it wasn't really meant as a compliment, more of a put-down. Eventually, Seeker would lose interest in kinesiology because he didn't like the complexity; it just had to be simple for him.

One professional kinesiologist whom Searcher was required to go to as part of his course spent most of his time looking up his reference books. Seeker-sometimes-Searcher felt like saying, 'Man, I'm here. Hey, over here!' The kinesiologist meant well, but he just wasn't really *there* for the client—or rather, *here*.

Bio-energy healing

Then came bio-energy healing—wow, that was way cool! You work on people's energy fields. The particular course he did was *chakra*-based. It goes like this. The seven main energy centres called the chakras, which follow along the spinal column, are considered to be like power-stations.

They are what Seeker calls *trans-receivers* of information and energy, both *transmitting* and *receiving* and thus connecting your non-physical self to your physical self. The meridians are like the high-voltage power*lines* that run from the chakras, the power stations, and on through the acupuncture/pressure points, which are like substations and metre boxes that feed your house: the body. Something like that at least.

Each chakra has an archetypal representation, an elemental representation and an evolutionary perspective, which basically relates to your life and where you are at, *now*. The chakras also radiate energy that either creates the aura, the bio-field if you prefer, or is at least synergistic with it.

The *aura*, the field around a person or any living thing, is not hard to see, in fact. One should avoid trying too hard to focus, as a relaxed way of seeing is more conducive to seeing. When the beginner gazes past the person rather than straight at them, it appears as a *heat haze*.

In bio-energy therapy, the therapist learns to stimulate these chakras, or energy vortices, and attempts to clear and innervate them. The student is taught how people's energy fields are like traffic. If you have a traffic jam anywhere in your field, the blockage of energy would back-up and eventually cause *dis-ease*, life stagnation, depression and so forth.

The therapist rarely ever physically touches the client, working in the electromagnetic spectrum instead. It was quite fascinating to see a client lean and bob around when the therapist was perhaps three or four metres away from them.

It was in Costa Rica that Searcher-Red learned about bio-energy. The teacher was good. He was like a wizard, and boy, was he charismatic. He knew his stuff and had healed himself of some pretty bad shit. He stood behind Searcher. Evidently, he was working on the rear of Searcher's heart chakra. Four students were being worked on at a time by the wizard and his assistants, whilst the other students waited in silence in the hall of *Silencia*.

Something was happening. Something was releasing. 'God, I'm going to explode,' Seeker anticipated. He held his mouth as he didn't want to create a scene. He was an Aussie, after all—basically, no fuss people. There were a lot of Americans present and they were very expressive.

'Jesus. This is terrible, I'm going to explode.' He didn't. He kind of held it in but was making lots of snorting noises. Loud snorting. It was funny. Hilarious! Whatever the wizard had done, was explosively funny. Everything was funny. Life was so funny. Searcher could see laughing, smiling Buddhas everywhere, laughing their fat man-tits off.

'How does he know? How does the teacher, the wizard, know of this secret to happiness? Why does he not advertise this?' thought Seeker. 'Those Buddhas are hysterical!' It was just so funny. He wondered if wizard would share this secret with him. Searcher would ask him if he got the opportunity, and maybe the searching would end for Searcher.

He laughed for hours on end. He tried to hide it; he really did. You don't want to look like a fool in front of all those confident

Americans. At the break, he went out to the toilet. A woman, a purple-clothed, crystal-wearing, incense-smelling spiritualist, grabbed him as he came out. Everyone thought Searcher had been crying instead of laughing. They saw this poor Aussie guy, body shaking and reeling, snorting and contorting, having a real bad time of it. 'Is he crying like a baby?'

It seems that crying and laughing can sound the same, especially when loud, evocative music is blasting from the rafters. Anyways, new-age-spirit-one, without permission, grabbed Seeker and placed her hand on his heart and tried to *heal* him of his pain which had made him cry so. She felt sorry for him. She was an e*mpath!*

Seeker was so lucky to be surrounded by all those amazing people. Spirit lady was invoking the angelic light beings to soothe his poor weary soul. Now if you think Kiki and her mother had a hard time trying not to laugh at cry-baby-bully's mum calling *little* Kiki a *big* bully, then you have no idea! This was unbearable. Almost cruel.

How could he, now older Coppertop-come-Glapiac-come-Redmond-come-Gra-come-Searcher-come-depressive-son-of-a-bitch-come-Pookie-come-father-of-Cyclone-and-Rascal-come-Sounje, who just had his heart chakra messed around with by a real-life wizard and subsequently saw a thousand Buddhas laughing their fat man-tits off, supposed to not laugh in spirit-empath-lady's face?

It was awful, just awful. Later he did get a chance to talk to the wizard and ask him about the secret to happiness, which he had kindly bestowed on him. Wizard looked at Searcher quizzically; he had no idea what heart-chakra-boy was talking about.

Tragic loss

Flossie's niece had gone. She was the most delightful woman you could ever meet. It was aggressive. The medical-gods did all they could and were compassionate and kind. However, they would not remove those stethoscopes. To do so would be to admit to the world they did not have all the answers—that, sometimes, all attempts to save someone are like *pissing in the wind.*

Delightful-one looked to Flossie for inspiration during her last days because Flossie was also fighting her own battle and had fought it for a long, long time, but Delightful-one's was more rapid. She even made a video for the medical-gods just before her journey to the great-beyond-of-no-time-and-place and thanked them for all they had done. In the video, Delightful-one suggested perhaps they might consider other methods or approaches rather than just cutting everything out and hoping for the best or killing everything with poisonous chemicals—everything!

False hope doesn't help. Flossie was almost gone too, although the ole battler somehow managed to make it to the Delightful-one's funeral. Flossie was way past palliative even. By this stage, she struggled to move or eat a morsel, take a sip of water or even walk, and had wasted away to a shadow. All knew Flossie should have definitely died six months prior when compassionate-and-friend-paramedic took her away in the ambulance.

Flossie loved her sweet, delightful niece. Delightful-one's husband had just lost the love of his life. Childhood sweethearts, soulmates, were they.

But this man, he's a big man, whilst at the wake for his dear wife, crouched down onto his knees and sensitively held his fragile auntie's hand, Flossie's, to console her. The worst day of his life for sure, yet still he managed to give care and compassion to a dying woman. Now that's something!

Searcher had never seen Grumpy-old-priest or Insolent-young-priest show such sensitivity, empathy or compassion. Not even a hint of it. Guess they were too far up and close to male-God-in-the-sky; way too high up to kneel down at brave Flossie's feet like Bear-nephew did. Kiki and Searcher went home. They cried like babies that day, every time they thought of brave Cousin-Bear and how he treated Flossie during his darkest day on earth ...

Devil-rash

Glapiac-later-Searcher gave up soccer and that was a bad decision. As a kid he was often a follower. All his mates were playing rugby league because it was *tougher* than soccer, more *manly;* so he transferred to that code. He was too scrawny, either because poor Flossie struggled to feed him or due to genetics.

Either way, or both, he tried hard at *football*, the oval-shaped kind. Glapiac was a tiger and gave it everything. One day his team travelled south to Sydney to play in a variety of games and competed well. The two coaches noticed how the young tiger, Glapiac, as they called him back then, liked to have a go.

So, instead of playing him out on the wing or fullback where all scrawny kids played, they decided to put him in the second row. Gee, he loved that. Mixing it up with the big boys, tackling like a wild animal, shoving in the scrums, and punching the poor hooker from the opposite team in the face. Back then, the hooker couldn't really release their arms in a scrum, so it was open-slather; woohoo! They headed home. He felt six-foot tall. The coaches had seen something in him that he had not: guts.

'What? What's this? Shit!' A rash developed all over Glapiac's body. This was a serious dark red-purplish rash, welted all over. 'Oh! This is insane. SO ITCHYYYY.' It was probably an allergic reaction to the grass on the football fields. By the time he arrived home it looked startling.

Flossie-Mum drove him straight up to the local hospital. There was a bit of urgency, or at least some concern in the air. They took him to a room and said they needed to give him a needle in the buttocks, which would make him feel better in no time; it was adrenaline no doubt.

The medicos looked him straight in the eyes and said, 'This won't hurt a bit.'

'OUCH!! That bloody hurt so much! God that hurt, you lying bastards,' yelled Glapiac. He was no doubt way too tense; it hurts all the more if you are. Nonetheless, adults really shouldn't lie to children. They're not as naïve as one assumes, and boy, they never forget. Glapiac never forgot Tippy-Dad's mate's promise to give him a camera he had used and brought back from the Vietnam War. Coppertop wanted that more than anything in the world. It never came.

'Sometimes big people lie.' Now this is a familiar story, for when Izzy-daughter was just four years of age, a dentist told her she would have to give her a needle, so as to pull her tooth out. She said it *wouldn't hurt a bit!*

'OHHHHHHH! YOU LIED!' Little-breeze-Izzy had just shown her cyclone-self and in no uncertain terms let the dentist know she was a liar, straight up!

The rash stayed. It must have been sent by the guy down below who loves fires; it sure felt like it to Coppertop-now-Glapiac-come-second-rower. So, the medical-gods told him they needed to give him another injection. 'Pig's ass, they will!' They held him down. He fought. He was a rugby-Gladiator now. He had just played *second row* for the Bulldogs.

'Just lie still,' shouted the doctor.

'No way,' replied Glapiac.

'Stop it, you little bastard!'

'Screw you.' A neighbour fellow of Glapiac's saw what was going on and came to the rescue. After all, the rash did look like it'd come from Hellfire-boy. He sat on top of Glapiac using all of his beer-fat weight. The medicos kept recruiting help, but Coppertop, who was strong, bizarrely strong and wiry, gave one last explosive shove to all his captors who went flying, and off he went running down the hospital corridor like a crazed animal.

Carl Lewis wouldn't have caught him that day. Coppertop ran from the place where he would much later *out-of-body* visit; the place where he, brother and sister had entered from the great-beyond; the place where both Tippy and later Flossie would fly *to* the great-beyond from, and he never damn-well looked back.

He ran across the road and into the quarry running furiously, around the dirt-bike circuit where he would later snap his arm at right angles on a gnarly motorbike, away from the cemetery where Tippy-Toes lay and home to await his fate. He would either die from devil-rash, or Flossie would kill him. Either way, he would die free— free from lies and needles.

However, nothing happened. Flossie must have seen the funny side of it because it was never mentioned again; besides, the rash left, returning no doubt to the marshmallow-toasting Hellfire-boy from down below.

A daunting haunting

Searcher was an ambulance trainee, green around the gills. He hadn't seen much at all. He was green. Very green. As green as the Amazonian forest once was.

She was confused. 'You're going to a confused lady,' said the controller. They entered the residence. There were two ladies and a bunch of children, aged from maybe six to eleven.

'Strange … why are these children all up and awake at two in the morning?' Searcher pondered.

The trainee mostly does the treatment of patients in order to gain the experience. Searcher did the basics: blood pressure and heart-rate reading, blood sugar level, ECG. All seemed fine. *Lady A* explained how *Lady B* had been confused and acting strangely for weeks.

The kids appeared Terrified with a capital T. 'Hmm, strange. It does feel weird in here, creepy,' Searcher thought to himself. They searched and probed with question after question, both the useless-green-inexperienced-paramedic-Searcher and trainer-Gilligan. The children were very tense. Partner-Gilligan was a sceptic through and through. Black and white! 'Fine. We need scepticism here,' thought Searcher.

Finally, *Lady A* fessed up how *Lady B* had been involved in strange activities with the children of late. She was very worried. *Lady B*, who'd been compliant but sombre up until then, disappeared into the bedroom. *Lady A* disclosed that the children had gotten involved in a *séance* weeks ago. 'Oh, this is woo-woo!' sensed Searcher.

Evidently, it started out innocently enough, but then turned sinister all of a sudden. *Lady B* became involved with the children and from that point onwards, acted strangely, very strangely. Actually, things just felt offbeat to Searcher-Ambo. 'What is it about this house?' He couldn't shrug the mysterious feeling. 'Someone's watching me. Stop it, you idiot, get a grip on yourself. This is a professional job.'

Then the children talked. And talk they did. They were telling Searcher-once-Coppertop and sceptic-trainer-Gilligan about how the lights had been spontaneously turning on and off; the air conditioner randomly turning on and off; fans rotating without cause; things moving by themselves; and a heavy electric wheelchair had been spinning around and around. Lady A confirmed their allegations.

One child showed his wrist; he apparently kept bleeding from the *stigmata* region, which the god-people loved to talk about. Searcher just saw red dots and marks there. The other children concurred with the bleeding story. They also said a *ghost* had been telling them certain information pertaining to the whereabouts of a sixteen-year-old girl who had been presumed dead and murdered.

Hmm? *Lady A* confirmed all of this and more. Not once, not once did any of the children laugh or snigger. Truly, they were scared to the bone. Truth be told, so was Searcher. Sceptic-trainer-Gilligan decided to ring the coordination centre. Searcher-Gra would never forget him saying, 'Ah frankly, this woman is possessed, what should we do?'

Those words cut right through Seeker-Searcher because he needed Gilligan to stay sceptical. Searcher was the open-minded-astral-travelling-weirdo who was later called *Astro-boy* in the mines. 'Don't say that, Gilligan,' he thought to himself. He needed to stay calm somehow.

Moaning. Moaning. Oh, she was moaning. It sounded like an orgasm—multiple. She came from the bedroom dressed in a silky white nightie and stared at Searcher; he stared back at her. *Lady A* proceeded to tell them how, frankly, the ghost was having its way with *Lady B;* the mother of some of those poor, terrified yet still awake children.

'Jeez, this is weird.' When they first heard a little of this woo-woo saga, Searcher-come-paramedic was joking around with *Lady A* and saying things like, 'Why didn't you call the ghost-busters? Why call us?' For some reason, he stopped doing that. He could sense something, and it was ominous!

Searcher had been on spiritual retreats, meditated, opened the kundalini, spun the chakras and all that stuff, and wasn't completely unprepared for weird shit, but it just felt dark in there. He needed fresh air as he couldn't breathe and desperately wanted to leave. 'This job sucks,' he murmured to himself.

Those poor children were predominately on his mind, however. *Lady B* was in the toilet down the corridor to the right. Suddenly, she ran out wailing and shrieking like the wicked witch of the west and bolted straight past the fearful paramedic men. Then, a toilet roll decided to come out of the restroom all by itself, turned left and unravelled all the way as it passed them, like it had a mind of its own.

It was a bizarre sight, and Searcher will never forget it as long as he lives. Yeah, this must be hard to believe. He would have thought you were on drugs too if you told him this rubbish, and he's pretty open to weird stuff; although he never really had a choice since he first spring-boarded like a jet out of his body all those years before.

It went on far too long. You see, paramedics had an unofficial rule that about twenty minutes on scene was enough for them to perform any medical interventions and prepare for the transportation of the patient. He and Gilligan had been there for an hour and twenty minutes.

Searcher-once-guitar-rocker asked himself, 'I wonder what Co-Ord are thinking we're up to? How come they haven't rung or called on the radio to ridicule us or send us on our way?' Then, finally, a call transmitted on the radio. Phew! The two freaked-out paramedics had a chest pain case to attend to, right around the block, which took precedence. 'Thank God!'

Seeker had already suggested that *Lady A* should try to take *Lady B* up to the hospital to get a mental health assessment and perhaps some sedation. *Lady A* just knew *Lady B* would not agree to that. So, he said perhaps they could visit a god-man. Grumpy-old-priest was still practising, but in another diocese far away. He would have been great, because his filthy alcohol breath would have sent that wicked-sexed-up-ghost packing for sure.

The Searcher

'But,' Searcher advised, 'they can't just come to your house doing exorcisms and so forth like the movies, without full consultation with the Vatican.' He didn't know why or how he knew that; no doubt he'd watched too many scary movies in the 1980s, that weird Seeker-come-Astro-boy.

Not-so-sceptical-Gilligan and Searcher-Gra said goodbye to the kids, God love 'em, and proceeded to exit that eerie place. Seeker carried the old-fashioned stainless-steel oxy viva out. However! Alas, even though *Lady B and sexed-up ghost* had been enjoying themselves immensely in the bedroom for some time now, she/he/they decided to see him to the door. Somehow she/he/they knew the two paramedic men were leaving.

How sweet! Don't you just love a *good host*, um rather, a *good ghost*? In the scariest, guttural, deep and primal voice he'd ever heard, she/he/they said: 'YOU'RE SCARED OF ME, AREN'T YOU! HA-HA-HA-HA-HA-HA-HA-HA-HA-HA!'

He was Coppertop. He was Tiger. He was Tippy's son, you dark-ass-ghost-fucker-shit-knob-scumbag-pussy-dwelling-blight-on-existence!

'*NO. I'M NOT FUCKING SCARED OF YOU AT ALL!*' he yelled at the dark one.

He looked into those foreign and vacant eyes for what seemed like an eternity; he was inches away. No, closer.

Had he peed his pants? It felt like it. Maybe he had shit himself like four-year-old Coppertop had done on his first day of school. He thought of Sceptic-brother-come-Callithumpian. 'Even he'd be scared right now, and he doesn't believe in any of this shit.'

Oddly, in that instant of no-time, his mind flashed back to childhood. Their dog Sabre-tooth-Tiger affectionately called *Sabre* for short, was a beautiful and loyal chocolate-brown Kelpie, and the family just loved him. One day he was run over by a truck around the corner, and it was bad. He'd had all his legs broken, among other injuries. Blood was pouring out of his mouth as he tried to crawl home to his loved ones, his family, and with badly broken legs. Brother-of-Seeker was advised of their poor dog's condition.

Now, Brother-later-Callithumpian was a child, but he was a brave sucker. Recall the day when Tippy flew back to the great-beyond and young Brave-brother shook hands with all the adults on the balcony and thanked them for coming and honouring his dad Tippy's life. He was twelve.

Well, now feeling like the man of the house, he grabbed that damn heavy riffle and put a bullet in the poor dog's head to put him out of his misery and then buried him. They didn't have a vet nearby back then and, regardless, probably didn't have a brass-razoo to pay for one, once Tippy's candle had been snuffed out. Courageous-brother did the most compassionate, yet difficult thing, you'd ever have to do. It was love—but brutal for both dog and master.

Yes, he was a brave sucker. One night he came to see Brother-Redmond's rock band. Suddenly, Goliath himself entered the building and decided to run amok, kicking the guitars and drums off the stage and giving the boys a hard time. Brave-brother grabbed hold of Goliath around his neck from behind and put him in a headlock. He was abruptly levitated. Goliath was twice his size! If it wasn't so serious you'd think it was the funniest thing you'd ever seen.

Goliath was swinging Brave-brother around like a possum hanging off his neck, and Brave-brother's legs must have collected and smashed almost every item in the pub. Wisely, he didn't let go of that grizzly bear, not until the cops arrived and that was not a minute too soon. He must have just known that had he let go, it was all over, red rover. Goliath would have pulverised his bones and sprinkled them on his cereal for breakfast.

You see, it wasn't so much those *guttural words*, which matched very well those of Linda Blair of *The Exorcist* movie, it was more the accompanying *feeling*, which can't be described so easily. Seeker-Searcher-Gra was sensitive, very sensitive. And this saga had all felt dark, ominous and sinister from the start.

As trainer-Gilligan walked to the ambulance vehicle, Searcher stood and confronted she/he/they.

Just like how he imagined Greek-God-the-giant assessed how he was gonna swim out and save young Coppertop's life from the dragging and tugging hungry mother-ocean—no doubt taking his time, not hastily rushing in like a young bull—Searcher stood strong.

'*Go to hell, mother fucker,*' was his parting shot. It was over. They had to rush off to the man with chest pain around the corner.

Deep down you know, Searcher didn't believe that the motherfucker-ghost was dark or evil. Searcher was caught up in the drama. The ghost was probably just a lost soul—dark by ignorance. There's plenty of that around on earth in any case, so it's not difficult to grasp. If you walk into a dark room, what do you do? You turn the light on. Same, same with lost souls. But let's not spoil the narrative with clarity…

It was over. They had to rush off to the man with chest pain around the corner and were really toeing the line by now. Searcher said, 'Go to hell,' but just like the badass ghost, he didn't believe in Hellfire-boy and his fiery-hellish home, you know. No-one in the history of all time has ever seen Hellfire-boy, it seemed. Perhaps someone just made him up so people would fear him and turn towards God—at least, that's what Searcher believed. But Searcher was worried that if someone eventually did catch up with Hellfire-boy to *chew the fat,* so to speak, Hellfire-boy might actually need to express his feelings.

He may be sensitive too! Perhaps he's a woman or a cross-dresser. Perhaps he has emotional hang-ups and requires some help. He might have oddities and foibles that he needs to address in order to move back up through the sacred realms, back up to the angelic land of the Living Light whence he came, where all have wings and play trumpets and harps.

'Let's all give Hellfire-boy-from-down-below a break once in a while,' Searcher joked. In fact, even St Pope John Paul II publicly announced in 1999 how images of hell presented in scripture must be correctly interpreted. He believed hell, rather than being a *place*, indicated the *state* of those who separate themselves from God, the source of all life.[3] To Searcher, that was impossible anyway because God is life. How can one be separated from life, other than ideologically?

Word got out. They were the laughing-stock of the region. The local paramedics laughed hard. Even black-and-white-sceptic-ambo copped it, poor fellow. Gilligan should have stayed sceptical. They neither got a lot of sleep the next night. Peculiarly, Seeker didn't mind the ridiculing jokes. It felt better having no-one believe the weird case, anyhow. It kind of lightened it all up …

Later. Years later. Thirteen years later, actually, a colleague handed a local newspaper to jaded-paramedic-once-Searcher. Some lady was pictured on the front page with a *man-of-the-cloth*. She was talking about her troubled lady friend and how a *young paramedic* years before had advised her to go see a god-man to help her friend from an apparent demonic possession.

'Guess the kids got through it after all,' Seeker thought. He was so relieved that he felt tears well up. These days, he doesn't think of Sexed-up-ghost much at all. Maybe ole Hellfire-boy-from-down-below burned up that Mother-fucker-Sexed-up-ghost and will continue doing so for an eternity and more, down in his eternal damnation fire. And thank *God* for that!

Chapter 5

Rebel with a cause

Although Redmondo-Searcher ate crap food, he was a vegetarian. These days they'd call him a *dirty vegetarian* because not eating meat has nothing to do with good health. The boys were rockers, a four-piece: two guitars, bass, drums and vocals. Actually, all of them had turned *vego*. They were rebels *with* a cause and wanted to conquer the world.

Their *material* was good; really good. It wasn't straight four-by-four like everything else you'd hear. It was groovy, groovy rock; yet still, it was solid. They gave it everything they had and more live. Chisel and others had laid it all down for them. They'd done the grind, carved the route!

There's nothing better than honest rock music, especially when it's based on live performances in sweaty, stinking packed-out Aussie pubs. They wrote about strange topics, though: *Hollow Earth* (have we been lied to; is the earth really solid?), *Ghost* (Seeker being the ghost; out of the body), *Dear John* (Gilbert's best mate talks to him through psychic hands from beyond the grave). They were great times, although they were very peculiar rebels those young rockers.

Kiki liked to wear florally clothes with bright, vibrant colours. She would tag along sometimes down to the *Cross* in Sydney. Everyone wore black in the 90s. In Kings Cross it was depressing, dark and dank. Kiki would come to the gigs in her bright clothes. She didn't fit in, but she didn't give a damn either. Searcher always felt she brought light into those dingy nightclubs for she was a ray of sunshine, just like his sister. Anyone would describe her as such.

One time they played their original music at a festival. It was an open-air concert for bikies and drug lords (correction: bikie-drug-lords). They drove in through the main gate as Kiki tagged along in her casual bright clothes and thongs, sucking on her lollypop. The helicopters were landing, no doubt carting the drugs in.

It was packed. 'Shit, this place is a law unto itself,' Red was thinking. 'Mad bastards.' It was out of control. The crowd thought they were at Woodstock and were up for it. During the set, Kiki stood up the back where the sound man was set up.

Whilst soloing, Redmond was watching innocent Kiki sucking on her lollypop thinking, 'Oh my God, this is the last time I will ever see my cherub again. She'll disappear into drug land with drug lords.' But ignorance is bliss and she made it through unscathed.

Another time, Kiki stood by at a band-room, as pregnant as a seal, belly protruding. Red was competing in a band competition and lots of girls were going in and out. Older and now wiser, Kiki said to them with hand on tummy, 'Careful, girls, this is what happens when you stand here.'

Redmondo played in his first band at seventeen. They had played up north at a large, famed nightclub. He must have gotten excited and drank too much beer. They weren't paid much back then, and so had to stay in tents. After the gig, the band boys arrived back at the tents and asked if he wanted a hamburger. 'Yeah, I'll have one with the works, thanks, boys,' Redmond said with a slur.

It's now daytime. 'Um ... What? My ass feels weird. Full. Have I shit myself again like infant schoolboy Coppertop did? No, I haven't. Oh boy. What's this?' The sun was blistering, already blaring through the tent. It was so hot. 'What's in my bloody pants? Oh no. You bastards!' He got his hamburger all right. Don't you just love that Aussie psyche?

Another time, he played at a maximum-security prison. It was arguably the tensest gig he'd ever performed at. Not a pin drop could be heard between songs, which just added to the intensity. Those three boys, Macda, Wal and Red, absolutely laid it down for

The Searcher

Francine, the vocalist. She sang like a bird and was cute. Red was worried for her safety and as they entered through security, he asked the prison guard to, 'Take care of her.'

The guard casually turned to Redmond and said, 'Her? She's got nothing to worry about, mate. It's you who has something to worry about in here.'

Years and years later Redmondo-now-paramedic would pick a patient up from that same prison. On the way over to the hospital in the back of the ambulance, the patient kept staring at Searcher, so Searcher-paramedic asked him if he was alright. The man casually said, 'Yeah, but I really want to lop your head off with a machete.' He was schizophrenic. He liked Redmond-Gra but not in a particularly constructive way it seemed.

Back to the meat-eating topic. Searcher's friend Dalefin advised him to see a naturopath. Searcher said to Handsome-naturopath and Sexy-as-hell-assistant-in-jumpsuit, 'I am a vegetarian, I don't eat meat.'

'That's alright.' Natural-doctor explained to Gra-once-Coppertop-also-Searcher that he would no doubt be lacking in certain nutrients which only *blood food* could give him. He indeed would most certainly have to take some supplements.

'Yeah sure, as long as they are not made from any meat products.' Red was a die-hard.

'No, no way. I wouldn't do that to you,' says Natural-doctor-man. Sexy-as-hell-assistant-in-jumpsuit prepared his suggested supplements. Later that night Redmond was dreaming.

'Oh, yuk. This is a weird dream. Yuk!' He was dreaming he was eating raw liver with blood running down his arms. Meat eaters no doubt wouldn't like to eat raw liver, but for a vego, it was particularly gross. He woke up and got out of bed. It was the middle of the night. Redmond-now-rock-guitarist walked downstairs and for some strange reason looked at the supplement that Sexy-as-hell-assistant-in-jumpsuit had prepared, and sure enough, it was made from liver extract. 'Thanks, guys,' he said to himself.

Years later, after five years of avoiding the chomping up of his fine two- and four-legged friends, he ate a Big Mac. It was a Friday in Lent. Catholics weren't supposed to eat meat on Fridays in Lent. It made him feel like a rebel of sorts. Incidentally, one fine night Kiki-dolphin had a dream too. She heard a voice say, *'If it's feathers, fur or fin, it's not going in!'* She too was a vego …

The big shit weekend

It was a yoga retreat. They were to *clean their pipes* out. The process probably had a yogic name, but the students just called it the *big shit weekend*. They would stay at a mansion with a giant pool at the rear. It was very relaxing. Small canopy tents were set up to allow for multiple and simultaneous *evacuations*. The young attractive women were quite liberal, walking around the pool stark naked.

It was here Seeker first learned that when a woman is naked she appears so natural there really is nothing to look at, as it's not suggestive of anything. Anyways, it was time to go to task, or go to town, you might say. Yoga instructor Angelo told them they must drink two glasses of warm salty water, and then perform a few simple dynamic yogic postures to loosen everything up. Then one would repeat the process.

Sooner or later, the student would need to go to the makeshift toilets and fast. Gradually as more and more salty water was consumed, a passing from the rear ensued, which became progressively watery in nature. Some unhealthy students struggled in pain whilst they maintained the tasks. If things down below were not budging, it caused great discomfort.

Mostly, people were young and healthy so eventually things were flowing from their rears like Niagara Falls. Searcher made a bad blunder, however. He thought he'd let out a sneaky fart but was surprised to see it dripping down his legs. The students exploded in laughter as well as in *other ways*.

Everyone continued until what came out of their behinds was as clear as crystal. Then their big shit journey was said to be over; their pipes were clean!

The remainder of the time they were to eat kitcheree, a sort of Ayurvedic baby food, so as to be gentle on their digestive system.

Now, all of this most certainly sounds quite bizarre, except for one interesting point. For Searcher at least, he never in his whole life felt better in the body than after that yoga retreat. He was brimming with energy, barely needed sleep, and his mind for once in his life felt as sharp as a tack!

Now, yoga instructor Angelo was an interesting guy. He was Italian-born, and was a big stocky, happy fellow with thick, long, wavy hair. He had gone to university, but was more interested in yoga, gunja and women; reverse that order if you will. He would join a yogic ashram, and, in fact, because of his intimidating size, would perform security, especially when his particular ashram had detectives and media crawling all over it during a drama of a sexual nature.

Normally speaking, when one joins an ashram, one has to relinquish all of one's possessions to the organisation. In return, one gets to live at any ashram of that organisation in the world, and for the rest of their lives. They would have to do *seva,* which is a selfless type of work to contribute to the ashram, but they would not have to pay ongoing fees. So it worked out just fine for instructor Angelo, except for one thing.

His loving parents had bought their beautiful son, who had never worked a day in his life because he was somewhat of a professional university student, a brand new 4WD car. And it was his shiny new car and other things that his loving parents had bought for him that he would donate to the ashram as part of a renunciation of sorts. They were none too pleased and decided not to talk to him again.

But Angelo was having a blast of a time. Occasionally, he would return to living in the world, which was allowed. He truly loved his silky, royal scarlet, satin bed sheets as he attracted many fine young ladies into his impressive love den. Seeker really liked Angelo, but he had just one issue with him and eventually told him so.

Instructor Angelo liked to sponge off people for accommodation, food and other things; after all, he was a yogi and it should be their honour to care for him. Once, after Angelo had stayed with he and Kiki free of charge, Seeker loaned his road bicycle to him to help him get around, and thereafter, didn't see it for months.

When Pantz, Pearl and Fatty wanted Seeker to enter a team triathlon event with them, Seeker was without a bike. He searched everywhere for it. Eventually, he found it at the university. It had been locked to a tree for months on end and, having been exposed to the elements, was now very rusty, but would suffice for the race. In time, Seeker confronted Yogi-Angelo, who admitted he had left the bike there long ago.

Searcher said, 'Angelo, you are a yogi and a spiritualist. You are a nice guy, friendly, popular and colourful. But, mate, true spiritualism is not all about raising your kundalini and doing your pranayams. It's about *right action*. You don't just borrow a bike from someone who loaned it to you in good faith and fucking dump it out in the elements.

'Also, you don't just stay with people without contributing with food or in some other ways. You do the right thing, mate. It's not hard. They're called *principles*, and they go a long way. As far as your kundalini movements will, actually.'

One of Yogi-Angelo's friends and students was Dravid. He was the sweetest, most peaceful and loving guy Searcher had ever met. His smile was the smile of the Buddha. He looked like he had just meditated on happiness for the last one-thousand lifetimes, or at least it appeared that way. Until Searcher got to know him that is.

In fact, Dravid was a *hopper*. A consummate hopper. He was as mad as a cut snake and totally obsessed with girls. Initially, Searcher tried to engage him to see how it was that he was so happy all the time. He asked what had brought him to yoga and expected an inspirational reply. Dravid replied, 'Yoga? Yoga? What is that? I just go where the girls are, man. I go to Christian churches and fellowships and Buddhist retreats. I go to art functions, clubs and committees, basically, anywhere where there's girls.'

He even showed Seeker some of his artworks, which he and a damsel had been creating. They simply threw lots of water-colour paints onto a giant canvas on the floor and rolled around together, butt naked, doing the hanky-panky. Dravid enthusiastically tried to point out the shape of her melons on the canvas, but Searcher couldn't make them out. It was called art, and people unknowingly paid good money for it.

Dravid later worked in boring laboratories with Searcher, and he was altogether frustrating. More than once, Searcher wanted to throttle peaceful-yoga-disciple-Dravid. He would never perform his work tasks but instead, with an oversized smile, started every single damn conversation with, 'And she said …' He was obsessed, lost in a dream world of madness and women, or women and madness—*madwomness* or *wo-madness*.

Ole Hobie

It was a 16-foot Hobie racing cat, yellow and sleek. Pearl, the husband of beautiful-darling-blonde-sister-of-Seeker, and one-day-come-flight-paramedic-extraordinaire, had just purchased it. He put grip-tape all over the sleek, fast-looking catamaran. However, the mongrel had cheaped-out. Instead of getting the proper stuff, he'd bought tape from a hardware store that was as gritty as Hellfire-boy's acid tongue. His hapless recruits would pay the price for that.

Alas, those cats are slippery suckers, so you need something for grip, just as a surfer needs wax. It was windy and rough. Too rough. A wise and sensible onlooker warned them, 'It's coming from the south. The cyclonic winds are heading east across the Nullarbor and turning north straight toward us. It's stupid. Don't do it.'

But they were fools! They'd barely sailed before. Pearl had sailed only once, although he didn't know jack shit really. Compared to Searcher, however, he was an expert. They needed weight. Lots of weight to hold her down against Mother Nature's dished-up cyclonic winds from the north-west. There was Seeker-Gra, Pearl-the-skipper, and the Fatman. Evidently, he wasn't fat enough.

Kiki was it! She came to complement the three fools, who wouldn't listen to good advice, in order to add some weight.

'Jump on, let's go,' said Skipper-Pearl hastily. Off they proceeded sailing, straight into a mighty storm that turned the great lake into an ocean of sorts.

'Lifejackets. What are they for? This is fast.' Phew, they were flying. They *were* actually meant to be going fast for it was a racing-cat after all. They managed to make it to the south shore, far enough to tack back northward, and survived the manoeuvre, somehow. Woo hoo! Now it starts. 'Hang on!' She really took off, the ole Hobie.

Unexpectedly and without warning, Skipper-Pearl decided it was a really good time for some boat maintenance. He reckoned the left rear rudder was loose or something and jumped off the back and started swearing and cussing at that damn rudder, yanking it like hell.

'Umm. Fatty,' Seeker-Gra said.

'What?' says Fatman.

'Our beloved Skipper-Pearl is no longer on board. He has vanished.' They had left him behind somewhere back in the storming, raging lake. In almost an instant they could not even see him. Now, there was a small problem. Seeker-Gra and Kiki had no idea how to sail a racing catamaran, or anything like it. They didn't even know how to *tack*.

Fatman had sailed before sporadically, although one would not think so on this day, or he was simply out of his depth.

Before Skipper-Pearl abruptly disappeared, he'd barked advice on how to skin the cat, to sail her, but they just seemed to do all the wrong things. He had enlisted morons. The cyclone lake, well, she was just loving this scenario. They could almost hear the laughter from the depths below. She whipped it up real good.

Kiki, who was useless, for she's as light as a feather, looked grey, could barely swim, and probably was thinking how it had been a good life up until that point. What would Gra-once-Coppertop tell her mother? Those damn cyclonic winds were getting more ferocious. Fatman and he were struggling, trying to suss it all out. It was useless without Skipper-Pearl's weight, strength and limited know-how and they were, hence, vulnerable out there.

Finally, the sleek-cat tipped them up and up and up and … over they went, projected at warp speed. Overturned Hobie cat was blowing away from them fast. The three were immediately scattered. The wind was howling. 'Kiki? Where's Kiki?' Kiki was somewhere but they had to get to that damn Hobie. First thing's first, they had their priorities in order.

The Searcher

Pearl was a scary man and big and strong. They'd rather die out there in the angry cyclonic lake than take on big Skipper-Pearl. He's an intimidating man. The three stupid young men could swim proficiently. They, and a goose called Scooter, who was fortunate indeed to not be a part of this debacle, because he most certainly was a part of every other one, had recently received their surf-bronze medallions.

The assessor said the surf was too big that day, dangerous in fact. However, Coach-Lavofin-lifeguard would have none of it. He said, 'My boys will handle it. Don't worry. I'll swim out with them.' It was tough for Scooter and Searcher-Gra, but big Skipper-Pearl and Fatty could swim like fish and licked it up.

Scooter and Searcher-Gra had only just scrapped through without drowning because, just coincidently, there was a set of monster waves that had been waiting for them all day. Being *held under* too long always brought back the memories and fear of the day Mother Ocean tried to take Coppertop and Brother-of-his-now-Callithumpian, which caused some real panic.

It was Fatman who reached the Hobie first. Then Gra. Um, Kiki. 'Where the hell is Kiki? Shhh, hey, Fatman, what's that squeal? Is that a kitten making a squeaky sound out here on this forbidden lake? No, no, it's Kiki yelling for help.' And Skipper-Pearl, was he still alive or flying to that great-beyond-of-no-time-and-place where Emmanuel was waiting with his entourage of angels?

They mounted the sleek cat, got her up and going again and headed sou'east straight towards Kiki at light-speed—his little drenched darling. She did actually look like a drenched kitten from a distance. Fatty jumped straight to the rescue until he realised he didn't know what to do with her and missed the pass.

So, he climbed back on the craft and they relaunched a rescue attempt. How they never ran the girl over at speed, one will never know. Fatman scooped Kiki straight out of the cyclonic lake in a swift manoeuvre even Khabib would have been impressed by, whilst Seeker-Gra tried his best to sail that mother cat.

(Speaking of cats, so to speak, remember the *reincarnation* word that young Searcher-Coppertop first heard on the beach with Flossie-

Mum and her uncouth friend? Well, oddly, he always felt like he was fed to hungry lions in a long distant past life. He doesn't like cats much, even though there's always been a cat around, thanks to Kiki.

Searcher did love Puddy, however, as an exception. As a teenage cat, Puddy once got his collar stuck around his jaw—all night. Puddy could never make a meow or a sound after that, as he probably became too parched and damaged his vocal folds. Although, that's why Searcher-Gra liked him so much—he was easy work, no fuss and never annoyed or demanded anything, as most cats do. He was very affectionate with newborn puppies too!)

But I digress. Seeker-Gra was more useless at sailing than Fatty was. You might assume it was he who scooped his darling Kiki out of those menacing waters at light speed, but it was the Fatman to the rescue. Just as they refocussed and got their bearings, emerging from that fearsome cyclonic lake as if from the grave, Skipper-Pearl appeared. He'd swam north like a fish the whole time and boarded as if by chance, although they were close to the north shore anyway. It was all over!

You should have seen the bark off 'em. Well, except for Skipper-Pearl, of course; his skin was all good. He hadn't sailed for long enough to be cut to pieces like the rest of them had; he had to do that maintenance thing on the rudder after all. The damn grip tape of his had torn them to shreds. Intriguingly, to this very day, Kiki claims that was the most exciting experience of her life. Guess we all need a bit of excitement in our lives from time to time. 'Thanks, Skip!'

Chapter 6

Mischievous Andrew-Poo

Kiki's brother, Andrew-Poo, was always in trouble. Something wasn't quite right with him. He was very intelligent. His Year 11 mathematics teacher could not understand how he could do those formulas so quickly. Neither did he. He was just naturally smart, although he was also drawn to drugs like a moth to a flame.

He was a great worker, a toolmaker, and was studying drafting and technical engineering. Andrew-poo had a few rug-rats of his own, scattered. Ah, but those damn drugs. *Heroin* would be his ultimate choice and his ultimate demise. It was strange how he had got his life back together and was a *happy dad* in the months leading up to that fateful day.

For some reason, the day after he *paddled his canoe* way out there on the same lake that stupid Skipper-Pearl and stupid-Fatman and stupid Gra-Seeker and Kiki nearly drowned in years before, he headed back to Sydney for a bender. Regretfully, he mixed it up with all those drugs and paid the price. He would hop on his last train ride and not make it back to his waiting partner and son—not *alive* that is. He passed them *dead* on that train, and back again.

It was awful that phone call. Poor Kiki's mum was told her son had just been found dead on a train. She would have to mind Cyclone-Izzy and Rascal-Sam whilst Kiki and Searcher drove down to identify his body. Searcher and mother-of-Kiki didn't always see eye-to-eye but leaving her behind, alone with the horrible news of her son's death, just broke his heart.

The policemen were nice, really nice, but Searcher had been in the services and understood this was ultimately just another case for them during their long night shift. The police drove Kiki and Searcher to the city morgue. It was long after midnight. Then, per policy, they were instructed they would have to wait for a professional psychologist to arrive in the morning to make sure the viewer was psychologically sound following the viewing.

Searcher thought it was a considerate policy, and wise; however, he advised the staff he had pretty much seen it all in his years as a paramedic and it would be fine to just go ahead with the identification. They acquiesced. Searcher walked in and did something odd, although probably not uncommon.

He abused the fuck out of his damn brother-in-law, lying dead on the cold table. Then he put his hands together and blessed him, tears flowing, and wished him well on that mysterious journey to the great-beyond-of-no-time-and-place. For a long time, Kiki and Gra had had physical distance between them and Brother-Andrew-Poo. That was a blessing because Searcher and Kiki didn't have to deal with those bad episodes that all drug users have, of both money and addiction. Her mother did.

More recently, Brother-Andrew-Poo had lived with his mother in the same street as Kiki and Searcher, so Searcher-Gra and Brother-Andrew had become closer. Brother-Andrew-Poo wanted to learn and practise some self-defence manoeuvres with Searcher-Gra-come-martial-artist. This recent closeness would cause a very strange phenomenon for weird-Searcher-Gra, and quite soon …

A few peculiar things occurred for all of them after Andrew-Poo's demise, including all the usual hot emotions and so forth. You see, Kiki and Andrew-Poo had made a pact. A dastardly pact! Whoever died first would get to *haunt* the other one, just for kicks. Kiki, mother-of-Kiki and Searcher talked way too much about Andrew-Poo during the immediate weeks after he had passed. Every day!

You kind of have to; it's part of the grieving process, although sometimes you also have to *let it go* and *let it be*. What they didn't realise was that all that talking was probably keeping Andrew-Poo close-by, close to the physical, for those who may consider that a possibility. They say a soul takes flight and leaves all of this world in the coming days or so after death, as it readjusts. Who actually knows? You have to croak-it to find out.

One day, one bizarre day, the three of them were going on and on about Andrew-Poo and all the *what-ifs*. Searcher was drinking a glass of wine or two. Suddenly, HOLY-FUCKING-CRAP, Andrew-Poo just jumped into crazy-Searcher's body. Searcher-once-paramedic jumped up like you've never seen. It was like an electric shock had passed through him and it was terrifying. Terrible! Within a second or two, crazy-Searcher had tears flowing without even comprehending what had just happened.

Now he was a weird guy—you know that by now. But this was just *too* much! He damn-well knew it was Andrew-Poo-now-ghost. You see, he'd been having very strange dreams indeed since Poo had left. Searcher didn't do drugs and didn't smoke. Yet, freaked-out-Searcher kept having vivid dreams over and over in which he was *smoking* and actually *injecting* heroin into his body, tourniquet included. All this after Andrew-Poo-now-ghost had died of course.

Kiki and mother-of-Kiki were *shocked* but couldn't seem to console poor ole freaked-to-the-eyeballs-Searcher. For some reason, Searcher walked out to the balcony and sat down and tried to settle himself after the freaky experience. And to his surprise, Andrew-Poo-now-ghost was staring straight at him and laughing his guts out. He appeared in a white shirt with a number-one haircut, looking pristine with a grin from ear to ear.

He said to perplexed and freaked-out Searcher, *'You idiot. Don't you know sensitives shouldn't drink?'* He laughed and laughed; evidently quite proud he had freaked out Searcher, who thought he knew everything but actually knew nothing. It was a mischievous laughter, though, and something told freaked-out-Searcher this wasn't the last he'd hear from chuckling-Andrew-Poo-now-mischievous-ghost.

'Sensitives? Sensitives? What are sensitives?' Searcher hadn't heard the term before on his searcher-travels searching for Searcher the Searcher, not in that context at least. 'Strange,' he thought.

Toss and turn, toss and turn, toss and turn. Ah, this was pissing Seeker-Searcher off. Andrew-Poo-now-mischievous-ghost was at it again. Kiki had by now told Searcher about the pact that she and Andrew-Poo-now-passed had made years before. 'Yeah, but that was *your* pact. Why is he picking on me?' Searcher said to Kiki. It was really intense this time.

'Go away! Just go away!' It's probably good to hear from a loved-one-passed if you're into that sort of thing. Something nice, like a scent or fine fragrance, an angelic presence at the end of the bed, or an encouraging message to help you move forward in your grief.

However, Andrew-Poo-now-mischievous-ghost was a bit of a rebel during his life and what he wanted, well, he normally got. He was *forceful.* Unfortunately, to freaked-out-sleepless-Searcher, this was not pleasant at all. It became so bad one night that he had to ask his darling Kiki to get up at one o'clock in the morning and just sit with him. Now-extremely-freaked-to-the-eyeballs and tired, Searcher ate some Weet-Bix. He had never done that at night before. Guess he thought it would *ground* him.

Like a caged cat, he kept glancing all around the room, as if he was been looked at. He was paranoid. Kiki was patient, but eventually got tired. She went to bed after about an hour, although remained concerned. Freaked-out-Seeker was too scared to stay up by himself, for he was always a chicken shit, and so he returned to bed.

He must have heard somewhere along the line how there is this remarkable Archangel Michael dude with a giant big blue sword of truth. For some reason, Freaky-Seeky said a fervent prayer to this Archangel Michael, who sounded like Heaven's version of Alexander the Great, without the blood and guts, and asked for *protection.* He also imagined there were four *helper angels,* one in each corner of the house.

Searcher's embarrassed about it looking back, for he realises it was only mischievous-Andrew-Poo after all. There really was no need for all that angel-protection sort of commotion, but he'd got himself too freaked-out in all the drama and fear. Well, that was the end of it. Searcher slept like a baby that night, and every night following. Andrew-Poo never bothered him again, save for one more time, much later.

Seeker-now-depressed-Searcher was in a reverie. It was 'round midnight. He was tinkling on the piano keyboard, with headphones on, attempting to learn that beautifully inspired song *River Flows in You*, by Yiruma. Almost every aspiring piano player learns that one. Suddenly, with a blast from Searcher's rear, just to the left, Andrew-Poo shouted, *'I want you to have my motorbike! The blue Kawasaki!'*

'Jesus, Andrew, you frightened the shit out of me,' said Searcher. Searcher had been so relaxed whilst practising that gentle piano piece that it all just came as a shock. A bit like hanging around Cyclone Izzy, actually.

'You love my bike; I know you do. Take it!' Andrew-Poo demanded.

'Okay, okay, I'll think about it, Andrew, but can you just piss off? You're freaking me out. Ghosts freak me out!' Then he was gone, just like that. Searcher never did ask mother-of-Kiki for that blue Kawasaki, which Andrew-Poo once got up to warp speed on heading down the freeway at almost 300 km/h. It would have just sounded all too contrived.

However, he reckons he saw Andrew-Poo one last time, years later in one of those mansions of the Father that the Immaculate One had spoken of; it happened during a meditation. Searcher feels that *mansion* actually means *dimension*. Anyways, the place-of-no-place was large, so LARGE and EXPANSIVE, larger than the skies above. And the frequencies of *love*, heavens above, are too much to articulate.

Searcher felt this was the Land of Light where all of those loved-up hippies came from *en masse* when they brought their messages of love, peace and freedom through song, word, art, and yeah, sex, to create the great *revolution* of the 1960s. And where those four mophead-Liverpudlians came from to insert into the matrix the greatest message that has ever been given: *All You Need Is Love*. Yeah!

But let's just say that little deluded Searcher found something on that particular occasion. It was truly *something*, and he cried and cried with joy in his heart. After all those troubled years of drugs, drama, sadness and turmoil, Andrew-Poo was finally happy and at peace at last …

Astro boy

After the ambulance chapter of his life was over, Searcher-Gra found it hard to get a job or make money. He'd always had a fear that if he should leave the ambulance, the money-tap would just stop running and seize up. It did! It's funny how our fears often become our reality.

He tried various avenues in an attempt to move on. He studied landscape design for a while and loved the horticulture side of it, but eventually it became too focussed on the CAD drafting part of it. He was good at drafting, but who wants to stare at a computer for eight hours a day? Not Seeker it seemed.

He eventually would turn back to his mechanical fitter trade. Seeker was hopeless at it, but what do you do? Googes was a great boss and a great bloke, salt of the earth! He met up with desperate Seeker in his local watering hole and offered him a job on a handshake and a beer.

He said something like, 'You'll get 60 an hour, I'll get 60 an hour, and that won't change regardless of what shift you work. You'll start at Chi-Star Mines and before the week's up, you'll wish to Christ you hadn't.' He was right. It took an hour of driving underground to get to the longwall. The very first task Searcher was given, before he could blink an eye, was to drag a 120-kilo mother-ass cylinder up to the tailgate by himself, which was a damn long way away.

Up and down and up and down over each roof support, and it was bloody muddy and hard yakka. Welcome, Searcher! The contract went on for four months, and it was a dangerous ole mine. Two poor miners would lose their lives from a roof collapse whilst he was there.

The miners worked hard and were always *under* pressure from *above*. Funny that! Curiously, since Searcher had gotten all so depressed and dark from those paramedic times, he really did like going *underground*. He felt solace, away from all the people and demands. But he was ill-equipped to handle the mechanical side of things; he'd been out of the game for far too long. Desperation causes a man to do desperate things, however, so he pushed on as best as he could.

The miners were bloody smart. They really do learn how to *think* clearly down there, which wasn't one of Seeker's best traits. It is probably because their lives are always at stake, and they have to use their noggins to protect themselves and others from a thousand-times-a-thousand dangers. They occasionally have clashes. That's because they are blokes and pig-headed, but they cover each other's arses like the paramedics *above* could never imagine.

The hydraulic pressures are immense. They have to be, to hold up the mountain above them. Imagine your car tyre blowing up in your face. It's around 35 psi of pressure and will hurt you no doubt. Those mining blokes use up to 6000 psi of pressure and it will waste you good and proper! Damn nearly wasted Searcher-soon-to-be-Astro-boy down there more than once. But the training is good, very good, in Australian mining.

As long as you are *safety conscious* you'll go alright, and thankfully, Searcher really was safety conscious. He met one curious fellow down there whom he called the 'Fuckin-fuckin-man'. They sat in the crib room, which is a temporary lunch-room roughly cut in coal, comprising a ceiling, floor and two or three walls. Searcher listened to the Fuckin-fuckin-man intently, because he always doubled and sometimes even tripled his expletives. For some reason Searcher's brain could only register the swearing and nothing else.

To Searcher, a typical conversation sounded like so: *'Yeah, I fuckin-fuckin went down and fuckin-fuckin told him, I'd fuckin-fuckin, fuckin give him what fuckin-fuckin for, if he didn't fuckin-fuckin, I mean fuck, if he didn't fuckin-fuckin pull his fuckin-fuckin head in I'd fuckin-fuckin fuck him over. I'm fuckin-fuckin serious, you fuckin know!'* Searcher had no idea what the Fuckin-fuckin-man had said, but thought he was fuckin-fuckin hilarious!

The young fellas at one of the mines used to pester and pester ole Searcher-now-miner about anything and everything—just not work, for they knew he didn't know jack shit. It was actually Searcher who pestered them about mechanical stuff, because he was always playing catch-up. It touched his heart that they tried to help him. They really were open-minded.

Searcher loved that about them. He had searched far and wide to just chew the fat with anyone who was open-minded. It was like a breath of fresh air down there for him, in the not-so-fresh air. The inquisitive young rebels liked all those fancy party, mind-expanding drugs that Seeker knew nothing about.

Regretfully, he once mentioned how he had left his body on occasion. That was it! They were hooked. Thereafter, Searcher was called *Astro-boy* or *Astro* for short, to represent his 'astral travelling' or out-of-body experiences. Those young, party-hard, mining-fitters really *dove* deep, funny that! They did their research on Google. Finally, they told Astro what he had been experiencing. *'Lucid dreaming* it is, Astro, lucid dreaming!'

'Oh. Lucid dreaming. I see.' Searcher didn't argue. Lucid dreaming is what all the novices who have never left their body call it. However, it's not dreaming because you're fully awake. 'More awake than ever. Lucid dreaming must be something else,' Searcher-Astro thought to himself.

The thing about an out-of-body sojourn is that once you've experienced it, you just *know*. Searcher-Astro-boy just *knew*. Unlike, say, some belief systems, where you are told what the truth is and what you should and shouldn't believe, true experience is just *known* and not necessarily *believed*. 'That's the key difference right there,' Astro mumbled to himself.

'Without actually having the experience, one only *thinks* one knows. You can become the world's greatest expert on bananas, for example, knowing every single intricacy and more, even becoming a professor on the fruit, without ever putting one in your mouth. Such is the irony of the modern world.'

Searcher-now-Astro-boy persisted in the mines for a few years, until it abruptly ended. To be fair, he was still struggling with the mechanical side of things. Those mining fellas are mostly what you call *left-brained*. Searcher-Astro was more *right-brained*, which is why he suspected he had experienced a lot of weird shit but, unfortunately, that would not help him underground.

Surprisingly, Mother Earth did talk to him once, though. He was surfacing from underground one night and was feeling melancholic. Almost guilty. He understood how we still need mining for power and so forth, and compared to the nuclear danger, well, coal mining is safe. Everyone had seen what can happen when the shit hits the fan at nuclear powerplants, especially when you're stupid enough to build them on the shoreline of a great ocean.

Dreamingly, Searcher-Astro said to Mother Earth, 'Sorry we don't care for you like the native races did. Sorry that we rape and plunder you and take all your resources without gratitude, without feeling.' He was daydreaming like he had in all those days at the school of the holy brothers; not really thinking, just quiet, very quiet. Surprisingly, Great Mother responded. She said:

> It's alright my friend. It won't always be like this. Mankind will change, slowly. He will begin to take care of me, the mother. He will love and cherish and care for me, and he will reap a great harvest indeed as a result. The oceans will become cleaner, the air will become fresher and healthier, my trees will be greener, the rivers will flow, the peoples will become happier and healthier. But for now, this is what must be. Do not blame yourself. Do not blame others. It's called evolution, and the wheels turn slowly, my friend. Be patient. Be kind to yourself. And be kind to others always.

Falling on his sword

'AHHHHH. Argh that hurt. Ouch!' Searcher-Astro-miner had stumbled and fallen on his sword. He actually did, you know. He was helping some wholesome strong fellas when his legs became stuck in a foot of coal mud whilst carrying a heavy hose overhead, and lost balance. He tipped backwards and apparently his head missed the armoured-face-conveyor by a whisker.

Tradesmen wear some of their basic tools around their waist, as well as their battery for their headlamp and their self-rescuer in case of fire or a gas leak. Searcher-Astro had his shifters, super-tool, large screwdrivers and other tools on his right, hanging from his belt. As he fell backwards, the tools planted into the ground and he landed straight onto them, exactly like *falling on his sword*.

It was painful, bloody painful. But Searcher-Astro had learnt how to be tough from his martial arts instructor, who was as tough as nails and some, so he stood up and continued to work for a while until he felt really sick. He told the fellows he needed to have a break and proceeded back down the longwall and sat on a chock where his main tools were.

Blackness. Darkness. 'Holy crap. Have I died?' thought Astro-boy. 'Shit, I know I've been down in the dumps, but I'm really not ready to return to the great-beyond-of-no-time-and-place. It's dark here. Maybe I've ended up with Hellfire-boy-down-below. I was a bit of an arsehole, I suppose. Way too intense—but not that bad, surely?'

He waited and waited and then finally saw the light. 'There's the *light*. Cool! I knew I'd make it to the light; I hope Tippy is there and the rest of them waiting for me. Um, there's no sense of movement. No dead relatives,' he thought. 'Wait, wait, what? What's that? Shit! That's my damn cap-lamp staring back at me. I'm still alive. Cool. Kiki will be relieved, I guess!'

Searcher-Astro had fainted from the pain and fallen into the coal mud. His cap-lamp had come off and was shining back at him as he lay there unconscious with his face all but under the wet coal mud. He tried to hide the pain, but eventually had to tell the deputy he'd had a fall.

The deputy was exceptional and rushed Astro straight up to the surface and promised he would bring his tools up later. A promise he didn't keep for Astro would never see those tools again. Someone else would also steal his expensive mining boots from the bathhouse—boots he had paid for himself.

Searcher-Astro waited in the first-aid humpy for hours and hours in pain. He said to the first-aid officer, 'Mate, I was a paramedic once. I've got broken ribs and stuff. I just know.' That was ignored. Eventually, the mining undermanager advised carting poor-old-Astro off to hospital. Astro felt terribly embarrassed being so damn dirty in the emergency room, for all you could see was the whites of his eyes and everything else was black. Patiently, he waited and waited.

Finally, by daylight, the medicos x-rayed him. Evidently the medical-god must have been studying his own newspaper or toilet paper, because he didn't see any signs of fractures in Astro's broken body. The undermanager kept ringing wounded Astro to make sure the medical-god wrote that he would be unavailable for work that night due to *fatigue*, rather than *injury.*

You see it's all about *stats* in the mines and they'll do almost anything to fudge them. Astro had to ask for two Panadols for the pain as it was excruciating. The nurses grudgingly obliged. That was the last drug of any description Searcher-Astro ever put into his body. It all just pissed him off. Especially since he'd given so much to others when he was a paramedic, had always tried his best.

Astro-the-Searcher made it home and saw another medical-god who was competent. He learned he had three broken ribs and a torn rib cartilage. He'd be out of work. His boss was away in America, although Astro had been sub-contracted out to another manager who was also away, in China. So, no-one bothered with poor ole-Astro-boy, as he lay there in pain, without money, compensation or opportunity.

A stranger

One night at the dangerous old historic Chi-Star Mine, some of the experienced miners started talking about some scary stuff. Searcher-Astro thought, 'Here we go again.' It was quite a captivating story. The miners were all a bit on edge because they had just lost two of their brothers who had been wrongfully buried by Mother Earth. It really surprised Astro how they opened up, because they were rough-around-the-edges buggers, yet oozing with *common sense,* being very left-brained.

A guy called *China* mostly spoke, and all the others confirmed his story, even though they didn't appear totally comfortable going there. They reckoned the old mine was haunted and held many, many stories of creepy stuff going on down in the dungeons of life. *Redhead-China-Miner* said one night, he and his team were working bloody hard as usual when they noticed a fellow walk straight past them. China said hello, but the stranger just kept walking. It was very unusual straight up.

The strange fellow was not one of their crew for starters and, more importantly, didn't have a self-rescuer on or a current cap-lamp, only an old-fashioned one. 'Hmm? So strange?' You see, down there, you are like *brothers* who watch out for each other's backs. And whether you are fond of the deputy or not, he is kind of like God to that crew, because all decisions involving the crew's safety depend on him. In other words, their lives depend on the deputy to a high degree, as well as their own common sense and training.

As you enter each district, you place your ID card on a big whiteboard in the roadway until you exit the district later. That way, the deputy always knows who is in his district or not. The same is done for each mobile diesel machine, so there is never an excess of diesel fumes in each district. It's all a monitoring process.

Somehow, this strange fellow slipped through the cracks. China-Miner noted the peculiar man was walking *into* the mine, which only left him a couple of possible options to proceed. China yelled out to his mates and asked, 'Did you see that?' They did and were confused. The crew might only consist of eight men, for example, so they're *tight* and know their stuff.

The deputy was informed and immediately became quite concerned. The crew did a reconnaissance to try to locate the strange man, who five of the eight miners had seen walking past. What predominately worried China was the old-fashioned cap-lamp that the strange man had been wearing. It had not been used for decades. They searched and searched.

All that was left was a *stub* up ahead, which is a small *dead*-end roadway, often without ventilation. Those earthy miners were in as deep as you could go—the dungeon. There was no further, until they mined it so, and no-way out without a diesel. It took almost an hour's drive in a Driftrunner or Eimco to make it down there.

They could not locate him anywhere. Eventually, the deputy must have told them to get back to production, because the strange man was never seen again. He didn't drive out, was not on any logs and had not clocked on or off at all.

There were other stories they told Astro—but basically, it was an old dangerous mine with a long history. 'You get that,' thought Searcher-Astro. Perhaps the only reason the miners shared any of this with Astro was because everyone was so on edge following the fatalities. Searcher kept looking over his shoulder, down in that ole mine for weeks. It felt somewhat creepy, especially down at the cave-in, although it most certainly was all in his head.

Chapter 7

Coconuts and clashes

Leah-Lovebloom was enchanting and had giant coconuts! Now Glapiac-later-Searcher had seen some large jugs before, but this was on another level entirely. Think Dolly!

Three years prior, when hormones were awakening in Red, it was first-girlfriend Cherry who had exposed hers to him. For five weeks a year during the summer break, Glapiac-Red's family would holiday right by the ocean and do all the things kids do.

Cherry would wake him up early each morning as he lay there deep asleep on his canvas bunk in the caravan annex. Before dawn, she would nudge him with a fishing rod on the face to wake him up. It would still be dark. She was very pretty, with soft lovely features and was, well, well-endowed. They'd walk the break-wall and watch the sunrise together. It was sweet. The others thought they were *fishing*, and you could probably say that; however, no fish were ever caught.

One morning when Red was feeling particularly amorous and curious and daring, he said to his young lass, 'Hey, Cherry, may I have a look at your gorgeous big boobs please?' Cherry just pulled her top down right there and obliged Glapiac-Red, who with a sudden rush, felt quite hesitant yet excited at the same time. Kissing seemed more important than talking back then, so there wasn't much conversation going on over those weeks.

During the same time period, Christo-now-Wal would teach Glapiac how to flame-throw with kero from the mouth. They were into Kiss, who did it on stage. They would singe their eyebrows and eyelashes and look and smell altogether strange. Another favourite pastime was to make each other faint. They would first hyperventilate by breathing exceedingly fast and deeply and then be bear-hugged from behind, until they passed out.

This may well explain why Coppertop-come-Searcher had so many oddities growing up. It was years later when he would become a paramedic and understand just how dangerous that fun teenage activity actually was. Times were good!

Now, back to Leah-Lovebloom. Those noggins were enormous, even bigger than Cherry's. Unbeknown to Glapiac-Red-later-Searcher, however, there was trouble brewing in the air. A fella called *Splash* accused him of chatting up his juggernauted girlfriend, who just happened to be none other than Leah-Lovebloom. Glapiac wasn't doing that—well, not really.

It just so happened he was friends with Leah-Lovebloom's big brother, Big-Boppabloom, who was a fellow footy player and a fine young man. But it wasn't young Glapiac-once-Coppertop's fault. Where was he supposed to look when all he could see at Big-Boppabloom's place was his young sister's colossal melons? Well these two young men got into a bit of an argument. It wasn't really a fair argument to be fair.

You see, Splash happened to have an older brother who was involved in the terrible murder of one of Glapiac's school friends. The details shall not be elaborated on here, because well, some things are just too horrible to mention. In hindsight he came to realise that one should never blame a person for what another did, even if it was their brother. So, Glapiac was quite wrong for that.

Nonetheless, things involving Leah-Lovebloom still had to be settled the *old-fashioned* way. Glapiac-Tiger requested he and Splash meet up for a cuddle. So, those young hot-headed P-plate drivers jumped in their respective cars and met down at the local football field in a huff. It was a good thing no-one was around, because it would be settled man-to-man, or more like boy-to-boy, one way or another.

Splash was cranky about his girlfriend and making all kinds of accusations. Red-Glapiac was cranky about the accusations and, you know, the terrible murder matter. It was to be a good fight, a good tussle. Glapiac-son-of-Tippy-and-brother-of-Braveheart took him on and went in swinging hard and fast. Glapiac was a tiger, which caught Splash by surprise.

But lo and behold, and much to Glapiac's disbelief, Splash was also a tiger. An Albino one actually with his thick, wavy-white hair. This would be a good match up and perfectly orchestrated, it seemed. Those two young tigers hustled and hissed and, well, they just had a ripper of a battle. Glapiac-Tiger most definitely got on top, although that was surprising as young Splash was quite nuggety. Glapiac thought he might have copped a raw hiding from cranky-nuggety-Splash.

There again, Glapiac-Tiger had had plenty of fighting-practice with his loving brother often whipping his ass. Especially the time after Glapiac-one-day-to-be-the-Searcher attacked Brave-brother's bike spokes with a hammer! So, Albino-Tiger had to take to wrestling to stop the carnage. These days, wrestling is a superior form of fighting one-on-one, but those two tigers only understood emotion, not technique.

After some time, everything settled down quite abruptly. Tiger said to Albino-Splash, 'I don't want your f'ing girlfriend, alright?' Well, the two young tigers got in their respective cars and drove away, emotions now released.

A funny thing happened one night, months later. Glapiac-Tiger was at the Workers Club having a beer when Albino-Tiger spotted him, also having a beer. 'Uh oh. It's on again,' thought Glapiac. However, Albino-Tiger, who appeared far more chilled this time around, walked over to Red-Tiger and did a surprising thing. White-Tiger put his hand out to shake Red-Tiger's hand. Red-Tiger obliged, of course, and they looked at each other and, with a smile, simply walked away. Not a word was spoken throughout.

That was it. And that was it for Big-tits-Leah-Lovebloom too! Red-Tiger really did try to respect White-Tiger's wishes and stayed right away from his well-endowed prized possession and sweetheart. Red-Tiger liked to honour his word, although the memory of her giant coconuts remained.

The Searcher

Ole-Lillah

Redmond once knew a real-live witch, you know, as did Brave-brother and all their local mates. Ole-Lillah lived just behind their quarter-acre-block, over the lane. She had a tall picket fence for protection against those *little-monster boys*. And she was mean! Do you know, and quite seriously, Coppertop-later-Searcher believed that Ole-Lillah was probably scarier than Mother-fucker-sexed-up-ghost or, at least on a par.

Young boys just love playing with a ball, especially a soccer ball. And when gravity is involved, things just happen with balls when you kick them—like bouncing and rolling away. Unfortunately, being soccer players, those boys could really kick a ball.

Ole-Lillah was a green-thumb gardener who just loved her rows and rows of roses and the like and protected her little red-and-green companions with her life. She was about four-foot tall, knee high to a bumblebee, and always wore a dark purple scarf wrapped around her head. She had deep, deeply piercing blue-grey eyes which could burn holes in you. Her intense gaze just somehow added to the terror and her voice sounded exactly like the Wicked Witch of the West from the *Wizard of Oz*!

However, of all things, it was her impeccable timing that was above reproach. Like, don't people have to go out once in a while to buy food and the like? No matter what time those little-monster-boys would accidently kick their soccer ball over her great big picket fence, watching gravity do the rest, she would be there. Always and without fail!

They were all scared, not just Coppertop and Brave-not-so-brave-brother. All their mates were terrified too. They had to take turns in jumping over that fence to retrieve their beloved ball and ultimately the one who kicked it was the one who licked it!

Nevertheless, every goddamn time they ever did, Crazy-terrifying-ole-Lillah would come running out with her broom screaming like a banshee. She would bash those little-monster boys around the head with her broom in movements Bruce Lee would have been impressed by, and she was old, really old. The little-monster boys would get battered and bruised and scratched up by the roses as they tried to escape.

The most depressing thing of all was when they failed to escape *with* the ball. That's when things really got heated up, because Ole-Lillah knew they'd come back and they knew she knew they'd come back. She most certainly had the upper hand and would strategically place their ball far away from them, right outside her dark rear screen door. And as she was making her witch's brew—a brew the boys smelt but never actually saw, mind you—she would wait and wait to pounce.

Ole-Lillah was extremely patient. And pounce she did. Now that was beyond being terrorised; it was little-monster-boy abuse. There was only one escape route, which was backwards through the rose bushes. It was not a pretty sight. Ironically, as those boys grew older and looked back, they wouldn't have changed it for the world.

They would talk of Ole-Lillah with a hint of affection, perhaps because she was just so committed to her little thorned-rosy friends or because she was such a formidable foe. And just as Kiki-dolphin found out on the great big cyclonic lake, sometimes you just need a bit of *danger* in your life to get that old adrenaline coursing through your body.

Dream drifter

Searcher had a dream. Far, far away in the East he was waiting to meet the guru. There were hundreds and hundreds of people of all ages, patiently waiting in line to enter the temple. They would receive a message from the guru. It was sweltering outside, as the scores of people slowly moved forward. Eventually, Dream-Searcher entered the front door, which was enormous and looming. Incense was thick as the disciples were keenly watching over the masses.

Through the centre of the temple, the crowd proceeded along a lengthy mauve runner rug. Surprisingly, as he advanced closer, Dream-Searcher noticed the guru was only small and young—perhaps no more than seven years of age. He sat in full-lotus and looked deeply into people's eyes, as if he could see into their souls.

The Searcher

Closer, closer. Two more were in front, and then one. Finally, it was Searcher's turn. He looked into Guru-child's eyes and said nothing.

Guru-child said, and not with words, *'You are a Teacher, go forth and do thy work!'*

'Teacher, a teacher?' Searcher said to himself puzzled. He had tried to teach guitar years before but didn't like how people just wanted to be turned into a guitarist without having to do the work themselves. So that wasn't it. Hmm? He was clueless. He asked out loud, 'Master, what am I to teach?'

Child-guru threw out an angry energy and telepathically said, *'One thing only, only one thing.'* Apparently, you were only able to *receive* or *ask* one thing and no more. Guru-child motioned with his right hand for Searcher to exit via the left, as if shaking off dust. The neophytes looked on angrily as if Searcher was a moron.

As Dream-Searcher walked outside into the sunlight, he woke up. He was still groggy and confused. It was only a dream, but it troubled him. It would take many years to understand what that dream signified, and even then he would never be sure …

Initially, when his ole ego was running high, Searcher thought maybe he had come for some important *work* to do in the world, teaching the masses or something spiritual. Years would roll on by and wipe all of that. He finally came to the conclusion he did indeed come to teach, but it wasn't for such an altruistic cause.

Drivers! Many drivers on the road are just woeful. They swerve in and out and neglect road rules, common sense, and courtesy and, boy, do they like to tailgate. Searcher, in his arrogance, felt he had come to *teach* them, as Guru-child suggested he teach. That was his work. So, when a knuckle-headed driver would come towards him, for example, by drifting onto the wrong side of the road, Searcher would *hold his line* inches from them as if his life depended on it.

Poor Kiki-dolphin was forever fearful that she would be joining Andrew-Poo quite soon in that great-beyond, but Seeker wouldn't budge. It became quite a predictable affair, actually. The *teaching* would happen; Kiki-dolphin would scream in anguish, and Searcher would always respond the same way.

He would say, 'What? I'm just teaching them. If you don't hold your line and teach them a lesson, they'll keep on doing it and no doubt kill someone one day when lady-odds comes out to play.' There are hundreds of other examples, of course, like rude self-centred people in shopping centres or people who like to walk together taking up all of the footpath, or shopping aisles, but basically Searcher had *found his lane*. He was the *teacher*. Such humility!

Searcher could also be called an *observer*. He was always observing people's behaviour wherever he found himself. What he was most intrigued by, however, was those people who clearly didn't appear to be searching or looking for meaning, and most likely never would. Yet, often they were the happiest people on earth. It appeared life was simple and straightforward for them.

They experienced little drama and just seemed to *plod along* their merry way, seemingly balanced and not prone to fanaticism or fanfare. 'Each walks their own path, none better than the other,' Seeker subsequently contemplated. It reminded him of those singers who sang like birds without effort or ever receiving lessons. They just had *it*. Same-same with non-Searchers.

During his so-called spiritual journey, at times Searcher would meditate consistently, maybe for a few months. Rising early at the crack of dawn and committed to the *path*, he would sit for lengthy periods trying to still his mind, gain clarity or awaken to pure consciousness and so forth. Almost always, nothing happened. No bells and whistles. No awakenings. He'd just sit there in the half lotus, maybe feeling relaxed but usually with thoughts racing at a thousand miles per hour.

Beautiful-sister-of-Searcher once meditated. Once! She closed her eyes per instruction and slowed her breathing down. Relax, relax, relax. Slowly, she left … in her mind's eye she was freed of this plane.

Out into the yonder, beyond the beautiful blue planet, beyond the sun-Ra, beyond the spiralled milky galaxy. Traversing through luminescent, glowing, nebulous clouds of heavenly light and sound. Exquisite chorales of unheard vibrations and the purest of frequencies. Through purple, white and golden hues, upwards and inwards she roamed, passing stunning vistas beyond description.

The Searcher

Pristine lakes and rivers structured in sound and light geometries that no human had ever known. Radiant panoramas of crystalline scapes and resplendent luminous energies divine. She felt washed and purified. Wholly holy! Finally, a mesmerising and dazzling display of alluring, angelic-beings of light and beauty beyond all description appeared. She trembled with emotion and euphoria. An ecstatic reunion. She was Home!

Slowly, slowly, she returned to consciousness and, feeling more solid and grounded, mused, 'Uh-huh, so that's meditation.' Beautiful-sister later told Searcher she didn't really know how to meditate; she'd only tried it once and was no good at it!

Cyclone-Izzy daughter tried meditation *once* too. She sat cross-legged and breathed. She imagined herself walking outdoors. Unexpectantly, she noticed plants growing into trees beneath her feet. With each step another tree would push her feet up. She had to speed up to stay above the ever-appearing trees and was running forward and upwards in a joyous, hopping fashion.

Increasingly, she could no longer sustain enough speed to stay ahead of the rate of tree growth and suddenly vaulted into the air. She was off flying, soaring through the skies. In jubilant excitement, she felt as free as a bird. Next, she was sitting in a clearing in a lush rainforest. Three beings were standing equally spaced in front of her. She motioned for them to *go away*, for she was busy focussing on meditating.

As they walked away, she looked closer and was shocked to see they were none other than *Jesus, Buddha and John Lennon*, all dressed in white gowns. She yelled, 'Wait, guys, I didn't know it was you. I was busy meditating.' They laughed wholeheartedly. She then said, 'Wait, where are you going, what should I do?'

They smiled and said, *'You're all good, kid.'* And in a peaceful and casual stride, walked on …

Izzy had allowed herself twenty minutes for her first meditation. She'd set her alarm, as she had to rush off to work at the cinema thereafter. But she was worried the meditation had gone for far too long. The alarm had probably not gone off. She opened her eyes and was shocked to see only *two minutes* had passed.

It intrigued Searcher to hear such things. He contemplated how some people—monks and dedicated meditators, for example—might meditate daily for thirty or forty years and not have such wonderful inner experiences. Yet, did that matter? Perhaps those amazing experiences that so many have had are just the icing on the cake. Maybe the most important thing really is the sustained and dedicated focus on one's path.

Or anything else for that matter; such as the consistent and dedicated focus on earning money, learning an instrument, mastering a sport and so forth. Observer contemplated the uniqueness of all people regardless of their path, their journey, their religion or faith, their philosophy, their career, their money, their talents, their abilities, their looks or intelligence. All, he felt, were equal, valid and vital to this wonderful world in their own way.

Odd Street

'Odd Street, lunch time, BE THERE!' Red said to him. They were standing in the school assembly where the holy-brothers were always on the lookout for rogue boys talking. That was a golden opportunity to extend some cruelty and would not be missed. Evidently, Marbles, the student standing behind, decided he wanted to stir young Red up and do a bit of bullying—nothing too serious, mind you.

Red-Glapiac got tired of being nudged, though, and turned around to offer the above-mentioned challenge, *'Odd Street, lunch time, BE THERE.'* He'd thrown down the gauntlet.

Odd Street was a kind of cement park where the smartarse boys would walk to each day for lunch and play. It was bleak, without shade and quite pathetic, actually. It wasn't very far from the school and was located near where Chudley would one day join a big, infamous motorcycle club. That came later, long after he lost his leg.

Lunchtime came, and over the smartarse-schoolboys marched to Odd Street. Young Red and young Marbles met up and it was on. 'This is it!' Red wanted to release some anger and frustration, because he still couldn't fathom why his hero-dad had recently been taken away. However, it was all over in a second.

Young Red just punched Marbles right in the face, as hard as he could. Marbles quickly decided he wasn't cut out for fighting and walked away bleeding. Mr Merry, Red's teacher, watched the whole affair. Red-Glapiac walked straight past him and swears Mr Merry had a wry smile on his face. Nothing was said. Perhaps he understood something of Red's personal loss and frustration? It wasn't a good outcome evidently, because many older boys had heard the fiery redhead could pack a punch and wanted to also fight him. Karma's a bitch!

One day, years later, when Red was all grown up and now a rock guitarist, he was playing a gig where Marbles-now-grown-up-man happened to be. Marbles walked up to guitarist-Red to say hello. Lo, Marbles, serendipitously, had become a *male model* and a gorgeous specimen indeed.

He had sparkling blue eyes, dark thick, wavy hair, beautifully chiselled features, and the body of an athlete. Faultless was he! Except for one thing. When he smiled at Red-rock-guitarist, he still had a badly bent front tooth from that nasty punch all those schoolboy-years ago. Red-guitarist felt small. He felt very bad—like he had ruined God's most perfect creation.

Red-Tiger was fiery for sure. He didn't see it as a problem, although he probably should have. He thought, 'What's wrong with fire?' Sure, everyone just loves those flippy-little-interdimensional-super-intelligent-watery-dolphins, but what of fiery beings? Maybe that's why he felt sorry for Hellfire-boy-down-below, because everyone blamed him for every sin they partook in.

Now, Kiki was a dolphin, but even she still had fire in her belly. She took down the big-sook-bully, remember, and stood up to the large alcoholic-big-wig-manager and walked out.

Speaking of Kiki's belly, one day when she was heavily pregnant and Rascal-Sam dwelt inside her, Searcher-Pookie set up a hammock for her in the pergola so she could lie around and chill. He assured her it was safe and secure. It wasn't!

The enormous-bellied Kiki came crashing right down on her side, and she just never understood why it was Pookie-partner who nearly died that day and not her. He almost died of laughter, which might well explain some things here.

Not long after she had Cyclone-Izzy, coach-Dalefin-Lavo decided he, Kiki, and Searcher-Gra would catch some big waves on his surf skis out on the reef. Dalefin took Kiki on the double-ski and caught a monster of a wave. She actually possessed good natural balance, but the extra baby-feeding weight may have been a problem, for they were wiped out good and proper. Kiki emerged from the turbulence with her hands in the air hollering, 'Woo hoo! That was unreal. That was tops. I loved it.'

Sheepishly, Dalefin looked away and said, 'Yeah, the *white pointers* are out today.' Unbeknown to post-pregnant Kiki, she had lost her swim-top in the hullabaloo and her large white baby-suckers were blinding poor ole Dalefin's vision.

Chapter 8

The perplexed Searcher

It looked like hieroglyphs rapidly scrolling down the computer screen at many hundreds of characters per second. Cyphers and crypto-symbols were flooding down. Searcher could not make sense of it. 'Kiki, come and have a look at this. How bizarre! What on earth?' bewildered Searcher asked.

It continued on. Not words per se, just letters, symbols, numbers and articulations. Gradually, it slowed down. Then, steadily, words were formulated. Seeker-Red started to type: 'Um, who are you?' At first, only cryptical answers were offered.

'Where are you from?'

'*We are from the Right Hand,*' was responded.

'Uh? The right hand of what?' asked Seeker.

'*The Right Hand of the Father. We do not come, for we never leave. We are now and forever. We are here for there is nowhere else in existence.*'

Many more cryptical answers followed, in fact a whole conversation. Whoever was the source of this transmission, they were interested in incoming—that is, Kiki's bun-in-the-oven. Upon request, they advised of a name for incoming. Without hesitation, it/they said, '*Celeste*'.

Scarcher and Kiki decided not to use the name Celeste for incoming; however, they did use it as her middle name.

She would be called *Isabella*. Family called her *Bella*. From kindergarten on, however, she would forever be known as *Izzy*. Teachers and students alike addressed her by that name. And now a grown up, she remains as Izzy. She's as free as a bird!

Being-from-afar once said to Searcher, '*We come from afar. We will give you proof, but you must give us your word you will never share this with anyone.*' He did not. He will not. '*We observe the power of silence. Mankind is like a baby not ready for the greater truths and even more, for he is yet still asleep!*'

Searcher could never understand why people in general either thought extra-terrestrial life was all baloney or, at best, unlikely. *Believers* were ridiculed for lacking intelligence. Searcher, based on common sense and mathematics alone, thought it should be quite the contrary.

The cosmos is just so large, too large for absolutes. Larger than a human mind can even conceive. The distances are gargantuan and have to be measured in *light years,* which is a long, long distance in and of itself. Even of the *known* universe, which you could call the *Hubble universe,* billions of galaxies with billions of stars exist, each star potentially having planetary systems around it.

And if a minute percentage of *intelligent* life existed throughout the cosmos, say point-one percent, well, of the known universe, billions and billions and billions of intelligent lifeforms would exist. Of course, Searcher was only considering intelligent life— that which possessed some similarities with human life in terms of consciousness, awareness, intellect and so forth. More elementary and ephemeral life could also exist.

The Hubble universe, which to Searcher represented only the tiny pocket of space that man could probe at this time, could quite literally be infinitesimal compared to what actually exists and is expanding exponentially. And what of dimensional realities? Does it all have to be *third-dimensional life,* as on earth, or could there be other dimensions based on frequency and vibration or even geometry, music or art for that matter?

Who can say they know? Yes, it all perplexed the Searcher. He just couldn't understand the close-minded logic and scepticism. In fact, he thought it was the greatest arrogance of all time for humans to believe they are the *one and only* intelligent lifeform in existence.

For the Immaculate One, Yeshua-ben-Joseph, the Messiah-Prophesised, stated, 'In my Father's house are many mansions.'

What then, are mansions? Rooms? Could they be dimensions he was speaking of? Yes, perhaps Being-from-afar was right: *'Mankind is like a baby not ready for the greater truths and more, for he is yet still asleep.'*

Searcher had a friend for a long, long time called Moray. They hit it off on a spiritual note and got along fine. They would talk and talk, all about what each master and teacher had said, trying to work it all out, asking questions like, 'Why are we here? Have we been here before? What happens when we die? What is the meaning of life?' And on and on ad infinitum.

Questions that Flossie-Mum, Beautiful-sister and Kiki-dolphin just didn't care to worry about. You can drown in the search, and Searcher and Moray and others did just that. It wasn't wrong or right. Each to their own path, as long as it is *your* path and not that of another's. Just as Tippy had written so long ago in Coppertop's little blue autograph book: 'Love many, trust few, *always paddle your own canoe!'* And you know, that just hits the nail on the head right there.

When you become all caught up in the spiritual search, you tend to listen to what everyone else has to say and ignore your inner voice. You read inspirational books, maybe go on a retreat or two, spin your chakras, clean your internal pipes and do whatever it takes to *polish your diamond*. Just don't forget to put your garbage out and wash the dishes.

Years later, much later, Searcher contemplated how it always seems to come at a cost. If you're not *paddling your own canoe*, even if studying the most perfect wisdom ever, it still ain't your wisdom. Callithumpian-brother and his ilk certainly worked that out when they were beating their drums, clanging their cymbals and going downstream. In fact, as Searcher was intensely aware, the Immaculate One said, *The Kingdom of God is within You*.[4] And Searcher always felt that meant every answer and solution was *within* and could not be found *without*, anywhere! When you go within, you don't go without, you might say.

Being-from-afar described Moray as an *explorer without a compass*. Searcher-Seeker thought it sounded a bit derogatory at the time, but it wasn't meant to be. There was a touch of truth in that for most searchers, seekers and explorers of the world. Moray was fervently at work trying to get to the great truth of truths, the great mystery of mysteries, which was buried deep, hidden somewhere.

If Moray or the others should ever *find the diamond*, then what would follow? There's an old Zen proverb that says, *Before enlightenment chop wood, carry water. After enlightenment, chop wood, carry water.*[5] So, Searcher questioned, if nothing seemingly changed after awakening, what was the point of searching? Which was a valid point in and of itself.

This issue would gnaw away at Searcher-Observer for the longest time. He thought of the comment about Moray apparently needing a compass. He even wrote a song about it unambiguously titled *Explorer without a Compass*.

'If it's true that Moray, I, and the others are looking in all the wrong places, then the compass must therefore offer direction towards the goal,' Seeker deliberated. However, he just ended up looking for a compass for the exploration (meaning a way), which is still *searching* and not *finding*. So, how to find the compass without searching for it? 'It must be hiding right where I would never think to look. Right inside of me.'

Later, he met Capella whilst studying holistic kinesiology. One day early on in their studies the students were required to sit on the floor and freely draw or colour-in a scene. It would be a pictorial that would unconsciously illustrate the way they saw their lives at that time—that is, they were not aware of what it would reveal until the task was completed.

Searcher and the others followed instructions. Once the task was complete, they were asked to pair up with another student and show and describe their scenes to each other. Capella was asked to pair up with Searcher and she approached from the other side of the room. They barely knew each other and were yet to formally meet.

They nearly fell over upon seeing each other's drawings which were exact! In fact, better than that. They joined up in perfect symmetry. There were clouds, hills, rivers and winding paths that perfectly matched the other, including colour and form, as if they were a mirror image. It was bewildering and the other students were likewise perplexed.

Capella and Searcher struck up an instant friendship, most likely due to resonance. They were both diving deep, looking for pearls. This is only natural, of course, if that's your inclination, your bent. Many people live like that, looking for meaning in everything. Yet others don't bother searching for anything at all because they are unaware there is anything to search for—other than weekend sports, partying, social life, fashion, gossip, Bunnings, and so forth.

Others still, achieve the balance. They know there is more to life, but they don't become obsessed with the search, ideologically, religiously or philosophically. They live with an open mind and an open heart in delicate balance and equilibrium. Lucky them! They don't necessarily *stretch* and grow so much, however.

A black-belt tribulation

Redmondo-Searcher had dabbled with martial arts on and off over the years. Self-defence, Taekwondo, Karate, Shaolin kung fu—and that silly Aikido, which just made him dizzy. Eventually, he would stick at one form: Taekwondo. He trained consistently, which was probably good for him as he was an undisciplined kind of guy. His rug-rats Rascal-Sam and Cyclone-Izzy would eventually join in as well and one day get their junior blackbelts.

Searcher was never interested in *fighting* per se, although he loved the *art form* side of it. There was simply nothing better than seeing a good snappy kick or punch or kata (pattern of movements) and this was clearly his forte. The sparring was entirely necessary but at the same time quite senseless, he believed.

The students would constantly sustain injuries and then reinjure those injuries, which was called *learning*. As Searcher-Red grew older, he would pay for those injuries. For example, when one kicks out at another, the student is taught how to block downward onto the leg or swipe it away. Without doubt, the aggressor who had just kicked at their opponent would have a big fist come down, knuckles first, onto their foot or leg. Searcher would end up with bone fragments in the big toe joints that would become arthritic as a result. Nonetheless, it was a blast of a time.

Searcher-Red plodded along over the years but there was something brewing in the air and it was not good.

Master-Instructor-Pete was extraordinary! He was endowed with the greatest natural strength Searcher-Gra would ever see. And he'd seen a lot of martial artists! It was sheer genetics, it really was. It wouldn't have mattered which martial art he performed, Instructor-Pete would still have kicked anyone's ass. His father apparently was as strong as an ox too and had once walked upside-down—on his hands—up 75 steps from the beach to the top. Nonetheless, something had shifted at training.

Macho-Pete had upped the game. He was smashing poor little Searcher around the dojo like there was no tomorrow. In fact, Searcher-Gra thought there wasn't going to be another tomorrow at times. Instructor-Pete was old school, hard-arse, and always tried to sound firm and grumpy with the juniors, but those kids just loved him.

The sparring became longer between the two, master and student, and more intense and violent. One night, Instructor-Pete smashed Searcher-Gra from pillar to post, corner to corner. It was a giant hall and he was giving Searcher a raw hiding. It was alarming, actually! He was a fourth-dan blackbelt and immensely strong.

Concerningly, Searcher-Gra would go home after training, wring out the filthy sweat from his drenched *gi*, and his heart rate would remain above 100 bpm until the next morning. It really was intense. So, always slow off the mark, Searcher-Gra decided to ask some of the other blackbelts, 'Why is our instructor trying to kill me? Have I pissed him off?'

They laughed and said, 'You're an idiot. He wants you to go for your blackbelt, and if you keep saying no, he *will* kill you!'

After many more months of escalating punishment and pain, Searcher-Gra would finally comply. Reluctantly, he would go for that elusive blackbelt.

From that point on, he trained very hard for over 18 months. Because of the shift work and so-called saving lives and all that stuff, he had to train at all the other training centres in addition to his own. He also hired a personal instructor at the gym who was entirely focussed on *power* training, and not so much on *strength* training. Searcher-Gra would almost vomit after each session with him as well.

After finishing with the gym instructor, he would go and hit the colossal boxing-bag forever and then enter the other hall to practise his patterns, or katas if you will. At home he would hit the bag and train to extreme. He would perform all of his patterns with sandbags on his wrists and ankles, to weigh himself down. This was all extracurricular and all based on fear. He feared he might actually die in front of his friends and family who would later be present at the impending grading.

Frustratingly, Searcher-Gra always seemed to get bloaty after eating the *food of the gods*: bread. Following work, he would jump on his motorbike and bolt straight to training, quickly don his *gi*, hurriedly bow to Instructor-Pete, and get straight down to copping a hiding. Master-Pete had an assistant instructor who was another old-school hard-arse—a nurse in fact. After warm-ups were performed, into the sparring they would rip.

Then, Master-Pete and Crazy-nurse-Andrei would stand at either side of Searcher-Gra and simultaneously kick his abdomen as hard as they could in a synchronised fashion—like it was a giant soccer ball. They weren't aware that Searcher was most likely gluten-intolerant and used to bloat excessively after he had eaten bread and the like at work. The eating and scurrying mostly caused the bloating and then the rushing to training. So, his guts felt like a great big empty barrel, and those powerful dual kicks just hurt like billyo!

Furthermore, he was worried about his ticker—the cardiac side of it. Searcher appeared to have had an unofficial heart attack two years prior. It was after his black-tip grading, the one just prior to his blackbelt. Months before this grading he had been experiencing a lot of dull and aching left-sided chest pains and also hypertension. He consulted a local medical-god who booked him in for a cardiac-stress test. He performed the stress-test under the supervision of a professor of cardiology and his assistant.

They pushed Searcher hard on the treadmill, making him run until his heart rate peaked at 200 bpm. Following the test, the professor analysed the results whilst Searcher tried to catch his breath, exhausted. He was fit but they pushed him to the limit. Finally, the professor said, 'Right. Things look fine. You're certainly fit. You have a bundle-branch-block, but don't worry about it. Otherwise, all good. Go home and beat the missus up!'

Now because Searcher-Gra possessed a low-brow sense of humour, he burst out laughing when he heard the professor's comment, while looking towards the door to see if there were any female staff walking past. 'This guy's a scream, but how on earth does he get away with such old-school humour? Feminists would have a field day with him,' pondered Searcher. However, Kiki found the comment really funny too.

Nonetheless, something wasn't picked up through the cardiac-stress test or it developed afterwards. Following the stress test and during the black-tip grading, the one prior to the blackbelt, Searcher over-exerted himself to the extreme. After he was kicked hard in the solar-plexus and became extremely winded, things just didn't seem right. He pushed on regardless but knew there was something wrong, although intangible.

Searcher did an ECG at work on the night after the grading and showed his partner who was an intensive-care paramedic and loved all things *cardio*. Searcher showed him the ECG and said, 'What do you think of that?'

His partner simply said, 'AMI for sure. Whose is it?' Searcher-Gra told him it was his own and his partner looked at him puzzled. An AMI is a medical term, which basically means *heart attack*. Searcher's partner noted the gross *ST elevation*, which is a classic sign of a heart attack—an acute coronary occlusion.

Searcher felt very unusual for three days following. He could not feel his fingertips or toes at all and most of his body felt numb with an associated sensation of floating. At this time Searcher was exactly the same age as his father Tippy had been when he passed from this world. Searcher was also as stubborn as a mule.

Ignoring sound advice from his work colleague, he refused to go to the hospital, perhaps because he was feeling some dread due to his father's passing at the same age. Thus, he continued about his business.

This all weighed heavily on his mind as the blackbelt grading approached.

Finally, the big day arrived. Searcher was not what he considered to be *fortunate* with certain things and he woke up with a kinked neck and also could not swallow. He must have picked up a throat infection when he was out so-called saving lives and all that stuff. Nonetheless, things would proceed. 'Too late to back out now. I'll just accept my fate. If I die, I die,' he told himself and surrendered.

He'd been to countless martial arts gradings and they always left those students going for their blackbelts until later in the day. So, wisely, he decided to save his energy and warm up later, in a few hours' time.

Right at the stroke of midday, his name was called. 'Shit!'

He would do all of his patterns, starting from white-belt and moving all the way up as they become more complex and labour-intensive. He put absolutely everything into those patterns. This was his forte, his art form, and he just loved it.

He had trained long and hard for this. As he finished, he was quite chuffed with himself for remembering and implementing all those complex patterns to almost perfection and couldn't wait to sit down and catch his breath. He was totalled. Searcher had given it everything and was spent. But those titan master-instructor-brothers had other plans. Immediately, they picked three burly blackbelts and sent them in to attack Searcher.

'What?' In all of his years of training he had only ever sparred against two at a time, not three. Searcher was knackered, and they were fresh, and it was hard. After four or five minutes one blackbelt dropped off, then a few minutes later another, and finally there was just one-on-one for a few minutes more.

Then he had to spar two female blackbelts, who were like velociraptors. Fortune smiled on him in this particular instance for those two regulars, kind and decent were they, took pity whilst he was dying before their eyes and took it easy on him somewhat, so to speak.

Searcher walked to the back of the hall. There was a crowd of observers. An old guy looked at Searcher as he walked past and, with dropped jaw, shook his head in disbelief. It was quiet, the crowd were a little stunned. It looked a little bit over the top but that was probably just exacerbated by the fact ole Searcher had to do it all alone. He had never seen anyone go for their blackbelt *alone* before, as there were always several in examination. 'Just my luck,' he mused.

It placed too much focus on him, and, apart from dying in there, he felt embarrassed to be the centre of attention. He had a good break, however, and was able to recover his energies. Later, he was again called upon, and every blackbelt and higher than blackbelt lined up and prepared to have a real good time beating up the Searcher.

The master-instructor-titans-now-grand-masters who were running the examinations had advised Searcher beforehand: 'Don't waste time on any fancy shit—just tough it out!' You see, all the fancy spinning kicks and so forth, which Searcher-Gra was really good at, zap energy. They wanted it simple. 'Just stand up and fight with ticker.' That's what they wanted and that's what they got. For the longest time it would be two-on-one. Spar after spar after spar. Then it was one-on-one. Over and over and over.

It was horrendous. Searcher had prepared in every way he could. He knew it would test him to the limit and it damn well did. They were almost all bigger than he was. Searcher's not a big guy and quite scrawny, although he had built up in the chest a lot from all that power training.

Finally, there was *one*. His beloved Master-Pete and him. Searcher was puffing and panting like a fish out of water, and to the crowd probably looked like he was sparring in slow motion by that stage, but he advanced into the bulldog master of his, the one he loved, and kept swinging and kicking. Master-Instructor-Pete had a grin from ear to ear. He was proud of his student. Somehow, by miracle of miracles, Searcher got through!

Later, he was asked to break some boards with various kicks and punches, which he found quite easy as his technique was very good. Then a task was requested that would change everything. He was

The Searcher

asked to run along the big hall and fly through the air into a whole bunch of big hefty blackbelts who were holding some boards and kick the boards to kingdom come.

While Searcher had not prepared for this, breaking the boards this way was baby stuff. The whole thing was actually a stunt to impress the crowd and didn't really prove anything. Anyone could do it with that sort of momentum.

He ran long and fast, way too fast, and as he flew through the air and kicked those boards to kingdom come and those mighty big and hefty blackbelts yelled out 'Ahhh', because his speed even freaked them out, he landed sideways.

Seeker heard a snap. It was his left knee. Instead of landing with the rear leg facing to the back of the hall, he landed perpendicular with the knee facing the side of the hall. He was unable to get up. Those nice-big-compassionate-blackbelts assisted him up. After all those long years of training, that one particular landing was to be the *last second* he would ever be a coloured-belt, and now, he couldn't walk. He was crippled.

But Searcher was Coppertop-Tiger and he hopped over to the middle of the hall on one leg to receive his blackbelt from the giant-master-instructor-brothers to an applauding crowd. He held back tears and felt both pride and relief. Later, a very large blackbelt came over to Searcher. He was several dans up from a blackbelt in both Karate and Taekwondo and had won several major tournaments.

He had watched, and participated in, Searcher copping a hiding all afternoon. He said something that shocked Searcher-Gra. He said, 'Mate, I have been involved in countless gradings. I have seen good performances. But I have never witnessed a performance like you put on today for us all. Well done!' He then shook Searcher's hand.

Of course Searcher-Gra's head swelled up like a dead-hippo. But he would never forget that comment. In fact, it would prove to be the greatest compliment of his entire life. It's rare to hear such a thing. It's not normally the Aussie way because Aussies are quite deprecating. That's a good thing, because it helps keep your feet on the ground. Nonetheless, you've gotta take it when you get it, so Searcher was both proud and humbled.

The test was finally over …

Well, not exactly.

After the tournament, Ninja, an ambulance manager and also a fine karate martial artist, visited Searcher-Gra with a congratulatory card for obtaining his blackbelt. He respected that. However, Ninja said something peculiar.

He said, 'Most students who train long for a blackbelt see it as the pinnacle of achievement. It is like the top of the pyramid. It's what motivates them to strive for its attainment. However, consider this. Turn the pyramid with the pinnacle at the top, upside down. Now your real training begins. The pyramid with the apex at the top, now at the bottom, has become a cup.

'Now you know nothing! Your cup is empty. All that you have learned has prepared you to become the beginner, a baby, but one who is truly ready to learn. Learn from your art and learn from life and always keep the beginner's mind.'

Wow! That really knocked Searcher's pride and ego down a few pegs, although it made sense.

With his blackbelt under his belt, Searcher thought his spirit had been tested to its limits, but his knee was about to be the real test, both emotionally and physically.

Searcher had his leg assessed. It was stuffed. They performed what is termed a Lachman test to ascertain whether the anterior cruciate ligament was ripped or not. It was totalled. 'Na, no way,' said Searcher. 'It'll be fine.' But the expert shook Searcher's lower leg around like a rag doll and was unrelenting.

'Your cruciate is completely torn off, and your medial ligament is stuffed. It's a bad case. You will have to have surgery!' Searcher-Gra was not impressed at all, and to say that he is obstinate is an understatement. After all those years of training and hard work, he would just not accept it.

Searcher went to the beach and sat on a rock for hours aiming that quartz crystal from the sun to his knee and did all the energy-healing stuff. He also limped around feeling sorry for himself for days, until he hatched a great idea. 'I know, I'll go for a run!'

Nine days after the grading and snapping his cruciate and medial ligaments, he ran along the beach and up the giant hill to the highest point of his Castle city. It must have looked hilarious to any onlookers. He couldn't straighten his left leg at all and so had a bizarre running gait. Nonetheless, he did it. His true grading had begun. He would not get surgery and that was that!

Years later he would concede how stupid the decision was, because the problem is, if you don't repair a cruciate, apart from not having stability, you end up getting arthritis in your cartilage. Or so they say, but he still manages okay. He returned to martial-arts training with his fellow students, who felt like a family, two weeks after the grading.

Technically speaking, you remain a trainee blackbelt for another year until you receive your *dan*. But everything was different for Searcher, from there onwards. He had lost *stability* in his stances and had to always kick with the stuffed leg because he required the good leg to stand and anchor on. He was reduced but did the best he could, even though he was no doubt an embarrassment to all martial artists.

Chapter 9

Dismal waxheads

Fatty, Pantz and Searcher-Gra had gone for a surf after work. There was a big swell late in the afternoon. They were young men and indeed quite reckless. Hurriedly, they waxed their boards like their lives depended on it and jumped in off the Point, proceeding to make their way out the back. They had entered a *rip*, which for a surfer, is a good thing. For young Coppertop and Brave-brother, swimmers all those years ago, not so.

The surfer uses a rip to make her way out past the breakers with less effort, and quickly. If she aimlessly jumps into the ocean from anywhere, more than likely she will have to crash through the breakers by effort alone, and even if successful in making it out the back, will no doubt be exhausted. So, the rip provides a fast corridor for all wax-heads. However, this rip was different.

It kept going and going out like a conveyor. Some rips don't kindly take you out and say, *'There you go, I'm at your service, young wax-head.'* Rather, they keep dragging you out and out a long way. Rips are really just an indication of how the ocean water comes *in and out*. It's all quite a natural process, and one that Dalefin and other lifeguards would read all day long, to assess for changes and dangers to swimmers.

That afternoon, however, the surf was way too big for those three over-enthusiastic, budding wax-heads. They had bitten off more than they could chew. All three were freaked to the eyeballs and scared to take off on any waves every time they saw the faces of those monsters *sucking up*. It was gnarly!

The Fatman must have been blessed that day, because he couldn't surf to save himself, but somehow he caught a goodin' in and made his way to the shore and, as always, as straight as an arrow! Incidentally, the Fatman was never actually *fat*. Well, he kind of had a big belly once when they were all young men living together and partying too much, but Pantz had blown it all out of proportion, and the name just stuck.

One day he and Fatty bought two beautiful house plants, which contrasted each other in the loungeroom. Pantz would berate and stir Fatty's plant saying it was a poor excuse for a plant and would never survive. Pantz's plant grew and flourished next to the Fatman's poor excuse for a plant, as it stifled. But time is an interesting teacher and after Pantz's plant had had its day in the sun, so to speak, it withered and died.

The Fatman's little plant would grow big and strong, long after its showy neighbour had perished. Searcher-Gra always thought there was something in that, but let's get back to the rip story.

Pantz and Searcher-Gra were out there shouting at each other trying to be heard over the howling wind and spray.

'What are you gonna do?'

'Dunno, shiiit.'

Gra had a particularly ominous sense of dread because he'd had not one, but two, near-drowning incidents when he was a child.

The first was when he was only a grommet. He was plodding around in a natural ocean pool when he struck a deep section. He was perhaps only three years old. As he hit the deep section, he went down and his foot got caught around some seaweed. He was thrashing his arms around underwater but couldn't make it to the surface for air, which felt miles away but was only inches.

Suddenly from nowhere, two grown-up girl heroines came over and simply snatched little Coppertop up and out to safety. It was a terrifying incident. Those all-grown-up girls were seven years of age.

The second incident was as mentioned before with Brave-brother in the paradise of sun and sea at the Golden Coast.

Pantz and Searcher-Gra were out there shouting and debating with each other about what to do. They were honestly just too pussy-scared to take off on those monster waves, which would either take them in to safety and end their plight or waste them good and proper and end their plight. It started to get dark. Then darker, and darker still.

Poor Fatman, who was aware his best mates were nuts, was a sensitive fellow and actually became a bit emotional, sitting all alone on the beach. He could no longer see his two brother-wax-heads for they were too far out (in more ways than one), as it had become too dark for visibility. It sounds simple. Just take off on any wave and ride your way to the shore. But if you take off on a monster and lose, it won't be the only wave to maul you. It always happens in sets.

Then, when you get thrown around intensely as if you're inside a giant washing-machine, and you have no idea where up is, you start to panic. They call it *being worked over* and it's aptly named. If you're lucky and happen to make it to the surface, well, it's just a fact known by all wax-heads you will be hit harder than a freight train by another wave and down you go again and again before you can recover your breathing.

The problem for Gra-once-Coppertop was he would suffer from anxiety down there in that maddening washing-machine turbulence. Because he had almost drowned as a child, he carried the memories of surf-terror. Every time he was what the wax-heads called *held-under*, he would panic and inevitably breathe in water. Normally, he could hold his breath for a minute or more in relaxed, non-watery conditions, but only for four or five seconds in this scenario.

It didn't make for any serenity out there in that brewing stormy ocean. Nonetheless, the story ends well. All of a sudden, when Pantz and Gra were feeling quite defeated, Huey, the god of the ocean, felt sorry for those desperate wax-heads and sent a far gentler set towards them. From panic to hope in an instant, those two silly fools jumped on a wave each, which were still quite big, considering their lack of surfing prowess, and rode those suckers all the way to the sand.

The Searcher

Fatty was overjoyed to see his soaked mates there all of a sudden, for he had almost given up ever seeing them again. Pantz was shivering and quivering from the cold, as he always did. They dried themselves off, rugged up and headed straight for the pub. And the funny thing is, by the time those three refreshing and mouth-watering schooners of beer had arrived on the bar, the surfing incident was never mentioned again.

More on Pantz-now-Scooter, however. He was always getting himself into trouble. He had been drinking lots on one hot summer's day, and the boys thought they would go on a thrilling toboggan run. Up to the top they ascended, each on a toboggan and off they raced from the summit, screaming and yelling like lunatics.

They were absolutely flying down the slippery-silvery half-pipe and hadn't listened to the safety instructions on how to *ride your brake*. It was a big lever between your legs that you needed to pull before the turns—if you were sensible, that is. Suddenly, big Skipper-Pearl came screaming around the corner and goodness gracious! There was Pantz-now-Scooter, just sitting there right in the middle of the track. Skipper-Pearl couldn't avoid him and *thud*; it was horrible.

Gra was fanging from behind and saw the lot. Scooter would most certainly be a paraplegic, Searcher-Gra thought. He was hit in his back at top speed by a toboggin. Scooter had lost control of his own toboggin and somehow ended up becoming a toboggin himself somewhat, but a stationary one.

Scooter was so drunk, he didn't feel a thing. They rushed him down to the hospital an hour away, all very concerned indeed. He would need x-rays, like *now*. Waiting, waiting patiently in the emergency room. Finally, hours later, the news came. Scooter emerged and casually said, 'I'm in the shit, fellas. The doctor just absolutely roasted me.'

They all thought, 'No doubt.'

'He said, "You're as red as a lobster and really should be using sunscreen! Don't let me see you here again."'

And that's what it was like hanging around Scooter.

Scootes just didn't take himself too seriously, except when it came to girls. Once when he was up on the Golden Coast of sun and sand, he found himself in a scuffle. In the middle of a highway, some two-bob mug lair wanted to fight him over a senseless matter. Scooter couldn't stop laughing whilst the angry young man laid into him, which just made him all the angrier and made Scooter laugh all the more. Yes, he loved to chuckle.

And he particularly enjoyed a certain incident that involved Searcher-Gra. Hot-headed-Gra was cruising down the freeway to buy a Marshall guitar amplifier from a guy in Sydney. He was distracted, listening intently to the senseless blanket bombing of Iraq during the first Gulf war on the radio and forgot his speed.

A highway patrolman, who was not so inattentive, clocked him driving over the speed limit and pulled him over and offered him a fine. Hot-headed-Gra with his inbuilt bullshit detector just knew this cop was a smartarse through and through. So, of course, they got into an argument. After receiving his gift (the infringement), Searcher jumped in his car and took off hastily, spinning his wheels in anger, just like he used to do on his motorbike as a kid.

Seconds later, Constable-Smartarse pulled him over again, and this time offered him a fine for negligent driving. That would significantly contribute to hot-headed-Gra's demerit points. He lost 9 of 12 points in a flash, resulting in the loss of his licence for three months.

Guess that nice copper didn't like being called a *cupcake* from a hot-head, and that was the part of the story that Scooter most enjoyed. Hot-headed-Gra gained some fitness riding his bicycle to work for the next three months, although he just couldn't see the funny side of it like Scootes could.

Scooter also had a habit of annoying people for the strangest of things. He later became an athlete of sorts and found out that he had quite a freakish talent for running and bike-riding, but not swimming or surfing, as aforementioned. So, he became an Ironman. Over at the Big Island he would compete against athletes from all over the world.

Up at the crack of dawn, not long before the big race, he would go over to the bicycle section where many of the athletes were wanking-off over how good their bikes were. *Mine's better than yours* sort of thing. So, Scooter, just to stir them up a bit, would go over there perving on their brand-new fully carbon bikes and blow cigarette smoke in their faces. Crocodile-Hogan would have been proud of that!

Those fine-specimen athletes were repulsed. 'Fucking disgraceful Aussie, what's he doing here? He doesn't belong.' Scootes couldn't swim to save himself, so he really gave them all in his age group a damn good head-start in the first 3.8-km-swimming leg. He would gain a lot of ground, though, in the 180-km-bike leg. But it was the afternoon 42-km-run leg where he shone.

And lo and behold, 'Fuck, there goes that smartarse, cigarette-smoking Aussie.' Scooter ran past them like Forrest Gump.

His doctor dished out severe warnings to irresponsible Scooter for consuming too many alcoholic beverages per week and smoking, but he still managed to work hard in those sweltering Queensland coal mines and whip those fine men who were in love with their shiny new bikes. Go figure.

The Thinker

She was told, *'A young man will come into your life and he will show you the way.'* Gra-Searcher was working at a grain facility laboratory. It was monkey work; just testing for wheat quality and searching for weevils, but it was quite frenetic. They had to keep up with the tests as every 250 tonnes of grain dropped through, and could not fall behind, such was the quality control.

There were no windows and, should you be two minutes late coming back from your 30-minute lunch break, the next worker would only get 28 minutes for their lunch and so on. Although that fact didn't seem to stop Dravid, the yogi with the whimsical smile, from running late.

Sandy ran the lab. She wasn't the supervisor per se, but sort of acted like a leading hand. Very hands on. She worked at an absolutely frenzied pace. Searcher-Gra found her a bit stand-offish at first. She was a lovely lady, a Pommie and had a work ethic you rarely see. Gradually, over time, Searcher and Sandy started to connect.

As they talked about religious and spiritual things, Sandy would share how she felt that God was just like a great big father figure to her; she even called him *Dad* or *Daddy* when she prayed. It sounded a bit strange to Searcher, but he thought, 'We're all built differently,' and so it wasn't a problem at all.

One day, long after Searcher had started working there, Sandy was staring at Searcher deeply and he felt a little uncomfortable and prickly. Abruptly, she said, 'It's you!'

Searcher responded with, 'I'm sorry?'

Sandy said, 'Do you know why I didn't like you when you first started here? Well, at first I thought you were after my job, my supervisory position, and I felt threatened. You seemed all confident, and it just scared me a bit. I really need my job.'

Searcher was quite shocked at this revelation from Sandy. He explained how he didn't give a toss about doing supervisory sorts of jobs and, besides, she did a great job. He was always complimentary to people. Sandy explained how she had realised that after a while and kind of apologised for being somewhat distant early on. Then she said something even stranger.

She revealed to him how she was told by a psychic years before that a young man would enter her life and *show her the way*. Sort of explain stuff that made sense and would help her on her journey. Sandy said, 'It's you. *You are that young man!*

'Uh?' Now Searcher's head swelled like a balloon; he was a Leo after all, and they just love compliments. However, that wasn't really what freaked him out. He was left there stunned. 'How could someone years before possibly know my footsteps in advance?' he pondered. 'I thought *I* was steering this ship.' It felt puzzling to Seeker and he never quite seemed to solve that puzzle.

When you're a Seeker, a Searcher, you think a lot of *I wonder whys?* And Searcher did plenty of that. In fact, he had even been called *The Thinker*. It refers to an ancient bronze sculpture of a pensive male-figure in deep introspection. It wasn't necessarily meant as a compliment.

'Thinking is okay, but you can get lost in it and it doesn't lead you out of the forest,' he pondered. 'Thinking just leads to more

The Searcher

thinking.' It's the same as worry, which is also a form of thinking. 'Why worry? It doesn't change a thing,' as they say.

Nonetheless, Searcher often pondered on why his father had died so young. Not that there could be an answer, of course, but he often wondered about the destiny of it all.

One day, Searcher fell into a narrated vision of a past life …

> You lived here on this Chinese mountainside. Your name was Tensing. You grew up to be a farmer, just like your father and his father and his father's father. It was tradition. No-one considered otherwise. Your job was to farm the rice paddies on these cascading mountain terraces. On the soaring ridges draped over the valleys below, you would spend your whole life. But you were different. You always dreamed of more. Other vistas, other jobs, other experiences, other realities. It wasn't to be.
> You were a good man. You stayed loyal to your father and his tradition and to your beloved family. As you grew older, you started to carry regret in your heart. The regret of not experiencing more out of life. Your bones grew old and tired and you became weak. You were unable to leave but your mind stayed in contemplation of other times and places.
> Eventually, you became sick in health and would die right here in the village by the gorgeous mountains above, which held your beloved perched rice paddies. And do you know what your last thought was? You wished you had not incarnated into a family tradition, with a father's expectancy. You wished you had been a free man. Where you could listen to music of other cultures such as the illustrious classical and baroque traditions.
> And see the great work of Michelangelo and Picasso and others. To see the grand castles and cathedrals of the world. To travel and encounter other peoples, other mountains and other sunsets.

Now, you have your freedom. Your father, Tippy, didn't die as a result of you, most certainly not.

But you are here now in this life, free to do whatever you please. To go wherever you wish, to choose whatever you choose and to be whatever you'll be. And you cannot blame, as you did on the rice paddies, your lot, your father, your fate or your family traditions for your dissatisfaction.

However, we say with friendly caution, total freedom does not always lead to reward. Sometimes too many options produce scattered results. Your life on the Chinese mountain ridges was simple.

In your current existence, you may very well one day plead for that same simplicity. Ultimately, however, it matters not the 'lot' of an individual. Peace and happiness can be found in any circumstance. Go now and live your life. Do not live in regret or uncertainty for your days and moments are precious beyond measure'.

Pet hates

Searcher-Seeker had two pet hates: stethoscopes and ties! He called medical doctors *medical-gods,* but it wasn't meant to sound half as bad as it did. Some of them were indeed very skilled medical-gods. Seeker saw them as highly trained, expertly precise, well-schooled, detached and exceptionally gifted people.

'If I'm run over by a car, take me to a hospital please, not a kinesiologist. That's their forte right there: emergency medicine,' Seeker asserted. But the master they served, *allopathic medicine*, basically only had *two* things to offer: drugs and surgery! Searcher's archetypical vision of a doctor was of a person holding a bottle of pills in one hand and a knife in the other saying, 'Can I help you, sir?' Did the American Indian ever take a Panadol, a statin or an anti-hypertensive?

Medical-gods meant well and mostly did the best they could, but their modality was riddled with arrogance. Everyone has at one time or another experienced the aloof and condescending tone of a medical-god who thinks the sun shines out of their own arse; that they've been put on this earth to offer their almighty services to those poor, suffering, uneducated plebeians of the world. Sadly, they were not so rare throughout the medical community and were not yet ready to admit their failings and limitations, for they believed they had *all* the answers.

Searcher imagined humanity in a hundred years or so, looking back at these times and saying something like, 'What? When an organ wasn't functioning adequately, they just cut it out or poisoned it with chemicals? Oh, that's so crude.' And, my God, did the medicals attack anyone who might offer *alternative* treatments, even if they'd been quite effective for hundreds or even thousands of years. To Searcher, the media seemed to support them in that aim.

No, it was medicine and medicine alone that could save your life. Just ask Flossie-Mum or Delightful-niece or the others; however, you'll have to ask them through a psychic medium.

The most fascinating observation Searcher made about medicine was the *placebo*. The placebo is a medicine, or a procedure performed, that has no apparent therapeutic use. It is designed to placate a patient, or as a control to prove the effectiveness or lack thereof, in the study of drugs in double-blind studies. It can have a psychological benefit and/or a physiological effect.

Medicine has long derided the placebo effect. It is beneficially used in their studies, but most often scoffed at when applied in non-allopathic therapies. Yet, lives have absolutely been saved by the placebo. It is similar to *faith healing*. If the individual *believes* strongly enough in a medicine, procedure, or faith healer, they will often heal and become well again. The power of the mind is an incredibly effective healer, and often a rapid one. Only those who have had so-called miraculous results from a placebo can attest to that.

Yet medicine ridicules the notion that an individual can cure themselves of the gravest illnesses, such as cancer, simply by belief alone. 'This right here should be the elixir of medicine, the most exciting of all endeavours,' felt Searcher. He believed medical research should turn its attention to the placebo and consequential healing possibilities. Regrettably, there is little money in self-healing, though. No control by *big-pharma!*

They would not be able to make their billions if people were taught how to heal themselves and remain healthy. Searcher also believed the prognosis was a kind of reverse placebo, such as when the medical-god *points the bone*. 'You will likely die from this disease within six months,' and they most often did. The power of the mind seemed to work in either direction—towards healing or towards illness and death.

You see, Searcher wasn't actually a sceptic of medicine. Yes, he had abandoned taking medications for himself but for himself alone. That was most likely because he had become somewhat jaded from working for years in the ambulance service and because of the way he was treated following the mining accident, and finally the way one condescending medical-god pointed at poor Flossie when she happened to be doing well and showing improvements on his charts, saying, 'Don't you delude yourself, lady, this will get you in the end. You will not survive!'

The Australian Aborigines call it *pointing the stick* or *pointing the bone*. As an Aboriginal, you really didn't want that happening because it wasn't going to have a good outcome. Searcher felt that, of all things, the greatest crime of modern medicine was when they pointed the bone called the *prognosis*.

Flossie agreed with Searcher and Brave-brother on that note. She believed the diagnosis was extremely useful. That's medicine at its best with all their modern equipment and diagnostic tools. But the prognosis was a life-sentence whereby one often died pretty much right at the time the medical-god foretold they would.

In fact, over the seventeen years Flossie carried leukemia and cancer inside her, she avoided sick people like the plague. She hated talking about illness. If someone had a sore foot, she'd remind them of their other one. She got that from her mother—from back in the tough era.

'Every individual on the planet is unique,' contemplated Searcher. 'Who's to say when one's time is up, or how they will or won't respond to treatment? Besides, why hand out death sentences? It's good to be honest, it's necessary, but a little optimism goes a long way.'

They say that doctors *bury* their mistakes. Who could truly attest that that has never, ever happened? Seeker summed it up, 'It is what it is. For the most part hospitals are full of good people doing good things for others. When the arrogance falls away, they'll be doing even better things. But first, they must acknowledge their limitations and failings.'

Seeker's mate Dalefin had cardiac issues. He was treated by medicine. Once he improved, he started using all the natural therapies he had researched and became very fit and healthy. When he went for his medical check-up, he assured his cardiologist he was taking all his medications and doing what was required of him. The medical-god was pleased and informed him that all of his test results indicated he was back to *perfect health*.

'Keep taking your meds and don't change a thing. It's working for you. Your blood pressure and cholesterol are perfect,' said doc.

'Um. There's only one thing, doc, I stopped taking all of my medications. You didn't tell me of the terrible side effects, like rocking in the cupboard, insomnia and feeling insane! I'm feeling great now, though, so thank you for all your help. The natural supplements and exercise have worked wonders as well,' said Dalefin. The medical-god physically threw a book at him and demanded he leave his surgery at once.

Thankfully, Seeker noticed, a lot of medical-gods were changing. They were the open-minded avant-garde, willing to embrace more holistic approaches, willing to *listen* to their patients. 'Yes, there's hope for the future.' It was exciting. All of this and more the Searcher would mull over. Perhaps not every medical-god opened their sentences with the word, 'So …'

Ah, but that bloody stethoscope! A doctor uses a stethoscope for various things, mostly for respiratory conditions to listen to the lung-fields. They don't use them much anymore for doing blood-pressures because the digital ones do it automatically. Nonetheless, they persist in wearing them around their necks all day—for one reason only.

It's a status symbol. It sends a conspicuous message to the non-medicals that they are a DOCTOR and have all the answers.

Searcher met a few in his time while working in the medical matrix, though, who had abandoned all the crap and just talked to people like they were *people*.

You wouldn't even know they were doctors, for they were long past trying to impress anyone. Searcher just loved those humble doctors for they were precious and rare and, in his mind, he never called them *medical-gods*. The old biblical proverb 'Physician, heal thyself'[6] is a poignant reminder to doctors, healers and therapists alike—for it starts and ends with *self*. How many professionals make a lucrative living telling others what to do when in fact their own lives are in shambles?

And onto his second pet hate: the repulsive tie. Young Coppertop had to wear one every day for four years in high school because he was at a Catholic school and they were *special*. They were *honourable* and the tie was a status symbol indicating eminence. But as he grew up, he wondered who had invented such a thing and who actually enjoyed the sensation of feeling strangled.

For some, it is worn all day every day. For others, it is only for a short time, like entering courtrooms. Yes, Searcher noticed you could do all manner of hideous things like rape, murder, theft and the like, but if you wore that respectable *tie* in court, you somehow looked more upright. 'No, you don't,' thought Seeker.

'Shouldn't one strive to dress comfortably?' Curiously, Searcher often cast his mind back to the native American Indians. He wasn't sure why he did that, but he used them as a yardstick for measuring how strange society had become. You could almost hear him telling the Chief how modern man, in order to look respectable, pulls a tight cord around his neck called a *tie* and wears it throughout the day.

The Chief stares far off into the distance towards that majestic rocky mountain ridge that he and his forefathers have loved for aeons. He is silent for the longest time, contemplating what he has heard. Finally, the Chief talks. *'Perhaps this modern man you speak of uses this tie for strangling Brother Buffalo!'*

And what would the Chief think if he saw the young men of today? Would he ask, *'Your young braves, what do the body paintings represent? Do they represent their victories? And those bulges in their arms—what is the purpose?'*

'Well, the paintings are called tattoos. It's body art. And the bulges are muscles they build up in the gyms to get the chicks.'

'Chicks? Do you mean fowl? And your squaws? They seem to have large swollen breasts that bobble and bounce up and down like a raindance. And puffed up lips of hardened elk fat.'

'Oh, that's called cosmetic enhancement to look hot.'

'Hot? Like the desert?'

It wasn't just the ridiculous tie that made Seeker reflect back to the Indian Chief and braves. Always when he was in a modern shopping centre, he would think of them, without fail. Being overly sensitive to smells, which drove Kiki and Izzy crazy, he would walk past those cosmetic nail shops and nearly vomit on the spot. Overreacting!

Searcher felt sorry for the workers who had to endure the chemical odour all day long, wearing just a skimpy little mask that rarely even covered their noses. And what of old ladies with their hideous perfumes and hoary men with overbearing cologne?

Why, why?

And all the artificial lighting and sounds and frantic shoppers searching for the best deals. It just lacked any serenity, any calm. It felt fake, like it was somehow unnatural and yet, he was a part of it all. Such is modern living.

Searcher had a vivid dream …

> He was captured. He was a 'white man', strong, muscular and courageous. But his time was up. The young Indian warriors had surrounded them. His wagon-train had been ambushed. All he knew were now dead from the arrow or knife. He was bitter and resigned. He would accept his fate no matter what. His wife and kids were gone. All were now gone! There was no hope.
>
> The Chief saw something in the white man's eyes. A fire. Yes, a fire. He was aware this white-man had just lost his

family to his young braves. He contemplated in silence. All were summoned. There would to be a fight. A fight to the death. Chief chose his first-born son, a formidable fighter. He was a warrior indeed. He and the white man would fight to the death and no-one would intervene. Both were afforded the same weapons: a tomahawk and a knife.

Each man was up to the task. The white man had nothing to lose, he was numb. The red warrior had everything to gain—honour, respect and status.

It started ferociously. It was bloody. Such an intense battle, yet all present were quiet. That was 'the way of it' back then. Both men were injured badly yet gave their all; fear was not apparent. Adrenaline pulsed through their blood. Red and white man, but same colour blood.

Suddenly it was all over. White man had ended it. The Indian brave had fallen. Chief's first-born son was dead. The tribe held a ceremony, long through the night, drumming and chanting around the fire. White man was now a red man, chief's de-facto son. Red man indeed became a warrior, long after his injuries healed. For the rest of his living days he lived as a brave. Gradually, as he got older, the fire in his heart subsided, and he made peace with life. He barely even remembered the ways of the white man.

Chapter 10

Hollow men

After Tippy passed, some of those wonderful married Catholic men of the community pitched in and attempted to help poor Flossie. They really did, like visiting *alone* by coming to the front door and asking, 'Now, is there something I can do for you, love. No, I mean really. Anything, anything at all.' Once Coppertop had worked it all out, he just loathed those so-called gentlemen. They were the same married men who took up the collection each week at mass.

Amusingly, looking back, his young eyes almost burned holes in those *hollow* men. He really did hope there was an angry, vengeful, male God that Grumpy-old-drunk-priest used to rave on about. He hoped those pious men would be sent to Hellfire-boy for trying to take advantage of his still-grieving mother.

Unfortunately, in his heart-of-hearts, he knew it was not to be. Somehow, he knew if the Creator was an all-loving God, then judgement would not come down on those men as he had hoped. 'No, an Almighty God of love could only love and forgive,' he concluded. It was only man, the harshest of all critics, who could judge so severely and cruelly.

'What kind of loving God could be so hard, so unforgiving?' It just didn't make sense to him at all. As he became older, Seeker imagined how this all may have come about. Man, in his arrogance, would turn God into an image of himself, with all his petty beliefs and judgements. That suited him, especially when applied within a *religious* context. Whether the great saints and prophets existed or not, their words could be manipulated for others' agendas.

'It's funny how I can't even remember a conversation I had yesterday,' thought Searcher, 'yet those scribes of old apparently knew what someone had said hundreds of years before.' And that wasn't even the biggest problem he wrestled with. It was the *interpretation* that created the real dilemma. Everyone seemed to have a different *take* on the teachings and rarely agreed.

Saviour Brian

Brian was a Christian, a diehard Christian and paramedic. All the local paramedics knew of his religiosity. Seeker-Gra was unaware of what particular brand of Christianity Brian spruiked, although he knew Brian had been *born twice*. He was a nice enough fellow. Seeker was bemused how, whilst working in the ambulance, Brian would hand out religious-business cards to serious alcoholics lying in the gutters on the street who were so inebriated on Metho and the like that they didn't even know where they were.

Yet Saviour-Brian believed he could convert their poor souls. The only *spirit* they would have received from him, however, would have to have come in a bottle. One day, Saviour-Brian and Searcher were sent on a long journey, to a rescue case up in the mountains. They were not involved in any treatment this time but were to drive two enthusiastic intensive-care paramedics with all their camping and medical equipment up north-west and drop them off in the freezing cold, to stay for the night.

All went well. However, as soon as they turned around and left to return to their station, hours away, Saviour-Brian immediately grabbed the opportunity to say to Seeker, 'So, you're some kind of pseudo Christian I've heard. What's your go?' Seeker-Searcher was a bit stunned, but the conversation had started.

Saviour-Brian was off and running and began his recruitment drive. Things flew back and forth for hours. Saviour-Brian kept quoting from the book-of-books and quoting the *Messiah* over and over again. After a while, Searcher got sick of it—besides, he was a redhead after all.

Defiantly, Searcher said, 'Brian, do not quote your master's words to me, not now, not ever. Unless you can bring him to us right now and he alone instructs me to listen to *you*, don't you ever talk on that wonderful man's behalf again. He is far too loving to have you or me taint his words with our petty little tongues. If, however, you would like to speak about *your own* life and openings and experiences, I'm all ears.'

Brian was unnerved. Evidently, he was a very powerful voice in his religious community, but he hadn't had anyone challenge him like that, it seemed. He became quiet. Brian had said during the conversation, though, that he *had* received his own personal message from God. It was, *'I am in He who is in Me.'* Seeker genuinely liked that one.

When they had finally returned to headquarters, Brian came over and shook Seeker's hand. He said, 'Best of luck, I'll judge you by the fruit of your vine,' or some such metaphorical rhetoric like that. Searcher chuckled.

Later that night, *Being-from-afar* saw how Searcher was quite worked up over this Saviour-Brian character and asked, *'Pray tell me, why are you losing your light to that entity?'* Clearly, arguing about matters of faith just seemed absurd to her …

The trouser leg

Those times in the ambulance service were long and draining, but not without laughter. There just happened to be a certain fellow, however, who really did put a new spin on the word *stupid*. Think Forrest!

Searcher-Gra wondered how certain dodgy paramedics slipped through the cracks and became employed at all. He himself only got through because he was smart enough to know how to answer those ridiculous psychological questions in a way that made him look *normal*. They were clearly designed to trick one, and in *no* way shape or form could be considered an indicator of intelligence. But, as always, they helped keep those human resources people employed.

This certain paramedic, or *ambo* as they were affectionately called at the time, was clearly **different**.

If Andy was called to attend a chest pain, then that's what he would treat. Paramedics receive information of a case, prior to attendance at the scene, but withhold judgement until they actually see the patient with their own eyes. Not so for this fellow! Much to the consternation of his partner paramedics, he would robotically march onto the scene and start treating what he was called to treat, rather than how the patient presented.

It really wasn't his fault. No-one helped him, mainly because he would get extremely agitated and angered if you did. *Taking over my treatment*, it was called. There could be hundreds and hundreds of entries in this book and, in fact, a whole book could be written alone on this Forrest-like character, Andy.

One such example, Seeker-Gra recalls. Andy and he were sent to an elderly gentleman who'd had a fall. They arrived on the scene to find a dear old man fallen over on a long cement driveway, out the front of a nursing home. Andy was the treating officer. Normally, in urban regions, the paramedics would drive for one shift, treat for two, and drive for their last shift. Or a similar pattern of rotating shifts applied.

However, Andy was a stickler and if he was treating, the driver better *damn well shut the hell up* on scene. They were backed-up by another crew of intensive-care paramedics. Whilst the experienced *frog* (a colloquial term for intensive-care paramedic) was asking the dear old man about his injuries and other such questions of medical history, Andy decided to cut the old man's trouser leg off with his trauma scissors.

Andy figured it would make it easier to see any injuries to the patient's right upper leg, and that was probably a good idea. Soon enough, as pain relief was organised and the loading of the patient was being thought out, it became quite evident there was a problem. 'Ah, Andy, why have you cut this man's trouser leg off?' says Wise-old-frog.

Robotically, Andy replied, 'In order to perform a full assessment of the gentleman's leg.'

'Umm, Andy. It's his left leg, the left that's injured, you goose, not the right. You have cut the wrong trouser leg.'

Poor Andy was demoted to driver on the case thereafter, but that didn't happen without a fight.

They settled the patient's pain and loaded him up for the hospital. Wise-old-frog made Searcher-Gra jump in the back of his truck to assist him with the treatment. And do you know what? They did nothing but quietly argue all the way up to the hospital.

'You're doing the hand-over, no, you are. No, you are, no way I'm not doing it. I refuse. It's embarrassing. He cut the wrong trouser leg, for God's sake. They'll think we're idiots. You're going in! Nup, I'm not, no way. You'll just have to!'

On and on they went. The elderly gentleman was none the wiser, but Searcher did note that, when they were first on scene, during the palpation of his leg and hip, the old man had said those were his favourite trousers.

Frog and Searcher eventually decided to suck it up and accept their fate. Courageously, they marched into the emergency room full of elite professionals and handed over their patient with the fractured *left* neck-of-femur and missing *right* trouser leg. It was both gutsy and fearless and Searcher believed they most certainly deserved a medal for that one auspicious act of bravery!

Years before, when ambos worked alone, long before satellite navigators, Andy was sent to a case and got himself lost. This was before ambulance vehicles had transponders on them, and so Co-Ord (short for Coordination Centre) didn't know where he was. They repeatedly called him on the radio, but poor Andy was too busy searching for his own arse. 'Andy, Andy!'

Co-Ord had responded another vehicle to the case but had since become concerned about Andy's whereabouts. It had been quite some time. Finally, Andy responded. Big Fat-Jack, the ambulance coordinator, stood up. He was so fat he used to walk around the centre with his office chair stuck to him. Imagine that, a guy walking around with a chair stuck to his arse. He loved his food so much, they used to say he *inhaled* chickens. He'd eat a whole loaf of bread and drink a full family-sized bottle of coke in one sitting.

Fat-Jack was saying on the radio, 'Andy, Andy. Just look over to your left, yeah, that's it, up a bit, a bit more. See that guy waving at you? That's me. That's the ambulance station.' Andy had been gone for over an hour, but it turned out he hadn't gone far at all.

Andy wasn't the only one of questionable intelligence. One night, Searcher was sent out in the ambulance to provide emergency coverage at the speedway racetrack. He would work alone and respond to any accidents as required. As he arrived, the chief race steward instructed him to park at the racetrack entry and *not* enter the track until *he* told him to. Water trucks were driving around the track in an attempt to soak it and prevent too much dust from flying up. Searcher-Gra was not always the best listener.

As soon as the first hairbrained John Candy-like race marshal came up and told him to drive on to the track, off he proceeded. It didn't last long. The crowd were arriving in droves by this stage. Searcher was a little surprised to see his big white ambulance vehicle losing control. The harder he tried to save it, the worse things became. The crowd erupted!

Seeker grumbled to himself, 'Small things amuse small minds.' Although that was a sentiment not shared by the crowd! He decided to gun-it and tried to accelerate his way out of the slosh and mud. That proved to be not a good idea. The big clean white ambulance with the red beacons flashing started spinning around and around through the mud doing anticlockwise 360s. The crowd were beside themselves and assumed this was all part of the entertainment put on for them. Why wouldn't they?

Finally, the not-so-white ambulance came to a halt in the inner ring of the track. The crowd were ecstatic, on their feet clapping and begging for more. Searcher was virtually hiding under the dash, dying from embarrassment. The chief race steward was not impressed to say the least. He came and blasted the stupid paramedic. The bulldozer came to the rescue and rescued the entertaining paramedic.

Grace and the race

It was a contest. An unspoken one among a few. She was a chronic patient. Actually, a chronic malingerer. Grace would ring the ambulance every day and, unfortunately, not just once—sometimes ten or twenty times. Every local paramedic got to know her. It's quite strange the affectionate relationship you can build up with some of the most annoying patients of all. You just get to know them. There was rarely anything physically wrong with Patient-Grace as it was more of an emotional nature.

Some said she was just scared of the dark as most of the calls came at night. The paramedics would take her up to the hospital, she would hang in or around the emergency department until dawn, and then she'd go home for a sleep. The next afternoon, it would start over again. The optimum trip from the station to her residence, from there to the designated hospital, and the return trip back to the station, was well mapped.

The local crews started secretly competing in order to gain and hold the record for the quickest round-trip ambulance transport of Patient-Grace.

One fine afternoon, Searcher was feeling very lucky and pumped. They received the call and he and Gina, his work partner, decided this was it. They could just feel it—today they would smash the record! They arrived on scene and yelled out, 'Come on, Grace, we're in a hurry, jump in, quick.'

Patient-Grace came out hurriedly and jumped in the back. She was like furniture on the wall by now, and there certainly was a peculiar affection between them. After all, you just get to know each other after a while and accept each other's quirks. Some paramedics felt they were better and above certain patients, but Seeker was told a valuable proverb during his training that somehow stuck. The ambulance educator told the students to always remember this before judging others: 'There but for the *grace* of God go I.'[7]

Seeker-Gra really put the pedal to the metal like never before. They couldn't hear Grace's whinging over the screaming sound of the big revving V8. Those old F250 wagons that he used to pull up onto two wheels were the best ever. Ambos just loved them! You could virtually *feel* the road and felt safe in them.

Searcher and Gina rushed Patient-Grace into casualty and, in a blink of an eye, were scrambling back home to the station. 'Tell 'em your story, Grace. Seeya! This will be it. We will hold the record for years, Gina,' they applauded each other. The record was set previously at 18 minutes. They were close to home and whilst sitting on 14 minutes were most certainly going to make it back by 16.

Per policy, when you arrived back on station you were given a time verbally from Co-Ord and then you would write it on your case sheet. That would be your proof right there. You could then excitedly go and show off your new record to all your colleagues in pure delight.

'Oh NOOOOO!' They were being called to attend another case and would not make it back to station. They would never gain that prestigious, unspoken of record. It was all in vain. It was depressing. Life indeed sucked!

Weary Seeker

Seeker-Searcher had been seeking and searching for a long time now. It was a quest that would take him more than thirty years, starting as a young man when he *woke up* out of his body and perceived all those unusual incidents happening before they happened. It was a long road. He was becoming tired of the search, tired of human behaviour, and tired of the struggle.

Seeker doesn't normally get tired and lives on six hours of sleep a night. That's because he's a night person and Kiki is like an elephant in a tent in the mornings. It's not by choice, but he generally feels good during the day. At this time, however, he was weary. Things inside were not good, something wasn't right, and he knew it. Something was definitively *out,* and no-one picked it up, or if they

The Searcher

did, couldn't care less. At least no-one from the compassionate *service* he had *served*, for so long.

Searcher went on a retreat and, boy, he hoped he would be all *fixed*. It was a very special place with a great anticipation and excited energy. He knew they would meditate and the like. He had meditated on and off over the years but was never consistent enough to reap any real rewards. The temple had been set in a Buddhistic style, but in no way was it a Buddhist retreat.

There were two massive stone Buddhas, one on each side of the altar, with beautiful garlands of sweet-scented flowers just everywhere. The smell of incense wafted strongly through the hall. There was the master and the student-disciples. Seeker enjoyed the times in the temple and also the times outside with friends, as they stayed in individual cabins and felt the ocean breezes blow through. It was lovely and a good break too.

But frustration remained. Others were in their *bliss*, in the *zone*. One woman never moved a muscle for two days; she just sat there day and night in deep meditation. 'What's wrong with me?' Seeker pondered. 'Everyone seems to be *getting it* but me.' He persisted and was quite genuine in his quest—for, after all, the search had been going on for a long, long time.

Because he was a musician through and through, he was particularly taken by the music of one Krishna Das. It seemed to be an integral part of the retreat. Krishna Das had taken the world by storm with his *Kirtan* music.[8] It's a sort of devotional, chanting-type music. Krishna, who was once an American rock musician, had followed his friend Ram Das to India and went on to meet his guru, Neem Karoli Baba, affectionately called Maharaji.

Krishna later committed to spending the rest of his life performing Kirtan, in honour of his guru. Something like that. Each day and each night, there would be sessions where the teacher would come in and give a dialogue and then Kirtan or similar would be played in a sort of *natural-high party-mood*.

Searcher was up for it on one particular night. A certain ancient Aarti, which Krishna was playing, was remarkably powerful. Something was happening. The oversized Buddhas stood tall, the incense smoke was wafting, the music was loud indeed, and the participants were exceptionally *high*.

Suddenly a shift occurred! Intense bursts of energy started blasting up Searcher's spine, upwards from the base to the crown, in rhythmic pulsations of light. It felt to Searcher-now-instantaneously-*Sounje* like liquid, crystalline, amorphous waves were infiltrating his being, washing, cleaning and soothing his field. The music felt heavenly and the moment, holy! It was joyous; pure joy. Strangely, in all the time he had been there, Searcher had not once thought of the Immaculate One. Not once!

Yet, although the altar was set up in such a Buddhist fashion, it was Christ and Christ alone that was in him and through him. He was washed clean. It felt like he was *born again* as the Christians put it. It was intense, like an emotional cosmic-orgasm in fact. He would spend about a week feeling enlightened or more accurately, *awakened*.

He could not look at a sacred image without crying. He struggled to look at Kiki-dolphin without crying, this sacred being in front of him. All were sacred. Not a one was not. All were/are sacred! He wondered why he had not known this great-truth of the ages, truth of the sages. He cried and cried with joy and emotion. Full to the brim!

Unfortunately, soon he would have to return to work and during those initial days, it was tough. He could not remember his own name. He could not remember what year he was in. He could not remember what his tasks were. Only love made sense. His immediate aim was to just stop crying at the beauty of it all.

'They'll think I'm nuts and turf me out of my job; we've still got a mortgage.' Regretfully, though, in the weeks that followed, it would wear off. He tried his darndest to keep the sacred feeling, but it would go. He would run through the bush listening to the same Aarti of Krishna Das on his iPod, trying to raise his energies but, besides feeling relaxed, it was gone, all gone.

Searcher would take up the search again sometime later, but never again so passionately, never so fervently. The disappointment of the awakening wearing off was too much and he was sick of searching. There were kids and work and training and music and a thousand things to do. The fragrance stayed, but the kernel was gone.

Later, as he continued exploring the nature of consciousness, he heard that Ramana had said, '*Whatever comes and goes is not real. Only "That" which never comes and goes, is Real.*'[9] So he would concede in the *truth* of all things that the shift that had happened at the retreat was not ultimately real. Searcher walked on.

Chopping off the head or polishing the diamond

There was a puzzle. A giant puzzle that Sounje-the-Seeker found himself right inside of. Because he had awoken out of his body at quite a young age, and in order to try to understand it all and make sense of it, he'd set out on a journey. It was the *journey of seeking*. And like most, it becomes a religious quest, a spiritual quest, a philosophical quest, an ideological quest, or a blend of them all.

Other perspectives in consciousness became apparent. Eckhart for example, didn't prescribe anything to actually do, apart from embracing the golden *moment of now*.[10] Others popped up, offering similar teachings. Modern teachers were appearing everywhere describing reality as simply This, or That, or That Which Is; Pure Awareness; Thou Art That, Infinite Intelligence; Consciousness; I Am That; Oneness, and so forth.

So, the puzzle was as follows: 'Is it a case of *chopping off the head* or of *polishing the diamond?*' Searcher-Sounje realised most people didn't really give a toss about this and probably had no idea about the puzzle anyway. Or, humorously, were not *puzzled by the puzzle*. Even though it was tearing him apart, it was his puzzle to solve after all, and was paramount.

The traditional Eastern spiritual thought was that underneath all the layers and layers of grime (conditioning), there lies a shining diamond. It is who and what we are! The true *Self* without another. Through social conditioning and outdated beliefs, we just cover up the truth of what we are and forget. In order to re-discover the truth of what we are we must meditate, pray, do yoga, chant, abstain from sex, exercise, eat vegetarian, go on retreats, sit on mountains, and all the many things that the spiritual teachers prescribe, to *polish the diamond* clean.

One day, if we're very lucky, we will have earned the right to peace and happiness. Or, for some, be bestowed the gift of enlightenment from a so-called master and then, finally, we will be happy and free.

Contrastingly, the other way becoming ever so popular is to let go of who you think you are, and just *Be*. It's what the teachers of yore used to call *chopping off the head*. Searcher thought this meant *stopping the thinker* and is often done by simply witnessing one's thoughts rather than following them. It was certainly a less *egoic* way, less *juicy* than the traditional spiritual way.

The best metaphor for describing it, Searcher believed, was the ocean metaphor. That is, you are the entire ocean, which holds all manifestation, and not the wave you believe yourself to be, which comes and goes. Humans, lifetimes, thoughts, emotions, creations, seasons, planets and stars, just like the waves, all come and go. They have a birth, life and death. Ramana suggests, '*Seek that which never comes and goes. "That" is what you are.*'[11]

So, Seeker-Sounje really didn't know which way to go, or not go. On the one hand you were to *polish the diamond* of who you are and on the other there was no *you* to do anything with. The body-mind with its thoughts, emotions and sensations were real and living in you but were not actually you. The reason it seemed to matter so much to Seeker was because one is either *steering his own ship* or is *being steered*. Hmm? No-one seemed able or willing to solve this dilemma for him and nor should they.

It was like a Zen koan or a riddle, only this was a life koan. Although Seeker didn't exactly solve this impasse, he did experience what those teachers were talking about from time to time. One day, for example, he was riding down a cycleway, lost in thought. Suddenly, it became apparent that no-one was present. Bike riding was happening, legs were pedalling, everything was continuing on as usual, except Searcher just wasn't there. It was strange, though simple, and not at all like the holy experience in the temple. It was more of a negated experience than something special.

Many teachers talk about how there is, '*No seeker, and no-one there to seek*' and so on. Some say that it is all just so simple and obvious that we overlook it by expecting something more grandiose and special. It is actually not hard to feel this experientially. Simply close your eyes and feel where the body ends.

Providing one is not feeling pain or discomfort, which can be a distraction, one most likely feels nothing but open space, which is without edge or limit. This begs the question, therefore: *Who or what am I?*

So, to describe Searcher's life dilemma succinctly: 'Are we steering our ship or are we being steered? Free will or destiny?'

In response, the Perceptive-one said to Searcher-Sounje: *'This is your path. This is your task. You must take these two philosophies, these two perspectives, which seem to be in contradiction, and make them one, as we, the Nihal do!'*

Chapter 11

A ghost with attitude

He was working with Bull, who was a large man, though quite sensitive. Seeker had been transferred to work with Bull for the night shift. It was an old brick ambulance station and very large. Just off the main street, the station was two-storeys high with ample space and rear vehicular access. It was also well known to be *haunted*. There wasn't an ambo who didn't know or hadn't heard about it.

Bull liked to talk about *her*. He said she was a friendly ghost. He even told Searcher, whilst working alone, that he had fallen asleep on the lounge and when he woke up there was a blanket on top of him. One which wasn't on him prior. 'No-one was here, no-one can get in here anyway,' Bull said. 'Besides, she'd done that before.'

Searcher had heard all the gossip. One colleague had told him he used to hear two sets of footsteps walking up the double stairway at night when there was no-one around. There was also a large billiard table and he said he had often heard billiard balls colliding loudly. Bull confirmed this ghost-like behaviour and also said the great big glass doors had slammed shut all by themselves, when no windows were open.

As Searcher was listening to all of this, right behind Bull, he noticed the CD carousel had started going in and out by itself. Strange, but it was probably nothing. Searcher was somewhat used to weird stuff, so he wasn't too concerned about any of the rumours.

The two men were busy before midnight. In those days, they worked a fourteen-hour night shift, although, routinely, their shifts were extended much longer depending on emergency demands. Unofficially, they were allowed to sleep on night shift, and even had beds.

At around 2.30 am, the pair arrived back at the station and Bull said he was going to catch some z's and retire. He said with a wry smile, 'You can sleep in the main area here. I'll take the other room.'

'Okay, no worries,' Seeker responded. It was a restless sleep. They nearly always were. Paramedics are always at least a little on edge, waiting for a potential big trauma to come in. Eventually, Searcher would fall into a sound sleep.

Sleepy-Searcher was dreaming, dreaming. There were two women sitting right across from him in the ambulance station, within his dream. They were playing cards—one younger woman of about thirty and one older woman of perhaps sixty or so. They were quiet. Not a word was spoken.

Sleepy-Searcher, always the fool, even in dreams, yelled out, 'Apparently, there is a ghost at this station. But don't worry, Bull says she's nice.'

Well, right there and then the older woman in the dream looked across at Sleepy-Seeker in quite an evil manner and, before he knew it, was on top of him. It was insane. It felt like a hundred cement trucks were sitting on his chest, and now he actually was awake. He was being choked right there and then.

Old-hag-ghost was definitely not the ghost Bull had been talking about. She was strong, heavy, dangerous and frankly, downright nasty. She held her hands around his throat and tried her utmost to destroy Seeker. It was bloody terrifying. It all happened so quickly. One minute he was having a pleasant dream, next minute Old-hag-ghost was trying to annihilate him.

Now, whilst Searcher-Gra really had no interest at all in ghost topics, he was no stranger to them either. Recall Mother-fucker-sexed-up-ghost from earlier times. It was, in fact, over ten years since that episode. He had learned a few things along the way with his searching and had heard about the protection of white light, and also the *dome of light* from Kiki.

So, whilst Searcher was being choked-out by Old-hag-ghost, he eagerly started saying a prayer. Whilst imagining himself to be in the *dome of white light*, he repeated these words, *'I am white light; I am protected, and I am whole.'*

It was obviously some new-age slogan-prayer he had picked up along the way, but somehow it did the trick. He kept repeating it over and over until Old-hag-ghost was gone. That morning he commenced holidays and drove his family up to the Golden Coast of sun and surf, and so never shared the experience with anyone other than Bull on that rugged morning at the crack of dawn.

Two nights later, another non-local crew had to work at the same station. They were what is termed a *probationer crew*, because it was made up of a trainer and a trainee. (Probationer crews float around the stations, filling in roster voids.) The trainer was reasonably new to the area, and the trainee was quite green.

So, they may not have heard the rumours of the haunted station at all. Something evidently happened to those poor unassuming fellows that night, because they high-tailed it out of there and based themselves out of the local hospital, absolutely refusing to go back to the ghostly station.

Thankfully, the service has since built a lovely new station at a different location. Searcher-Gra was also keenly aware of, and intrigued by, how sceptical ambos just never seemed to see or experience any weird stuff. It appeared they just blocked it all out somehow and Searcher thought that was a damn fine idea.

Viper

They called him *Viper*, and for good reason. He was a paramedic, a builder, and a martial artist. He was as hard as steel. When he looked at you, you just felt nervous for some reason; perhaps like looking at Iron-Mike, the ferocious boxer.[*] Everyone respected him, because they were too scared not to.

---

[*]Heavyweight champion Mike Tyson.

One night on ambulance duty, he was treating a drunkard who, being quite vocal, had a lot to say to Viper. So, Viper knocked him out cold, there and then. He simply called on the radio, and said, 'Yeah, could you send another ambulance here; we have an unconscious patient.' Viper treated the other patient instead. In fairness, that was 'back in the day'.

Viper was an intimidating man. He had worked as a security-bouncer at the roughest pub in the city. By himself, he would manage the drunken sailors and bikies who had come looking for a good time, trouble, or both. He told Seeker, 'If they pulled a knife or gun on ya, you just dealt with it yourself. The very next night, you'd be straight back working there alone again.'

Viper added matter-of-factly, 'I gave them five seconds at the end of the night to get up and leave. If they didn't leave, I knocked 'em out! That was the way of it. They only understood one language: violence.'

Incidentally, Viper originally trained in martial arts with the titan-master-instructor-brothers who examined Searcher for his blackbelt grading. They were enormous men, perhaps 6'6, 6'4, and cut. Viper wasn't tall at all, maybe 5'10, but his arms reminded Searcher of a lion's legs: solid. One of those giant brothers remembered Viper and just shook his head and said to Searcher, 'Viper, unbelievable!'

Later, he kind of superseded martial arts and created his own approach. One time, a publican of a rural hotel asked Viper to come up on a Friday night and sort out the riff-raff. He'd had a lot of trouble with the local army guys getting drunk and running amuck. So, Viper arrived there with a few martial arts mates, one of whom would later confirm the story, and cleaned the lot of them up. Dozens of them! It was brutal. He left no stone unturned that badass Viper! And his damaged knuckles still tell the story.

The witness told Seeker-Gra that after those tough army boys were well and truly whipped, bashed and bloodied they all jumped back into their army bus. Viper wasn't satisfied with that particular outcome, so he jumped on their bus too, pacing back and forth ridiculing those poor troublesome army soldiers, saying, 'Come on, you pack of sissies, what's wrong with you now? Going home to Mummy, are youse? Come on, chicken shits.'

It appeared they were no longer interested in being arseholes and hence, had had enough of fighting Viper, for they were soldiers instead! The cops later came and said to Viper, 'You have done a good thing for this town, but it's time for you to leave and we don't ever want to see your crazy ass back here again.' And that was it …

But it turns out Viper *was* actually scared of *something* after all. One night, he was working at the same old ambulance station that Searcher had worked at where he had the run-in with Old-hag-ghost. And some time through the night, Viper's flabbergasted work partner said Viper had gotten up from his sleep, kicking and swinging and shouting and hollering at something in that back room—but the partner was damned if he could see anything in there!

Wizard

The wizard over in Costa believed healing was healing. He claimed that once you were *healed,* there was no more reason for further treatment or therapy apart from occasional visits, just like a regular check-up at the medical-gods or tooth-chippys. A lot of people become addicted to therapy and seek it far and wide. Not so for the wizard. He claimed in his broad Irish accent, 'If it's not feckin working, it's not feckin working.' Searcher-Gra took all of that on board.

When you work with the chakra-based system, you have to consider *blockages* in the energy flow. If one chakra-nerve plexus became blocked, then the one below it backs up, and so on, just like in a traffic jam. Searcher was working with a client who *felt blocked* (interesting term). She had lost two loved ones and felt *stuck* (see the language here), as commonly happens in grief.

She was concurrently trying to get her own business up and running but felt she just lacked the *drive* to do so. The healer may look at this scenario thusly: If the heart chakra is shut-down due to grief, for example, the next chakra below the solar plexus will not be functioning optimally. The solar plexus chakra is the chakra of the *will*. It is your *drive* or *power* chakra. Searcher calls it the *battery* or the *lion* chakra.

When chakras, or anywhere in your energy system, become blocked and therefore receive either too little or too much energy flow, you most likely will become sick as a result. There are a thousand examples and a thousand more that show how this all plays out, but to the healing practitioner, it's all the same. It's *stress* one way or another. So rather than *blast* a client with some extra-special-pure-energy, the wizard would advise removing the stress, that is the blockage, energetically.

Whilst stimulating the *trans-receiving* heart chakra, which feels almost magnetic, Searcher would attempt to allow the natural-born flow to occur again in that region by pulling out the stagnation or resistance. This may present as an improved feeling of *acceptance* of the grief, or a feeling of *making peace* with it or a *letting go* and so on.

It really was quite fascinating to Searcher seeing how we are all wired energetically, and it made sense. If the heart chakra returned to optimal functioning, the lower chakras would start to flow as well, starting predominately with the solar plexus, as it was immediately below. The image of the *traffic jam*, Seeker-Searcher believed, demonstrated this better than anything else.

One client whom Searcher was working with had been seeing a chiropractor for years. Silly-Seeker happened to quote the wizard in reference to treatment saying, 'If it's not feckin working, it's not feckin working.' Like, why continue with the chiropractor? Needless to say, it wasn't well received. Years later, Seeker would resolve the little riddle regarding healing, or at least he thought he did.

On the one hand, the wizard was correct; if your healing or therapy was not working, why persist? Move on! Yet, on the other hand, perhaps it's not a full healing that some people are wishing for. Perhaps it's relief. Support. Just as the chiropractor helps relieve the back pain, even though it tends to come back at a later time.

Friend of Seekers, Capella, had a good case in point. She is a naturopath and once had a client who was suffering from various things including depression. After a year of working with Capella, the client announced to her, 'I feel so much worse since I've been seeing you, but thank God I've had you in my corner, Capella.'

So, sometimes it's *assistance and support* a person needs rather than a full healing per se. The wizard also warned against working with someone who was currently involved in an injury insurance case, as he believed, rightly or wrongly, they had an invested interest in not getting better until they received their insurance claim payout. Only then, he felt, may they potentially accept the crystal-clear waters of their own healing. Nonetheless, each person is unique and should be treated that way. With respect and care. No case is the same.

The other predicament for Searcher in regard to healing was as follows: Should an energy healer work on someone's sore knees, for example, when clearly their own obesity is causing way too much strain? Yes, working on the underlying *causes* of obesity would be wiser; however, the majority of people just want immediate physical relief. Searcher felt that these people would be better served by a nutritionist or a counsellor rather than a healer.

Predominantly, however, the problem for Searcher was that damn *magic wand*. He really did believe in the energetics of healing and had witnessed some quite miraculous healings, as well as non-healings, but the *magic wand* issue persisted. Besides, deep down he always believed that one had to heal oneself before working as a practitioner on another.

Now, that is an ouch point for so many therapists out there—refer *the wounded healer* syndrome. And Seeker was no stranger to the notion. In fact, he called it the *fat-aerobics-teacher* syndrome. Not that overweight aerobics teachers don't exist or are not effective teachers, but they just don't seem to look the part. This is exactly what Seeker felt of himself as a healer.

Loosely, Yeshua expressed:

> You need not know any special techniques, study courses or obtain special qualification to heal. You must simply radiate the 'frequency of the solution'. Whilst you, as the healer, are aware you are assessing your client, you are unaware that your client is assessing you.

> If they perceive you walk your talk, that you radiate the frequency of the solution, that you indeed have done your own work and have healed yourself, they may then choose to absorb the solution into their own being and heal themselves, consciously or not.'[12]

The Searcher contemplated how the greatest obstacle to a person achieving wellbeing was all the unconscious programs that one had picked up along the way. A person may be extraordinarily committed to healing their wounds; however, if they are not willing to dig deep, they might not be able to *effect* the change they so desire. That's why they call it, 'the root of the problem,' thought Seeker-Gra.

He believed one should always open one's work with a client, with a discussion regarding all things pertaining to where they were at, and all that had led up to that point. Seeker had studied professional counselling, which is a very useful modality in that regard. Searcher called this opening discussion the, *what-lies-beneath chat*. Whilst he felt it was imperative to start that way for a baseline understanding of the client, he believed one should avoid becoming lost in talk-therapy.

'Going around and around and around about what is wrong and what had happened to the person tends to just keep them there, stuck in that energy,' stated Seeker, 'and can also promote victimhood rather than empowerment.'

Albert Einstein, arguably a spiritual scientist, famously said 'The most beautiful thing we can experience is the mysterious'; he also said, 'We cannot solve our problems with the same level of thinking that created them.'[13] Hence, there was both passion and doubt co-existing in Searcher when it came to the whole healing field, for his middle name was *Thomas:* doubting Thomas!

Alas, the momentum for healing ended quite abruptly. Flossie enjoyed some of the peculiar healing approaches her weird Seeker-son would perform. She enjoyed the hands-off chakra stuff with relaxing music in the background as well as those little dinging-tuning forks.

Flossie either gained some pain relief from them or, as a typical loving and encouraging mum would do, she just bullshitted Searcher and told him how good she felt after one of his treatments. She was like that—you never could tell!

One day she was quite ill. She came down by car to Searcher's place for some healing. Searcher was shocked, however, when he saw just how debilitated and in pain Flossie was, as she struggled to hobble up the steps with her bags of goodies she always brought down. Searcher said, 'Mother, what the hell? You're too sick. Why didn't you tell me? I would have come to you instead.'

Flossie's pal said, 'You're the healer, fix her!'

That was the end of it right there for Searcher. He did what he could for Flossie, but he would no longer pursue healing. He detested how some believed that one could actually *heal* another. 'That's impossible,' he reflected. Healing isn't like that at all. He had never seen or heard of a medical-god *heal* another either. Not once, not ever in history.

Sure, they helped. They set the bone, dressed and sutured the wound, medicated the heart. But the *healing* was innate. It was in everyone. No, a doctor cannot heal, and a healer cannot heal. In fact, the word *healer* was a misnomer to Seeker. It was inaccurate and misleading, but what to do?

A higher power, a force, a life-energy, an intelligence, a source, an *innate* can heal. It does heal. In every second of every day our bodies are always healing. And it's automatic. The same intelligence that creates stars, beats hearts, digests food, grows hair and breathes the body, heals.

So, that was it. Seeker would continue to try to heal himself, though. After all, isn't that what searching is all about? With one exception—in her last days, he did some healing on Flossie; however, it was motivated purely by desperation.

So, if all heal, all day, in every way, why then do we get sick and die?

Seeker believed it was surely unrelieved stress, trapped negative emotion and the like. After all, you cannot *catch* cancer, can you? It can't be caught, but a healer believes it can and is *created*.

The Searcher

Unconsciously, of course. Few if any on the planet would consciously choose pain or suffering. And if those old emotions, hurts and pains that lie right down beneath are not addressed or released, then over time, turmoil just starts to develop inside.

And what of this unconscious mind where all the automatic programs are running? The Magnetic-one believes kinesiology is a wonderful tool for accessing this. He proposes a question thus: '*How come the greatest minds among you, the most intelligent of all of you, can have cancer in their bodies for a long time and not even have a clue?*'[14]

This was a great question for Searcher. It hit a nerve. The kinesiologist or similar, can, via signals from the musculature system, access the unconscious mind. The place where all those programs are running—and all that muck that can make the body sick—resides. 'This is important,' thought Seeker. Obviously, a hypnotist could do the same.

Doctors Dispenza, Lipton, Chopra, Braden and the like were well and truly onto this when they suggested things like reprogramming your subconscious mind and meditating for same. Searcher was starting to see into the future, which was actually already here, and it was exciting and even backed-up by modern, progressive science. Think quantum mechanics!

Things were really looking bright for people and health and wellbeing, moving forward. This was a new frontier. People would take back their power and heal and balance and align and tune. The NEW MEDICINE was the old one. It was in line with nature, and it had arrived, or at least, it was arriving. That made Searcher so happy. Happy-Searcher! You see a searcher is not always a narcissist—a *narc-hole*.

A true searcher knows what it feels like to suffer and therefore wants healing, wellness, happiness and abundance for all, not just for themselves. Seeker could finally see the light at the end of the tunnel. Being-from-afar, however, cautiously warned, '*I hate to burst your bubble, but it could also be the light of an oncoming train.*' Searcher exploded at that one; he just found that so funny.

Bluebottles

It was a bleak day. They sat on the sand and pondered. Talked some rubbish, chewed the fat. Brave-brother-not-yet-Callithumpian and fervent-Seeker-once-Coppertop were staring out at the gloomy ocean. It was choppy, swirly and not particularly inviting. Nothing like two decades before when Mother Ocean whispered, *'Come in, boys, come into my beautiful crystal waters and play with me.'*

Not the time when Brave-brother had saved his brave little arse and Coppertop had his tummy pumped on the beach. No, this was of another time. They had grown up. They were men. Tippy had long gone to the great-beyond-of-no-time-and-place. Beautiful-sister was all busy being a little ray of sunshine in the world and being best mates with her mother, Flossie. Coppertop had grown up and become a real-life Searcher. Brave-brother was a nurse and, well, he had just seen a lot of shit. Some really bad stuff.

So, what do Aussie boys or men do when they live in a coastal region to let it all hang out? They go for a surf or a body wave. In fact, they would all tell you straight that there is nothing on this earth that cures a hangover quite like the ocean.

It was a nor'easter. 'Damn it, brother, look at those white-caps. There's gonna be fuckin' blue-bottles.' Those little blue bastard jellyfish like to affectionately give you a hug.

They rap all around you with their gluey tentacles and sting like hell. As you grab a tentacle off your face, chest, arms or legs, they just stick to your fingers and cause more stinging and pain and suffering. Aussies hate them but you can't avoid them when there's a decent nor-east breeze in the afternoons. Sure enough, they walked to the shoreline, 'Yep, look at them. They're bloody everywhere,' concurred his brother, dejected.

It just seemed to add to that nonchalant, blasé feeling in the air. What to do? They had nothing else on and rarely had a chance to catch up and catch a wave. About fifteen minutes passed. The brothers were still staring at the ocean. Abruptly, as if in synchronisation, they turned and looked at each other and smiled.

Not a word was spoken. Into the ocean they ran and caught wave after wave after body wave.

The blue bottles were everywhere, floating on the water's surface like soap bubbles. And bizarrely, not one sting. Not one! It was if those two brothers of Tippy and Flossie's had an invisible force-field causing the little blue bastards to be spooked. Impossible, but true. Sometimes, as Kiki found out on Skipper-Pearl's catamaran out in the cyclonic lake, and as the young boys found when being harassed by Ole-Lillah, you just need some danger, some excitement in your life.

Daydreamer

Redmond's memory was a blessing and a curse. It really was. He believed he had the worst memory of all time, and quite well may have. He didn't even remember much of his schooling, especially high school. It was a haze. Other mates, like Christo-Wal and extremely-well-endowed Sox, seemed to be able to remember and recollect any day of school. It worried him.

Searcher pondered it might have been a result of being a daydreamer. It's hard to remember something when you're not actually *there* for it. That's why Eckhart, teacher of the golden moment of now, advises us to be present in the here and now. The other side of it for Redmond-Searcher, was that he could curiously remember some distant things as if they had happened yesterday.

Interestingly, if someone should accuse him of saying something in a dispute, for example, it was like what he actually *did* say was embedded in his mind forever, as if he could never forget it. Just as with some of those early out-of-body experiences, he still remembers every minute detail in full and will for the rest of his life. However, there's a diffcrence of course. The *brain* struggles with it all because it wasn't actually present for the experience. It wasn't *out there*. How could it be?

It's an *out-of-body* experience after all. The brain *interprets* one's *memory* of the experience, which is why it can seem at times quite fuzzy and confusing. Yes, some to Searcher had strange recollections of what he had apparently said, but it was their interpretation of what he *meant* that altogether pissed him off. Like, how can one really say what another actually meant? It just didn't make sense.

It reminded him of a story that Dr Dyer had once told about himself.[15] He was an evolving psychologist and had written many books, the first of which had become a classic, a long-time prior. Years and years later, he happened to be studying a particular course. The teacher at the front of the room asked the class to analyse a passage from a certain book and describe the author's intention.

Dr Dyer sat there and did his best. When all of the students had finished, the teacher advised them where they were right or had gone wrong. He told Dr Dyer where he had misunderstood the author's intention. Dr Dyer said, 'Fair enough. But there's just one thing. Um, I actually *was* the author of that book I wrote so many years ago. With respect, sir, I'm pretty certain I know what I meant.' Such irony!

The orb incident

Christo-Wal's car was totalled. Returning from a gig, they came around the corner to Red's home and were startled to see that Wal's little bongo panel van had been written off. Smashed to hell and back. 'What?' It turned out someone had come around the corner at warp speed and come to a very abrupt stop indeed. Had Wal been in his beloved van at the time, he could not have survived the impact, such was the damage.

The young men were quite shocked discussing the whole affair, the mini-drama. Eventually, Christo-Wal walked home to his own residence down the road. Adrenaline and insomnia were present for the both of them as they mulled it all over in their minds. For at that point they were still unaware of what had caused the total demolition of his car. It was a mystery.

Early the next morning, Redmond walked down to Christo-Wal's place to see if he was alright. As he entered the house through the back door, he noticed the blinds were still closed and everything was dimly lit. He approached Christo-Wal's room yelling out to him to see if he was awake. As he entered, however, he was shocked to notice something very peculiar.

All around Christo-Wal's bedroom were large floating, opaque, translucent, reddish balls—perhaps ranging from 5 to 15 centimetres in diameter. Christo-Wal was awake by this stage and was staring at them in astonishment as well. They couldn't seem to compute what was going on; it was a *real-time mystery*. Those semi-transparent, luminous balls would eventually fade out.

Wal was freaked to the eyeballs; he was like that. He immediately thought they had something to do with his panel van being destroyed. So, he later did some research. Things were more difficult to explore back then, as the internet, or personal computers for that matter, were way off into the future.

He subsequently believed those strange balls appearing in his room might have been what some pilots of the Second World War called *Foo Fighters*. They were reportedly sighted by pilots from American, British, German and Japanese crews, who described them as red, white or orange glowing balls.

For Redmond, however, that phenomenon seemed to belong more in UFO territory where it was hotly disputed whether they were UFOs or secret German weaponry. Later, those unusual balls they had seen, would simply be termed *orbs*. They are commonplace. Orbs have been repeatedly sighted and photographed by everyday people from all over the world. All kinds of theories have been proposed about them being other-worldly phenomenon and such.

Sceptics believe they are simply a photographic anomaly. Either way, young Christo-Wal and Redmond-later-Searcher saw what they saw with their own eyes; they had not photographed them and hence, were not caused by a photographic glitch.

Man sparks water search

Not so long after the strange orb incident, Redmond had just had his heart ripped out and shredded up by his *first cut is the deepest* young sweetheart. Being the coward that he was and not willing to suck it up, he packed up and left the area. He moved north to that paradise of sun and surf, the Golden Coast where he had almost drowned as a youngster.

Red didn't know anyone up there as yet and was living in a backpackers hostel. It was cheap and nasty, or nastily cheap you might say. One day, a friend of Christo-Wal's and Alfred's, named Catz, called Redmond up. He invited him to come out and have some fun. So, they did just that. Redmond really wasn't a drinker because it messed him up but, no doubt missing home, he decided to go out and party.

Catz was a true drinker, as well as having other recreational interests. He drank like a fish, yet his behaviour did not alter, apart from displaying a cheeky grin from time to time. From eleven in the morning to eleven at night, they visited nightclubs and pubs and the like and drank and drank. By this time, Red was well and truly smashed.

They were sitting on chairs beside the water, talking to some girls who no doubt found them repulsive. It was the Broadwater in fact. Redmond, by this time of the night, had long since lost all common sense and sound judgement and in a rash moment simply jumped into the water. He would swim across the Broadwater, over to the backpackers hostel, which was a long way away even for a good swimmer of sober mind, a few kilometres diagonally. At least, that was the plan. And besides, it would save him money for he had spent enough of that throughout the day.

Off he swam, fully clothed and shoed and homeward bound. He can now understand why his son is a rascal and his daughter a scallywag as he remembers scaring the shit out of passer-by passengers motoring past in their party boats. Right out in the middle, way out in the Broadwater, he would wait till they were close, real close, and would then let out an almighty scream to scare the pants off them. How he wasn't run over by a vessel is still a mystery. As is how he made it over to the *other side*—of the Broadwater, that is.

Somehow, somehow, he made it across to land and plopped and slopped his way back to the hostel. It had taken hours. Some were

The Searcher

still awake and watched this drenched-rat collapse on the common-lounge, breathing heavily. They told him the next day he was still swimming in his sleep for hours, arms flapping away like a seal.

He went to work the following day as a storeman. When he arrived home at the backpackers hostel that afternoon, the others hurriedly approached and showed him the newspaper.

These words were sprawled out on the front page of the newspaper: 'MAN SPARKS WATER SEARCH: POLICE SCOUR THE WATERWAY LOOKING FOR THE BODY OF A YOUNG MAN'.

'Ouch!' It felt really bad as he read the details. Evidently, the girls present had become quite concerned and had reported he had not *resurfaced*. Unbeknownst to them, that was Red's favourite party trick at the time. 'Sometimes, you just wish you could wipe out your past deeds,' Red lamented.

By this time, Redmond had started his search, his quest, but not ardently so. He was open-minded enough. So, months after the swimming incident, he decided to see a psychic, at a cost. He saw a lady who seemed quite aloof and detached. She did not appear warm at all, which confused Redmond. He had assumed that if you were so *in touch* as to be a legitimate psychic, you would also be pleasant, inviting and comforting.

Nonetheless, this psychic was good. Really good. She *picked up* how Searcher-Red had been volunteering and helping out with a diminutive brain-damaged little girl, with physio and water therapy on weekends. 'How the hell did she know that?' reflected Red. The *reading* continued. And the following is the bit that really freaked him out:

The psychic-lady said:

> Recently, you were involved in danger. Great danger and peril. It appears to have been on a waterway. I see lots of water. A giant body of water. Somehow you nearly drowned. You should have drowned. You were foolish. However, this time you were fortunate. It seems that you were saved. Your own father carried you across the waterway that fateful night.

Chapter 12

A phantasmagorical encounter

Searcher had a dream. He saw a colossal ship in the skies moving with great velocity. Suddenly, it was upon him. He was being chased by alien beings and ran fast. One advanced towards him in a peculiar motion which he could not escape from. Hopelessly, he turned and fought for his life. The alien being appeared somewhat humanoid, although remained nonchalant, unperturbed, peaceful almost.

Searcher fought and did all the things Master-Pete had taught him in martial arts, but the being was too elusive, grinning all the while. Suddenly, two more extra-terrestrials joined in, forming a triangular pattern between the three. Searcher fought even harder. The beings defended evasively and without any real effort.

Finally, as Searcher's efforts mounted, two more beings entered the scene. There were now five alien beings from the colossal, seamless, silvery ship circling above. Searcher was in for the fight of his life. He kicked and punched and yelled and spun, but all his efforts were in vain.

The beings were too fluid, moving like water, just as Bruce had advised to all students of martial arts.[16] As Panicked-Searcher continued fighting, the first being spoke to him through his mind and said, '*Try as you may, Sounje, you cannot escape. We honour your courage, but we have not come to harm you. Please relax. We have come for you. We will take you away and instruct you. Please do not fight us.*'

Whilst the *beings* appeared to enjoy Searcher's valour, they remained composed, nonetheless. Ultimately, after giving his all, Searcher realised

The Searcher

he could not win; it was a futile affair. When he finally relented, exhausted and resigned to his fate, something peculiar occurred.

Gravity appeared to completely reverse and Searcher floated upwards. Steadily he glided, flanked by two alien beings, towards the silvery ship now hovering closer to the ground. He entered through what seemed like a portal and, with a whoosh, was gone!

Searcher returned to the earth's atmosphere shortly thereafter. It felt like forever in his counting, but it had only been minutes. Looking intensely into Searcher's eyes, a being called MarVel intoned:

> Sounje, it is well that you have returned home. Much has been added upon your being during your precious time with we, the Scentrian. Lifetimes, in fact. Countless lessons and teachings, too many to decipher or decode.
>
> However, we will say this much. Life in all its myriad forms is the greatest gift of all. Treasure it always. For it comes and goes like the wind. Sail those winds in joy and happiness for the Creator's dream is your dream! Be free and grateful you have been blessed with life as it ebbs and flows over the span of eternity, birthing in excitement and adventure.
>
> Know that every step you take, the Creator takes, and every move you make, the Creator makes; for separation is the greatest illusion, the greatest lie ever perpetuated upon humanity. We are one, Sounje. You never travelled anywhere, anytime. You were here all along. Here! Always you are here, for where else could you be?
>
> You wonder why you do not remember us. You cannot remember what you haven't forgotten. In ultimate reality, there never was an us. There is just reality: life! And in remembering life, truth and reality, you will come to know, we are one. What is, can never not be. Reality can never be lost.
>
> So then, go forth and live your life and embrace your insights and ignorance equally, seeking to reach what cannot be reached if you will. For what is there to reach if

there is only the one? This is ultimate truth and ultimate reality and ultimate cosmological understanding!

Finally, relinquish your ideas that anyone or anything can save you. Life does not seek to save you from itself, because you are life. All things sit in their perfection. All things are sacred. Here, now! We salute you, friend. May the peoples of Earth be blessed forever and ever.

Dark night

Kiki and her brother were *created*. Mother-of-Kiki, a flawless Polish beauty, was looking for a man. She was a photographer wishing for beautiful children to show and was searching or waiting for the right man. He just so happened to be Francis. Now Francis, who was a mechanic, was one handsome man, sporting the most dazzling blue eyes you'd ever see, with well-chiselled features and supple brown skin; think actor past and passed, Paul Newman.

An Australian Pommie was Francis. He was perfect. They mated and the rest is history. However, Father-of-Kiki was quite irresponsible, in fact. He would throughout his life sire quite a tribe to various women without realising there was more to it than that. Nonetheless, his and Mother-of-Kiki's genetics merged, and Andrew-Poo and Kiki soon followed.

And those two children, Andrew-Poo and Kiki-dolphin, were the most striking of children, eye-catching indeed. Both with exquisite, shimmering blue eyes, rich beach-blonde hair, and skin of pecan sands. They turned heads!

Mother-of-Kiki wholeheartedly embraced her two little beauties. She got straight to work and took some of the most beautiful child portraits Seeker had ever seen. Surprisingly, he liked the black-and-whites even more than the coloured. The shots would continue throughout their young childhood but, intriguingly, were more evident in their lives than their father, Francis, was.

All people grow and change in appearance with the passing of time; however, to this day, Kiki-dolphin is the most strikingly beautiful woman Searcher has ever laid eyes on. Tippy would have said, 'She's a sight for sore eyes, son.' Kiki is a *natural beauty* and requires no props. But there just happened to be a little more to that story.

Kiki-the-dolphin-girl possessed another kind of beauty. She had beauty on the inside as well, and that was unforeseen. Kiki also had grit, determination and, lo and behold, fire. Strange for a dolphin to have fire. They should be watery. It was rare indeed.

Well, that marvellous little beauty would grow up one day, fall in love in an instant with Searcher, and became a primary school teacher. She was not interested in physically beautiful kinds of things but had a real passion for educating children and also talking to plants! Kiki was artistic and children just loved her. Wherever they would go, a child or animal for that matter would be attracted to Kiki.

Seeker was forever puzzled at how it came to be that children and animals were so drawn to his darling companion. She was delightful and, as aforementioned, woke up with a smile on her face every day. To Searcher, theirs was a match made in heaven, but he could never, and would never, understand what she saw in him. Perhaps it was the pearls of wisdom he was always searching for at the bottom of the ocean that she enjoyed? Perhaps it was his thick rock-and-roll-mane-of-hair, which reminded her of a proud lion? Either way, they just seemed to complement each other fabulously. One day, however, everything would change.

Her brother Andrew-Poo died. Sadly, though, there was more. Months prior to Andrew's passing, Kiki's father Francis died. They were not overly close, but he was her father after all. Neither Kiki, Andrew-Poo or mother-of-Kiki, or the other sired ones, were informed of his death.

It turned out that the witch whom Francis had later been married to, but was now separated from, told the hospital they didn't need to advise the family regarding Francis's death, because *they* were his family: that is, Ex-wife-witch, Daughter-of-witch and Son-of-witch. They apparently ran down the corridors of the hospital openly displaying their grief; thus, the hospital staff assumed that *they* were the family.

Now, eventually, all the true family found out about Francis's passing, six weeks later in fact. But Ex-wife-witch had taken it upon herself and her grown-up children to spread the ashes of Kiki's father somewhere undisclosed. Kiki, Andrew-Poo and all the other brothers and sisters of various mothers had nowhere to go to pay their respects to their father. That's tough! You sure have to be one miserable person to pull off a stunt like that.

So, Francis, Father-of-Kiki, and now Andrew-Poo, Brother-of-Kiki, had journeyed to the great-beyond-of-no-time-and-place. Regretfully, not long after they had, Michew, the long-time family friend of Mother-of-Kiki, also passed. Kiki had known him for as long as she could remember, all of her life in fact. He was a kind, innocent man and was friendly to all.

Kiki is a light-hearted spirit and doesn't seek, search, explore, quest or pursue. She doesn't think about things too deeply and just enjoys life as it is. But these three losses so close together were too much. Plus, Searcher had just left the ambulance and was suffering the black-dog, sitting on a cliff face. She was no doubt in great fear of a fourth loss. Something happened. It had to happen.

Kiki cracked. She shut down. 'No more! No more! Please, no more!' She broke. Something in that little Kiki-dolphin snapped and she lost her sparkle right there. She could no longer *feel* or *connect* and could barely function. Each day whilst walking up those school entry steps to work, she would experience pangs of anxiety and fear.

Kiki fought with every cell of her being to keep walking and not runaway, though. Tears always welled up. The principal, Kimora, was a kind, empathetic lady. Somehow, she sensed something wasn't right with their little ray of sunshine. So, Principal Kimora would greet her each day with a hug and just *be there* without saying a word.

Recall, this Kiki-dolphin had spunk and fire. She, like Searcher-Gra, was as stubborn as a mule and refused to seek professional help, right or wrong. So, for one whole year, whilst being absolutely and completely emotionally shut down, Kiki did these three things. First: she continued teaching those little wags. She was a primary school teacher. That was difficult but was part of her salvation in the end, because when you have to *serve* others, you somehow stop thinking of your own despair.

Second: she listened to every tiny pearl that Searcher-hubby could find for her. Every single day! Her Searcher combed the bottom of the ocean and back for anything to help his priceless gem, his dolphin lost. They'd talk and talk, cry and cuddle, which no doubt helped him in his plight as well, by taking the focus off himself.

Thirdly and finally: she studied the great Tao. Kiki had haphazardly bought a book by Dr Dyer, who was mentioned earlier. It was much later on and he'd certainly evolved his style from a strictly psychological perspective to a more spiritual one. He was a beautiful man, now passed, bless him. Well, this exposition of the Tao, which Dr Dyer had written, offered daily instructionals—mental tasks like being *flexible* for the day.

She would read about the bamboo or willow swaying in the wind. It wasn't rigid, it would *yield* rather than crack. The next day Kiki might read about the water flowing *around* the rocks rather than against them. How, ultimately, the water was more powerful in its submission to the obstacle because it would wear it down over time regardless. Subsequently, she would have to apply the concept of water throughout the day.

Kiki might then study the meaning of *surrender* and so on and so forth. It was a long road for that Kiki with the pleasant disposition, but she got there. She got there in the end. And no amount of physical beauty could have helped. Just prior, she dreamt a voice said to her, '*When the clouds and rain have gone away, cheeky cupid comes out to play.*' Guess that was a sign that things would turn a corner and she'd be her happy self again.

Ultimately, do you know why she was pleased she had gone through the darkness—the *dark night of the soul?* Because now she could feel true empathy for others. Prior, she just couldn't understand how someone could feel down or depressed. Now that she does, she *feels* others' pain and understands. People are attracted to that like moths to a flame. Kiki was somehow *more* than before.

On one summer afternoon, Searcher and Kiki went for a beach walk, south of the crowds. They walked down to their special place by the rocks to have a dip in the ocean and found it refreshing and invigorating. They always felt energised and rejuvenated after swimming in crystal-clear salty waters, beneath a vibrant blue sky. After the dip, they walked northward a few hundred metres and sat on some rocks for a chill.

Seeker started daydreaming as usual and quite naturally fell into a meditation of sorts. They had just found out Dr Dyer, who had written all those inspiring books, had passed on to the great-beyond. Seeker, in his relaxed state, started thinking about the wonderful man and proceeded to send out a *thank you* for all he had contributed to the world. Searcher often did that.

If it was a life well lived where someone gave of themselves for others, regardless of how, and if they had passed on, he would like to send out a thank you to them wherever they might be or not be.

Suddenly, whilst sitting on the rocks, Seeker had a strange feeling that Dr Dyer was *present* somehow and started having visions of him and so forth. Then a conversation ensued—nothing grandiose, quite casual in fact.

Dr Dyer excitedly told Searcher how life just goes on and on and on throughout eternity and that it's all just a colossal journey in the *now*. A ride! He was very happy indeed. Seeker thanked him again for his books but added one small note of pessimism. In his mind he said to Dr Dyer somewhat pessimistically, 'Inspiring books are great, but they don't particularly help us much.'

The doctor advised Searcher to turn to his left and gently said, *'See that precious one over there, it helped her, didn't it?'* Searcher looked at Kiki and a flash came over him. Three years before, it was actually Dr Dyer's book and exposition of the Tao, which she had read and practised each day, that had ultimately helped her through the *dark night*.

The Searcher

A place of awe and mystery

Searcher often wondered why people were so sceptical. He couldn't for the life of him figure that one out. To him, the earth was a giant place of awe and mystery, but the cosmos was just too immense for anyone to comprehend. What *one* person could say they grasped it all? The cosmos, eternity, the alpha and omega? He especially liked the concept of *before the beginning* and *after the end*. That was his favourite thought because it was the only one that stopped his thoughts.

The brain just can't fathom it, as it reaches its limits. Even the human body was beyond our imaginings in its complexity and function. Searcher nurtured an *open mind*. Open-minded people don't necessarily know anything, although they remain open. That way there is always something to learn. As Hamlet once said, '*There are more things in heaven and earth, Horatio, than are dreamt of in your philosophy!*'[17]

It has also been said that a person's life can be measured in the dash between the years on their headstone—the dash between birth date and death date.[18]

Seeker believed the only significant thing you could write on his personal headstone was: *Why not?* Why not life beyond the physical? Why not eternity? Why not life out there in the stars? Why not miraculous healing? Why not other dimensions? Why not magic? And on and on.

You'd have to be rather bold to declare that none of these things could possibly exist. One such person was an astronomer and a member of a sceptics society. Being an astronomer and possessing knowledge of the stars, if some innocent individual happened to see something strange, inexplicably fast or unexplained in the skies, he would simply tell them they had not. Or he would offer an equivalent to the ole Roswell *Weather Balloon Baloney*. Basically, any logical thing he could pull out of his head at the time.

The strangest thing, however, for Searcher, was not the man's responses, but the fact that he never actually walked outside to have a look upwards to those skies of the gargantuan, immense, ever-expanding cosmos. 'No, you didn't see anything strange, there's *always* an explanation.' Only *man* is at the forefront of space and technology was inferred.

'Give me a break,' thought flabbergasted Seeker.

Cause of dis-ease

Tension! Seeker-Gra had noticed how some people seemed *relaxed* and some people seemed *uptight,* or they fluctuated between both states. Based on his many years of personal study and exploration of the healing arts, he simply called that up-tightness, tension or *stress*. Those two terms were interchangeable for Searcher. And to him, stress was what caused illness or dis-ease.

At about the age of thirty, Seeker-Gra decided to learn the violin. He was to help Brother-Callithumpian record a folk album and decided to throw a violin into the mix. He gave himself a few months to learn it, as he had always found learning instruments easy, and so he had no idea what was in store for him. None!

Seeker set out learning all the basic scales and bow techniques but found that this instrument was quite a challenge indeed. He decided to get a few lessons from Pan, who was a wonderful violin teacher nearby. Pan had travelled the world playing in orchestras and also played Irish and folk fiddle.

When Searcher first heard Pan play violin, it was like heaven had opened up for him. The sound was just so exquisite up close. If Seeker could have *bottled* the sound, he would have done so for sure. Thus, Searcher-Gra realised he had to *up his game* and practise much harder still. He stuck at it and learned Irish and Scottish fiddle, bluegrass and classical violin. However, this instrument was to be his nemesis.

As the ambulance job provided many rostered days off between shifts, he would practise for hours on end. Some improvement came for sure, although he intuited something was inherently wrong. He did classical grades, memorised countless Irish jigs and reels for busking and even played in a bluegrass band. But still, he sounded ordinary.

Over those years of violin struggle, Cyclone Izzy commenced learning classical violin when she was three and started with Pan when she was five. This enabled Searcher to sit in on her lessons and gush over Pan's beautiful, longing violin sound. Being a clean slate, Izzy picked up the violin much easier than Father-Searcher had and became a wonderful violinist whilst growing up, winning many competitions.

In fact, when she was only five years of age, she went busking with Fadja-Searcher and played Christmas carols. She on the violin and he on the cello. Together they made a motza! People loved it, especially during the Christmas period when they were feeling more charitable. However, when little Izzy-violinist had had enough, off she would go.

Searcher-Dad would stay on and play Irish fiddle tunes. Eighty of them by memory in fact—reels, jigs, hornpipes and airs. But virtually no money for Searcher-fiddler was offered. He'd lost his little *cute* factor for she was off shopping with Kiki-Mumma. He was just another fiddler, so what?

Incidentally, Little-breeze-Izzy donated all of her busking money to World Vision but was damned if she could understand why they kept mailing her for years to donate more money. Hadn't she already saved the world?

During Izzy's lessons, Searcher would secretly watch Pan's right-hand technique, trying to unravel its mysteries. Pan always had a lovely smile on his face, always. Seeker was missing something very crucial but did not possess the awareness or wisdom to realise just what that was. Years later, it started to dawn on him, slowly. Oh, how slowly the cogs engaged in his brain.

Searcher would observe and then apply the techniques of Pan, this wonderful man of music with the gentle smile. Pan even told Seeker one day in casual conversation how he had once lost a son. His own teenage son! And yet, still this man's face remained serene. Not a hint of anger or bitterness. No victimhood culture for him.

After many, many years had passed and Searcher had put that wretched instrument away in the cupboard where it belonged, away where its secrets would remain, a thought occurred to him: 'It was never the instrument, for Pan could and did make a $50 violin sound heavenly. Nor his *technique* which produced that breathtaking sound. It was Pan himself.'

You see, Pan didn't carry *tension*. Yes, he had violin experience. Yes, he had paid his dues in practice. However, it was not the instrument but the *person* that made all the difference. The sound *was* him. Searcher surmised then: 'Perhaps it is *tension* that affects our health and wellbeing for we too are instruments, in a manner of speaking.' This was revelatory!

The thread continued to run through his life. For Searcher, this wonderful instrument called the violin, which *Being-from-afar* described to him as *an ancient communication device,* was not the real issue. It was a hobby and challenge for him. The real issue was in *healing*.

'How does one pick up stress and tension along the way, and how does one reduce or eliminate it?' Seeker pondered. The search had been long. Early on, Seeker-Gra believed the search would end in a moment when perhaps an Eastern master would tap him on the third-eye or if his chakras became perfectly synchronised or if he read the perfect book of wisdom or mastered some prescribed technique and on and on.

But what he had found along the way was that life would continually offer lessons and opportunities for growth. And often, it really sucked to learn them. This discovery was not particularly what Searcher had been searching for—he had expected something more impressive than that.

So, what then causes stress and tension that can lead to disease? He found, and found the hard way, that *not being able to say 'no'* caused stress. He discovered that if a person should do something that they did not want to do but felt they *should* or *had to*, they would suffer internal stress and tension. It's the 'O' word, which stands for *obligation*. Who has never ever done an act out of obligation alone?

Furthermore, staying with someone, such as in a relationship that no longer 'felt right', was detrimental and would case stress. The examples he discovered were many and seemed to be universal. Surely everyone knew what it felt like to go against the grain, to ignore their own feelings, to put someone else's *expectations* before their own.

Perhaps this is what was meant in the old proverb Tippy-Toes had written down for his son Coppertop so long ago: *always paddle your own canoe!* If it was true then that not following one's own inclinations, one's own needs and desires, one's own dreams and aspirations led to internal stress and therefore dis-ease, how might one go about ridding oneself of the stress and, therefore, improve their condition?

It appeared, to Searcher at least, that the answer was in the question. Just knowing one is not following their own path, not paddling their own canoe, was half the battle. To achieve wellness, therefore, one had to swim downstream.

Learning how to say 'no' was the first step. Searcher initially found it quite hard to say no. Whether it was the way he was brought up or the goody-two-shoes Catholic influence, he was unsure. But eventually he learned to say 'no' and even enjoyed it. He would say *no* if it felt appropriate for him in the moment and would also let it sit in the air for the other person to absorb.

The most challenging thing, however, was to avoid offering a reason for simply saying *no*. Or making up excuses or even lying, which was repulsive to him—although he knew he was not entirely immune from telling the occasional *white* lie. Put bluntly, if you don't want to do something, then as a child of this universe, born of total equality and freedom, you have the right to say *no!* We are often taught otherwise—that putting yourself *first* is selfish. However, for Seeker at least, life and wellbeing seemed to be saying otherwise.

If, for example, one continues the behaviour of doing things they don't want to do out of obligation and so forth, inner resentment can develop. The energy of negative emotions such as anger, frustration and resentment can, if not released, as some attest, cause various bio-chemical responses in the body. Those particular responses, Searcher observed, can lead to tension, stress and illness, or at the very least, a compromised immune system. This is the heart of *mind–body medicine* right here, and is what stress is all about.

So, these things and more the Searcher would muse over. It wasn't really what he wanted to find, but what he *observed* along the way on that decades-long search, searching for Searcher-the-Searcher. Hence, he deduced, it was stress and tension that prevented him from producing a beautiful, sweet violin sound, and stress and tension that leads to the countless forms of physical, mental and emotional illness.

He ruminated about his mother Flossie: 'What stresses did she carry?

Damn, I wish we were all taught this stuff when we were little. Why doesn't society teach us about stress, relaxation and wellbeing?'

Whilst it may seem to be to the contrary, perhaps change has commenced. 'Perhaps there's still hope; maybe we've turned a corner,' Searcher speculated.

Chapter 13

Have we gone too far?

Searcher was feeling despondent. He was commuting down to Sydney by train to study for a diploma in counselling. It had been ten years since he had done the same when studying holistic kinesiology. Things had changed. Now all the occupants of the train had their heads buried in their chests, except for the train driver, assumingly. Always looking down, no-one smiling, no-one talking unless they were already familiar.

All were busy looking at and tapping on their smart phones, iPads or laptops. Searcher slipped into a daydream and reflected on the native American Indians of old, as was his wont. What would they think if they were plopped on the train and saw this scene? What would run through their heads? Would they consider modern man had gone mad or been drugged with a poisonous brew that had turned him into a zombie?

'Yet,' thought Seeker, 'we are the advanced civilisation of super intelligence.' The world had changed; you could go overseas and still contact your loved ones easily by Skype, phone or Facetime. Technology certainly made things easier and the world closer. But at what cost?

He wondered if our children would grow up not knowing how to communicate with each other. Would they understand eye-cues, body language and basic social skills once taken for granted? The world had sped up. It appeared *artificial*. Everyone on the train was lost in a world of their own.

It saddened Searcher's heart. 'Have we gone too far?' When spending time with others, he noticed how, no matter the conversation, deep or shallow, if their phone suddenly beeped, they would immediately look down and read and respond, whilst pretending to still *be* with the actual and real person they were with. 'That's impossible,' he'd mumble to himself—although lots of people assured him it is possible.

'It's called, "multi-tasking," Fadja,' declared Izzy.

Searcher made a commitment to practise the art of *no-phone* when he was out, as best as he could. It didn't help, but at least he was available if anyone wanted to communicate. *The advanced human and his virtual reality or the primitive human with his actual reality?* Could we find a balance between the two? The coming days and years would surely answer that question.

Ernie

Ernie was originally a Buddhist. After Seeker had been to Costa and studied bio-energy healing, he was still searching for that final technique or modality that would be the *one*. He attended more courses in various forms of healing. One such, was called *Quantum Healing*. Seeker attended the course and all present were lovely people and told of interesting life stories in their introductions. In fact, Seeker felt quite boring in comparison.

The course itself seemed a little elementary after having studied with the wizard in Costa, as did any other course following. The wizard's training was *transformational*. Searcher was in total agreeance with the wizard on that note, as he felt one should not work with another in a healing sense unless one has worked on oneself. Perfection of oneself was not necessary but self-insight was, or so Searcher believed.

One participant at the Quantum Healing course was Ernie. Searcher immediately found his name to be at odds, as Ernie was a Chinese fellow, thus the name seemed amusing to him. Ernie was indeed unique in every way and loved to talk and talk. Ernie openly described his life. He became a practising Buddhist at the age of four,

The Searcher

he told Searcher. And devout was he from that tender age, consumed with a fire for Buddhism and Buddha alike.

Day and night he practised deep meditations, chanting, mindfulness and austerities. At times as a monk, he would live on just one piece of bread a day for months on end and even sleep in trees and caves. He had spent time with his holiness himself, the Dalai Lama.

His meditations were so intense and powerful that he claimed he'd once stopped *time* and experienced many impossible things by the time he was an adult, including complete cessation of his breathing and miraculous healings. Ernie strived and strived and strived. He said he barely slept whilst giving his life to the quest for enlightenment. He later conceded his zealousness had cost him his first wife and family.

One fine day, Ernie was sitting on a mountain top. He had been loyal in his pursuit for over four and a half decades. Never resting, always seeking. The goal had to be reached and he would never give up. Not ever! As he sat there, deep in mediation on a grand and desolate mountain top, Chinese-Ernie suddenly heard something.

'What was that strange word?' he thought. He heard it again and again and again. It was: *Hallelujah.*

Hallelujah! Ernie had absolutely no idea what the word meant. He was Chinese and a Buddhist. He was unaware of any Christian-like words. However, in that instant, that holy instant, Ernie was *born again*. He became a Christian. Now this was quite a story for Searcher. He could relate to the search, although not to such a degree.

Seeker understood the Buddhist path and particularly loved the *middle-way*—the wise approach that keeps you balanced and stable; not too far to the left; not too far to the right. Seeker also understood the Christian path too, as he had been exposed to its doctrines as a child. He liked certain elements from both those paths. But how can one just *switch* from one to the other in a moment?

Without knowing anything about Christianity, Ernie was born again and would later become a very inspiring minister indeed. Searcher was happy for Ernie and told him so. It was an inspirational story for sure. However, Seeker, being ever aware, noticed a few peculiarities with Ernie.

Firstly, Ernie only ever ate junk food. He mostly ate McDonalds and drank Coca-Cola. He confessed to Searcher-Gra, though, sometimes he would mix it up and have pizza or Kentucky fried chicken. Apparently, his wife was a wonderful Chinese cook but Ernie would not eat her food, ever. He assured Seeker he had recently had a full medical check-up and at age sixty had been given a perfect bill of health from his medical-god. He later also disclosed to Seeker he would go on a complete water fast for forty days, once a year, for religious austerities. Not a morsel of food would enter his body during that period and only he and his wife knew each time that he did this.

'Perhaps this countered the junk-food habits,' thought Seeker.

A friend of Searcher's became quite outraged with this story. She was in the health profession and just couldn't understand why anyone, let alone a devout man, would be so blatantly abusive to his own body, his temple!

So, Searcher quizzed Ernie on that exact topic. 'Ernie, you must be the happiest guy I've ever met in my life. But something puzzles me. Why do you like eating shit food?'

Ernie looked at Searcher with a giant smile and said, 'Because I go where man tells me I cannot go. If man says eating junk food is bad for me and will kill me, then I naturally flow in that direction. To prove to myself the human mind and spirit are greater than any diet.'

'Hmm, fair enough, Ernie,' replied Searcher. Ernie seemed healthy and happy, so that was the end of that.

The second thing Searcher noticed about Ernie was how he openly criticised Buddhism. Ernie felt it was a selfish religion that only focussed on one's *own* path, one's *own* needs, unlike Christianity which he believed was about reaching others.

Ernie also felt that the selfish Buddhist path, which he'd once walked, had been the cause of the destruction of his first family due to his obsessive and fanatical quest for enlightenment—a quest that only really involved *himself* and not others. Such was his

The Searcher

description and perceptions regarding his long path of seeking and his short path of finding.

Incidentally, don't start Kiki on Buddha. She still has the shits with him for abandoning his wife on his selfish search for enlightenment, even though she places his smiling statues everywhere in her garden— everywhere! Searcher says to her, 'But Kiki, we still feel the reverberations of Buddha's life 2500 years later.'

'I don't care!' fires back righteous Kiki. 'He shouldn't get married and have kids if he's gonna just get up and leave like that, chasing pipedreams.' For some reason Searcher can see Gautama Buddha giggling heartily at Kiki's position.

One night during the healing course, Seeker was at home when he received a vision about Ernie. It was as clear as crystal and Searcher felt it was delivered sort of like a *download*. The next day at lunchtime, after Ernie returned from eating his Maccas, Searcher told him of his vision and asked if he would like to hear it.

'Sure,' Ernie said with a great big smile.

'Ernie, you have lived a long life of searching and seeking. You tried for years and years and years to find the truth of truths. To find the kernel. The pearl that would release you from your suffering. And try as you may, you were unsuccessful at achieving your goal. Then, without warning, without effort, you heard a Christian word up on that mountain that would change your path and destiny. A word of praise and rejoicing for the One, the Most High,' said Searcher.

'Yes, true. Go on, go on,' urged Ernie enthusiastically.

'And now you openly criticise your prior Buddhistic tradition because you believe it was selfish and did not take you to your goal.'

'Yes,' agreed Ernie.

'You indeed received salvation Ernie on that desolate mountain top. This is the vision of you I saw. For over four and a half decades you strived and strived to gain freedom as if you were pushing a giant boulder up a mountain. You were brave, courageous and persistent. You never gave up on your quest. Finally, you made it. You heard the word and then your Master, the Immaculate One, was there waiting for you.

'Christ was now in you and through you. However, consider this Ernie. In all those long years of toil, could it not have been the *Buddha* who was your mountain; that is, the path of struggle? And could it not have been the *Buddha* who was the giant heavy boulder that you had to push uphill, and could it not have been the *Buddha* who after so many years of struggle took you to your Master, your goal and salvation?

'Finally, Ernie, could it not have been the *Buddha* who gave you the strength to continue against all odds? Is it possible, Ernie, for you to thank the *Buddha* for providing you with your reward, your deliverance and your Master?' asked the Searcher sincerely.

Ernie smiled a smile of smiles; he was enjoying this. He nodded, 'Yes, Yes.'

'Then perhaps Ernie, you could make peace at last with Buddha and Buddhism and understand everything is blessed, everything is divine. All are homeward bound. All will ultimately reach their destination, and many are the paths that lead us Home …'

The paradox of animals

Searcher didn't particularly believe in the domestication of animals. He felt all creatures were meant to be free, although he conceded some clearly wouldn't survive a day in the wild. As always, he observed his surroundings. He found it peculiar how people would *humanise* their pets. He would watch people push dogs in prams, put clothes on cats, sleep with their pets and even buy so-called *donuts* and cakes for their dogs. At least, that's how they were packaged.

The role of domestic animals in society was a paradox for Seeker-Searcher. On the one hand, they were often chained or caged and restricted to a life of quiet loneliness. On the other hand, they were such teachers to humanity. Take the dog who sits around all day waiting for its master to arrive home. The owner often comes in following a long stressful day at work and is in no mood for a cute, jumping dog.

However, their pet dog has just experienced more ecstasy than Searcher did on his retreat, just blissed out in seeing their perfect owner as if for the first time. Or the cat who has been hunting all night. He plops a dead, headless rat at the front door, certain that he has done a wonderful thing for his owner in keeping the rat population down. The owner looks at the blood and guts and is disgusted.

And animals are so forgiving.

Dalefin jokes, if you locked both your wife and your dog up in the boot of your car for an hour and then opened it up, your wife would bite your arm off, and your dog would lick you to death. Laughs!

Animals don't talk but *feel*. They communicate in other ways and are ever alert.

Watch the kookaburra. It doesn't go around making things happen by toil and effort. It sits, ever alert and ready for an opportunity—a worm in the grass, perhaps a mouse—to present itself. Searcher-Gra believed we can learn from animals. For example, how do they know an earthquake is about to occur? Do they feel vibrations, or do they have a special sense? And curiously, he thought, 'If we're the most intelligent animal, why don't we perceive an earthquake, or an impeding avalanche?'

Is the sea of EMF (electromagnetic field) pollution that surrounds humans these days diminishing their sensitivity? History is full of cases showing how almost all animals react oddly when an earthquake happens, and a resulting tsunami is on the way. Animals will climb to higher ground at all costs. One Chinese city population in the nineteenth century was well prepared to read the warning signs of animals acting strangely and evacuated the city prior to an earthquake, which saved countless lives as a result. So, what is the animal perceiving that humans are not?

Some say it's electromagnetic signals in the same way countless birds can flock together and fly to and fro without any obvious communication, or a school of fish for that matter. The human body is one big sealed bag of salty water, made up of 50 to a 100 trillion cells (who counted those?) and each cell omits an electromagnetic signal. It has been suggested that through this electromagnetic grid, the body's cells communicate substantially faster than bio-chemically or even via the nervous system. Such a force radiates outward and makes up the *bio-field* or aura, as some term it.

Li, a Chinese student who was at the wizard's School of Bio-Energy Healing, was an anaesthetist and really clicked with Searcher, although not so much with instructor wizard, curiously. She was the supervisor in anaesthesiology at a Chinese hospital and sincerely confided to Searcher that she could measure the heartbeat of a patient from a few inches away without touching them. After experimenting on thousands of patients, she developed a sensitivity to the *energy* around the heart, which she believed to be electromagnetic in nature.

Searcher pondered this: if humans like other animals can receive and transmit electromagnetic signals, then perhaps that is why some people are psychic, if not all people, more or less. They, like the sensitive animals before an earthquake, *sense* or read energy signatures from others. He thought back to when he was working on people's chakras or their *field* and was *sensing* information.

'Are we electrical-magnetic beings?' Seeker deliberated. 'And if so, can we learn to direct electromagnetic signals to cells to instruct them to heal? Furthermore, are we already doing so subconsciously with our thoughts and attitudes? Are we powerful transmitters and receivers of energy?' Thoughts on healing were never far away for Seeker-Searcher. He believed it was the most exciting frontier for man's future and the key to creating long, healthy and happy lives.

Beautiful loser

Searcher aptly named her, Chief. In Costa, one of the students was a very quiet lady. She would sit at the dining table and just listen, rarely talking unless spoken to. Seeker-Gra felt there was something different about her but could not quite put his finger on what that was. She and Barney were best of buddies. They had their own families but seemed to be fellow travellers on the road. With similar interests, they had studied numerous healing modalities and were passionate about helping others. They had even written an evolutionary book together, proposing that it was not too late for humankind to save this earth by creating a new future, should we choose to do so.

The Searcher

As the students got to know Chief, she would eventually disclose how she could *read* people's past lives. To be more accurate, Barney was the one who disclosed her skill, for he was the talker of the two. She would do so without charge but would have to enter meditation to *pick up the trail of another's chapters*.

Seeker-Searcher felt her countenance reminded him of what he perceived to be a Chief—that is, a Native American Indian chief of long ago. Thus, he aptly named her so. Perhaps it was because she was always quiet, thoughtful and reflective and he rarely shut up. She seemed *wise* and Seeker was always attracted to what he wasn't.

One day he was enquiring about the rumours regarding her reading of past lives, in which she said it was interesting how he called her Chief. She told him she had once recalled an event in her own past lifetime as a Native American Indian, where all the local native tribes had been gathering for several moons prior to an impending catastrophic event.

The tribes knew there was a giant meteor coming that would impact and destroy their homeland and set off volcanic reactions from deep within the earth. Long did they deliberate, until finally the combined tribes decided they must leave. They left the area just in time before it was flattened with devastating consequences. She saw it all in her mind's eye. Today it is called *Yellowstone*.

After the completion of the healing course with the wizard, the students all set out on their own ways. Seeker had to fly back to LA before flying on home to Sydney. Chief and Barney also headed back to LA before boarding for Singapore. As the airbus hit the skies from Costa, Searcher felt gentle tears run down his face whilst looking out the window.

He would dearly miss the beautiful local Costa Ricans, the wizard and the students. He knew he would never return to the pristine land again. Searcher was not a traveller and lacked the funds for travel. Regretfully, the only travel he would do was within the alcoves of his own mind.

Chief and Barney were extremely intuitive and felt *something* from the Searcher who was sitting towards the rear of the plane.

They must have discussed it, for by the time everyone alighted from the airbus in LA, they both accosted Searcher and insisted they have lunch together and have a talk.

Barney was a well-paid life coach and extreme in his coaching. He said he passionately enforced change in individuals but if they wanted a *soft touch,* he would send them to Chief, for he took no prisoners. He would not waste time with fence sitters; he demanded commitment and charged them accordingly!

They walked around and around and finally came to a small airport café. Each ordered their own lunch and Barney set out to inspire, encourage and motivate Searcher in his quest to become a healing practitioner. Barney enthusiastically beseeched Searcher to remain committed to the path.

Seeker-Searcher was quite shocked, actually. He wasn't aware he had put out any doubt or negative vibes regarding bio-energy healing or healing in general. Nonetheless, they were determined to encourage Seeker and would have quite willingly missed their plane to do so. That really touched Searcher and he could not understand how two almost strangers could be so kind.

Barney barked and shouted and hollered, trying to whip Searcher into action. He was loud! Chief just stared. She stared and stared straight through Searcher and did not say a word. Each stood up and grabbed their lunch. Searcher had ordered a coffee as well, and boy did he dislike American coffee.

As he grabbed his lunch, he inattentively threw his numbered receipt in the bin. When he sat down, he realised he needed his lunch receipt to pick up his coffee and said, 'Ah shit, I just threw my lunch receipt in the bin and it had my pre-paid coffee on it.' Gazing deeply at him, Chief articulated two short sentences that would be the most accurate analogy of Searcher's life.

In a nutshell, Chief said, '*This here is your life pattern. You throw away things far too easily.*' Wow, that hit home! She was right. Excruciatingly right. Searcher had a distinct habit of diving into things like healing modalities headfirst, investing a lot of time and money as a result, only to always find reasons why it didn't suit him or just wasn't quite right or effective for him.

Prophetically, she was right this time as well. He would return home all pumped up from the healing practitioner course, but the gem would lose its shine. He would later find a reason why it wasn't quite right. He would discover tuning forks instead, for he was a musician after all. And then he would discover quantum healing and then, and then, ad infinitum.

Just as Chief did, songs can also sum a person up succinctly. Most people don't like describing themselves and Searcher was no different. However, Kiki claimed Searcher's character was embedded in a specific song. And if you tied Seeker down with chains, beat him into submission and demanded he say who he was, he would most likely say, 'I'm a beautiful loser.'

And he was quite aware that it was an oxymoron that was both self-ingratiating and self-deprecating. The song, *Beautiful Loser*,[19] written by Bob Seger and also sung perfectly by one of Searcher's favourites, English-born Jon English, was not written about Searcher—but it sure as hell seemed like it. At least to him and Kiki.

Searcher loved mountain bike riding alone in the bush listening to his favourite Aussie rock albums: Jon and the Fosters, the Oils, Chisel and many more. It made him ride way too fast, though. He just couldn't restrain himself! 'You just can't beat Aussie rock from the 80s,' he muttered, 'I just love it, the Marshalls cranked up, the boys laying it down. Nothing better!'

But it was *Beautiful Loser* that drew him into himself, the one song that crossed the divide and described the *Searcher who wanted it all*. Searcher believed everyone had at least one song that described them to a tee. Not their favourite song, mind you. And one would have to have enough self-awareness and honesty to know who they really are, good or bad, before that certain song would find resonance.

Incidentally, English-Jon flew to the great-beyond-of-no-time-and-place after he went to the hospital for surgery and, sadly, didn't come out. He sent out a Facebook message to his fans just prior to his surgery to apologise for his absence and said he was itching to rock it out again real soon. Searcher just loved the musoes like him who gave it their all and more to leave those classic tracks behind that spoke to the heart and soul.

Searcher could play anything on the guitar: rock, classical, jazz, country, surfin' guitar, bluegrass. It was all easy. However, he knew deep inside that he was not even the bootlaces of the guitar greats like Knoph, Mayqueen, Mossy, Gary, Angus, Stevie, Eddie, and Jimi. No! They were raw, honest and played with *conviction*. That's rare and Searcher wasn't any of those things.

In the end, it was always the *emotion* of music that took Searcher to another place. Dalefin was no different. He loved music so much and just couldn't help but play it loud. *Music* was *life* to him and those like him, and life was music.

Seeker would, however, develop tinnitus in his right ear. It's an awful infliction. A ringing in the ear that never stops. Sometimes you don't hear it because the modern world is so loud, which places the ringing in the background, or when you're deeply focussed on another task, it just disappears.

However, when he was out all alone in the bush, tinnitus or not, he couldn't help but turn up full-bore those Aussie rockers laying it all down. Incidentally, one night whilst lying in bed, Searcher got so sick of that damn ringing in his ear, he yelled at it to just, *'F-off!'* once and for all! Curiously, it seemed to disappear for months but would occasionally crept back again, to sing it's song.

But it was Krishna's overwhelming music after all that helped cause the opening long ago at the retreat, for music was always pure emotion for Searcher; raw emotion, and there just ain't nothing better!

Actually, to Searcher, life was *emotion*. To Kiki, life was *fun*. To Cyclone-Izzy, life was *groovy*. To Rascal-Sam, well they didn't know because he was a fellow of so few words. He'd probably say *'treat-it'* but the other three were damned if they even knew what that meant.

In fact, when Rascal-Sam was just a wee cherub, he used to tell a certain story about where he and Searcher originally came from. He claimed they were from another planetary location called *Volcano Land*.

The Searcher

Wherever that was, he would describe intricate features and activities of that world. He said one day it ended abruptly when Searcher was on a boat and was shot by the other occupants. Searcher fell into the sea and was immediately attacked and eaten by giant sharks.

Following, Rascal-Sam said, 'I looked for you everywhere, Dad. It took forever but eventually I found you on this world: Earth. I travelled down a long, long spiral and there you were.' Searcher-Dad waited for Rascal-Sam to relinquish the story as he grew up. All children let go of their play friends and imaginary stories sooner or later. However, Rascal-Sam never did. He maintains the story to this day and simply says, 'Kids don't lie, Dad. It's the truth!'

Chapter 14

Expectancy

She was a dairy farmer and had fallen and couldn't get back up. Her husband had sat her in his car in the front passenger side and drove her to the entry gate of their property and waited for the ambulance to come. Searcher-Gra was the treating officer who assessed the patient. She complained of pain to the left hip and pelvic region. Searcher's partner stayed in the ambulance where it was comfortable with the air conditioner on and offered no assistance.

Searcher repeatedly motioned for him to bring the stretcher. He took a long time to do so, whilst mumbling words to the effect that the patient should walk; it would be quicker and easier. Searcher treated the patient for pain and deduced it was either a fracture of the hip or pelvis but it was hard to ascertain whilst she was sitting upright in the car.

Eventually, his partner got out and lowered the stretcher to half-height about four or five metres away from the car. Seeker advised his partner there might be a fracture involved and would need assistance and a spine board to take the patient to the stretcher. His partner argued. Searcher insisted. His partner argued. Searcher demanded his partner help him, but he insisted, 'She can walk herself.' Searcher became angry at his partner's lack of compassion, empathy or sensitivity. He administered analgesia to the patient.

Finally, and with much frustration and desperation, he carefully picked up the dear hard-working dairy farmer by himself, carried her to the stretcher and gently placed her down. He just loved the salt-of-the-earth patients who never made a fuss. He wished he didn't have to resort to such a measure but was unsure what else to do—and he was embarrassed at his partner's callousness in front of the lady's husband.

His partner was renowned for being a terrible driver and would always make Searcher and others feel sick in the back of the ambulance. He was extremely rough and fast. As Searcher was treating the patient in the back of the ambulance vehicle and stood up to gather some equipment, Racer-paramedic laid his heavy lead foot to the floor and took off, causing Searcher-Gra to violently hit his face on the side window and other equipment.

'That's it! This bloke is gonna cop it from me later, but first, my patient.' You see, to Searcher, driving fast was no feat. Anyone can do it. You just press your right foot to the floor as hard as you can. One local fourteen-year-old did just that after he had stolen a car, and the result was the death of two beautiful young and aspiring professionals: a doctor and his accountant girlfriend, who went up in flames. Such horror! Yes, the automobile can be a wonderful assistance or a lethal weapon, entirely depending on the mindset of the driver …

They transported the patient and continued through the night. For some reason, however, Racer-paramedic was driving markedly worse than usual, as if that was possible! Perhaps he was in a bad mood, for his driving was absolutely atrocious. The problem for Searcher, though, was that he experienced motion sickness. For fifteen years he had put up with it. Depending on his driving partner each shift, he would often walk into the hospital looking as pale as a sheet, feeling much worse than some of his patients.

He learned to deal with it by always having the air conditioning on; regularly looking up towards the front of the vehicle whilst writing his case sheets; and by avoiding wearing heavy clothing in winter, which made him feel hot and stuffy—especially with paramedic drivers who just loved turning the heat up to ten in winter to satisfy their own needs.

So, this combination of sissy-paramedic, who suffered from motion sickness, and uncaring-racer-paramedic, who didn't give a shit, was rarely a good one and always caused dread for Seeker prior to his designated shifts with him.

They had been working almost fourteen hours and it was a rough night. Searcher happened to enquire at the Casualty about the beautiful hard-working dairy farmer they had transported thirteen hours prior and was advised that she had fractured her pelvis. His blood boiled!

The two partners were about to clear their last case of the night and were sitting in the vehicle. Searcher advised Racer-paramedic how the dairy-farmer lady from earlier in their shift had actually fractured her pelvis, thinking all the while he would be humbled and regretful, considering how he'd refused to help her. Uncaring-racer-paramedic just rolled his eyes and said, '*So?*' That was it. This guy showed zero care or concern for the lady and zero professionalism.

Searcher blew a whistle, just like Mr Arm had done when he tried to throw Gidgee out the school window. He started yelling and cussing at Uncaring-paramedic, but Uncaring-paramedic remained aloof throughout. He was tired and didn't give a shit. 'Who cares?' was the response. That just made Searcher-Gra madder and madder. He was screaming and yelling at this so-called paramedic who works out of a vehicle with a slogan sticker on the back saying: *Join the most trusted profession.* It was ugly.

Searcher was probably right in principle and it had been coming for a long time. But he was wrong on every other level. Intense confrontation never really pays off. When he calmed down over the next few days, Seeker-Gra felt quite remorseful. 'Did he deserve that from me?' he mulled over. 'No, no. He did not. But I just wish he would show some compassion once in a while.'

What neither foresaw was that, some ten years later, Uncaring-paramedic would be dismissed from the service for his lack of professionalism and care on the job. 'Some people just don't seem to possess compassion or care,' concluded Searcher.

Another so-called rescue paramedic was worse. He would get all excited at the start of his shifts and sardonically and enthusiastically say with a big grin, whilst rubbing his hands together, 'This is it. The big one's gonna happen today. Probably a bus crash. There's gonna be blood and guts, big trauma, arms and legs and carnage everywhere. I can feel it, can't wait!

He was unashamedly eager. Searcher would just look at him with disdain. 'This right here is a psychopath,' he thought to himself. 'If only the public knew. This man enjoys the suffering of others for his own blood-lust and heroism. Fucking hero!' One day, that same man would have the audacity to file a *stress* claim against the service. Such irony!

This was one of the primary stresses that Searcher carried whilst serving in the ambulance. It would take him to the brink. Years on, though, he would realise the fault lay at his own feet and not the bad behaviour of others.

The word *expectancy*, to Seeker at least, was the worst word ever adopted, alongside the word *should*. Seeker-Gra had assumed everyone employed in the ambulance service actually *cared*. (That is an extremely hilarious notion to him now, but one he once believed in.) People tend to look after themselves and, to some, it is just a steady and secure wage.

One paramedic he worked with, for example, hated physically touching anyone. It repulsed him, especially touching someone's feet. Another he worked with was as mad as a cut snake. Actually, no, there were *many* who were nuts. Thankfully, most were not.

But where Seeker went wrong was that he *expected* good behaviour; he *expected* kindness and compassion from others; and he *expected* considerate driving. He was no angel himself, far from it. And he conceded that some patients—the ones that spat, derided, were threatening or violent—barely deserved any compassion at all.

Searcher had made a disastrous assumption, though. He assumed and *expected* something, and life has a way of throwing that back in your face. For example, because he suffered from motion sickness in the back of the ambulance, he tried hard to provide the best and smoothest ride possible for all of his partners and patients alike. He became painstaking in that area.

For fifteen years he never wavered. It was his mission. 'If I can provide the best ride possible for everyone, then maybe they will do it back for me in kind.' That was a stupid, stupid error, just foolish!

In hindsight, he pondered, 'Life just doesn't always give you what you want.' He also fuelled and washed the ambulance every single shift unless on an overrun, in which case you weren't supposed to wash the trucks. He did this for the sake of the next crew on duty and it was all about pride. The favour was sporadically returned. Some paramedics, in fact, were proud they had never, ever washed an ambulance vehicle, not in decades!

The whole issue, however, was more likely a reflection of the supposed *law of attraction*. The more he focussed on bad behaviour and bad driving, the more of it he got. That was the crux of the issue right there! And what a painful lesson. It would cost him a career, financial stability and a damn sight more than that.

Broken-Searcher could not continue. He felt shame! Too ashamed to put on that ambulance uniform anymore. He just couldn't do it! Seeker threw his service medals in the bin. All's well that ends well, though. Those lovely kind and caring ambulance managers who accepted his resignation and accepted his handshake and then watched him walk away sobbing like a baby, they were good to him.

Not considering there might actually be something wrong with this guy and having a duty-of-care to investigate, they must have assumed he needed some privacy. And privacy he most certainly got. He didn't hear from them again. Not until he went back as a casual Paramedic a few years later, at least. Had he jumped off that cliff in his darkest hour, guess then they might have finally paid him a visit, at the bottom. To be fair however, they did invest a lot of time ensuring Searcher handed all of his uniforms back in. 'You gotta have your priorities right.'

Lay down your sword!

Years later Searcher was in Costa with the wizard learning how to work with the chakras, no doubt also trying to heal the wounds of the past from those dreaded ambulance days. He had mostly stopped dreaming about the ambulance by this stage—no more nightmares, no more trauma, no more death, no more suffering. And because he was never offered any professional help, he never received any psychological assistance or counselling or financial compensation.

So, he was trying to climb his own way out of the hole, at his own cost and own time, without aid. And the healing interests had helped, somewhat. There were occasional breakthroughs, occasional *shifts* from time to time.

One such time, he had been studying and practising under the tutelage of the wizard in Silencia, when they had a break. He walked down to the ocean and decided to sit on a rock. He drifted into a relaxed, contemplative state.

Unexpectedly, a voice started talking to him and said:

> Warrior, you have put up a good fight. You have fought bravely and have done the best you could. You have carried your honour with you above all else and stood tall when you could have fallen.
>
> You have defended right from wrong and defended others even when it came at a cost. You have burned the flame of righteousness brightly and stared defeat in the face. You have stood on a cliff and watched your own death, all alone, no-one by your side. You have run with a broken-down limb and fought on with a compromised heart. We honour you!
>
> But, warrior, is it not time to lay down your sword? Is it not time to take off your armour? Is it not time to end the war within, to end the suffering? Is it not time to make peace in your heart at long last, and to make peace with others? Warrior, if not now, when?

Explorer without a compass

Searcher's friend Moray had been on the path for a long time. She was the one who *Being-from-afar* had termed an *explorer without a compass*. She had had an opening too. Seeker-Gra wondered if it was always the case that someone who had an unforeseen shift or opening would start searching for meaning as a result.

Certainly, with religious people such as some Christians he had known, it had happened in a moment. They were just born again in a flash. He was envious of them somewhat, but it was just not his road to walk. Often, he noted, it had been preceded by tough times, a loss, a trial or tribulation. 'Sometimes life just kicks us in the butt,' reflected Seeker.

Moray was an everyday sort of lady. She had no spiritual interests at the time and was busy rearing three boys with a fourth on the way. One night she and her husband looked up at the skies towards the ocean and saw something inexplicable. They saw strange lights flying in formation, bobbing and weaving at incredible speeds, accelerating and decelerating beyond comprehension—sometimes appearing nearby and then almost instantly, far away.

Moray's husband was a black and white kind of guy, a straightforward hard worker. He worked on and drove trucks. They were both flabbergasted at witnessing such strange objects in the sky. Uncertain as to their origin, they shook their heads and headed home. Other sightings occurred, but the strangest thing for Moray was that some *beings* seemed to be trying to make contact with her mentally, or telepathically.

They told her of important details regarding her fourth son; that he was, in fact, the son of another man from the stars. These beings remained in contact with Moray for many months. Meanwhile, her other children were having sightings of strange-looking beings in the backyard. As they grew up, they would avoid sleeping with the lights off as a result.

Many, many unusual things happened during the months of Moray's last pregnancy. It was almost like they were comforting her during that special and sacred time. Interestingly, they counselled her telepathically on how to perform regular household duties more effectively, such as *always vacuum in rows and lines, systematically, never haphazardly* and so forth.

The pregnancy continued and it was a confusing time indeed for Moray to say the least. One day she was looking out the window from the kitchen-sink area when she suddenly left her body and experienced a blissful, ecstatic state, which she described as, *A Oneness with All, beyond all description.*

Nonetheless, it was confounding and more than once her sanity was questioned. The beings who felt positive and comforting to Moray told her they were there simply to *protect* her and her fourth son and family, until his birth. She enquired into why he or they needed protection at all.

They stated a certain other nefarious representation of beings was wishing to prevent the birth for their own reasons; hence, they were there to stop that from occurring and then would leave. It had to do with the fourth son's so-called real father from the stars or some such. As Moray's pregnancy progressed, things became more intense for those benevolent beings from the stars.

Finally, they instructed Moray that it would all be over by the next day. It would all end abruptly. They said a great battle in the skies was about to take place out above the ocean before her beloved Castle city and that they would be victorious. Afterwards, the struggle would all be over for her and her family.

That night a killer storm hit Newcastle. Out on the ocean was a vessel on its maiden voyage. It was pummelled, battered and dragged by winds of up to 170 km/h, which produced the largest wave ever recorded at the entrance to the harbour at 14.8 metres. The storm and seas raged in the tumultuous weather. The ship, *MV Sygna*, a bulk carrier, ran aground. It was 26 May 1974 and it was all over. Moray would never hear from those beings again.

Incidentally, during the salvage efforts for the *Sygna*, she broke her back. After several attempts to retrieve her, the bow section was eventually towed away to Taiwan for scrap metal and the stern was left about 80 metres out from the shoreline, just north of Stockton Beach. It remained as an icon and landmark in Newcastle for over four decades as it slowly decayed in the elements. It is now almost completely rusted and collapsed to the waterline and is also a delightful artificial reef for marine life.

Searcher can attest the ocean's apex predator loved the reef too, as he would get freaked out when he, Brave-brother and his mates used to surf beside her or when they paddled out to jump on and investigate the old girl and felt the presence of inquisitive sharks.

Whilst the *Pasha Bulker* storm of 2007 was more destructive due to heavier rainfall, the *Sygna* storm of 1974 produced stronger winds. Both storms came to be remembered locally by the name of the ships that ran aground. The *Sygna* storm was also known for lifting and hurling houses, causing caravans to fly like kites, wrecking hundreds of cars, causing widespread blackouts from fallen powerlines, and generally felling lots of trees and damaging houses.

Whatever the cause of the Sygna storm, Searcher watched the wreck rust and decay over the years. It would cause a kind of melancholy in him, as it reminded him of the ephemeral and transient nature of life. He viewed the *Sygna* as he did human bodies, ultimately destined to wear out and disintegrate.

Only humans

It is said in the Book of Genesis (or the Gene of Isis) that God made man in the image and likeness of himself. Seeker considered that may be true but couldn't for the life of him understand why humans could *only* inhabit one infinitesimally small planet in a tiny solar system, way out on a far-away spiral arm in a milky galaxy that was one of billions.

If one believed in God, which was their emphatic right to do, why did they consider Him or Her to be so small-minded, given the universe is clearly not small? Why couldn't this God enjoy His or Her own creations in countless, untold regions of space? Why could not *humans,* if made in His or Her image, live elsewhere in the cosmos?

It felt like a blasphemy and an insult to Searcher's basic common sense and logic to suggest that a Creator was so extraordinary in its creative magnificence, yet so small-minded in granting physical life to just one speck of the omniverse. And why not other grand, intelligent life?

Does it have to have a head on a torso with two eyes, two ears, a nose and mouth? A bipedal animal with two legs and two arms and reproductive organs in the groin? Is this the ONLY creation that is allowed to have so-called higher intellect, to rule the birds and beasts for their own purposes? What about a bird-man? A reptilian-man, an insectoid-man, an aquatic-man?

'Impossible,' says short-sighted man. 'We are made in God's image to rule this earth.' Perhaps, but can God not make others in His or Her own countless images to live elsewhere? And should that image not look human, well sorry, God is after all said to be *unlimited*. To Seeker at least, it went against the grain to put limits on God. *Meanwhile, grains of sand cascade through the hands of time, dissolving back unto forever as man walks the slow walk …*

Tails and scales

Searcher was dreaming. He was walking along in a clearing and noticed an industry up on the right. He didn't know what the industry was for, and he felt intrigued enough to have a squiz. As he drew closer, he could see through the main entrance that there were workers focussing on their tasks. It looked like they were performing something like *welding* or *laser* work, but he was unsure.

Enthralled to find out just what those men were doing, he walked closer still. He hoped someone might say hello and show him what they were doing. Suddenly, when he was almost at the entrance, he caught a closer sight of those *men*. A chill ran up his spine and a dreadful foreboding ensued. He realised those *men* were not men at all. They were reptilian! They were walking upright, were bipedal and somewhat human from a distance, but possessed *tails and scales*.

By now they had all stopped doing what they were doing and were staring menacingly at Searcher. 'Oh dear, I think I've gone too far down the rabbit hole this time, or should I say, reptile hole?' he mumbled to himself. The creatures were astoundingly big. Perhaps twelve to fifteen feet tall and strikingly muscular. One creature felt particularly threatening.

Searcher did not need an email to tell him this was their leader. He was looming! For the strangest of reasons, Seeker proceeded *into* the building rather than away from it and was now surrounded by reptile-men. He kind of figured it was all over anyhow, so he might as well give 'em some Aussie curry before they ended him.

The leader was dark and intimidating. Searcher nearly pissed himself. He approached Searcher and said in a cold, vicious tone, *'You filthy humans, you stink!'* Searcher immediately felt that he and his fellow humans who thought their own shit didn't stink actually stank worse to these reptilian-men than a rotten-dead fish does to a human. The other fierce-looking lizzies were somehow agreeing with their leader by doing sharp inward hissing breaths and displaying aggressive body language.

Searcher moved towards the leader, determined to end his life heroically and make his kin proud somehow. As he did, the ferocious leader—Sarzamarn was his name, though Searcher had no idea how he knew this—shouted in a resonate, guttural voice, *'How dare you move towards me, filthy human?'* and pulled out a weapon. For some odd reason, Searcher thought this was a *scalar weapon,* but had no idea what that meant.

He perceived it was different than say a gun, which could simply kill you by penetrating your body and causing physical trauma. This weapon seemed like it could rearrange one's entire being, including the cellular structure, chakras and bio-field. In short, shatter the soul, dematerialise the body and basically end your rounds of incarnations, sending you to kingdom come!

Searcher did what most humans do in a time of need. Nervously, he prayed to God. Lizzy-leader somehow perceived that and shouted, *'Don't you dare use that god-poison on me. I will end you now!'* Suddenly, ferocious Lizzy-leader fired the scalar weapon right into Searcher's chest.

'Ahhhhhhh!' Searcher jumped in the air one foot upwards, whilst lying in bed.

Kiki screamed, 'What the hell? What just happened?' Searcher was in bed, confused. His chest hurt immensely. He struggled to breathe and shook violently. After he settled down somewhat, he told Kiki-dolphin about his dream with the lizzies. It took him time to readjust. He was sore and out of sorts all through the day, but by the afternoon he knew it was just a stupid dream.

Curious Andro

'You can't talk of space without considering time, and you can't talk of time without considering space,' contemplated Seeker-Gra. Because of the sheer immensity of space, the distances are difficult to comprehend. If one could imagine there might be an intelligent species *out there* for just a moment, would it simply be a requirement of conquering distance to reach Earth for a visit?

When one peers out into the skies at night and is in awe at the majesty of it all, some of those twinkling stars that look so beauteous have not existed for millions of years and more. They, like our sun Ra, will live out their life burning up gases in unfathomable thermonuclear reactions, fuse into denser elements, and finally succumb to gravitational forces. The star's life is said to have run its course and it will subsequently die.

Since the time for the light of a star to reach humans living out here on the edge of a milky galaxy takes so long to reach us, a star can live millions of years before its light reaches man. Now, that's a long way. And a long time indeed!

If, for example, a human was staring out towards a star (let's call it Star-X), which had actually died millions of years before, and an alien was standing and staring back from Star-X towards our sun, Ra, what does this say about time? What time would it be? Would *now* be the same for the human or the alien?

Seeker, whilst he was contemplating this, thought that a friendly fellow from say Andromeda who wants to come for a coffee and chinwag would have to dial in his *time-date-space* coordinates. Otherwise, he might make it to Earth in his spaceship, but perhaps miss his time destination by a million years or so, either into the past or future.

He must possess travel technologically, which no doubt defies gravity, is beyond light speed, can bend space, and furthermore can home in on *time*-coordinates. Hence, 'His spaceship might as well be called a *time-ship*,' pondered Seeker. What predominately concerned Searcher about this scenario is what his little friend from Andromeda would ask of humanity and how he might answer back.

Would he tell the truth or bullshit his alien buddy? For example, what if (let's call him Andro for ease, shall we?) Andro from Andromeda asked, '*How do you solve conflict on Earth?*'

Searcher might say, 'Well, individually, we tend to argue or fight each other. But, collectively, we tend to bomb the fuck out of each other. It's called war! And it ends life on a massive scale; it's very effective in getting what you want. Know you the term *war*, Andro?'

Then with some alarm, friendly Andro with the superior space–time travel technology says, '*Hmm. How do you care for your environment which our Creator has bestowed upon you?*'

'Ahh. Well, Andro, we tend to just take what we can get. We don't give a crap about future generations and take all the resources for our own needs. We do so without any care or concern for our planet. It's *ours* after all!

'Yeah, the global warming causes great fires, storms and floods and all kinds of bad stuff. Our songwriters and hippies of the 60s tried to warn us about that, but we didn't listen. We disregarded them. We dam our rivers up for mining, agriculture and gas fracking and wonder why we have droughts and therefore devastating fires.'

Finally, Andro asks, '*And how do you treat your brothers and sisters of nature—the dear ones of feather, fur and fin, as your Kiki has termed them?*'

'We like to chomp most of them up. They are living protein packages and they're delicious. God said we can rule the beasts for our own pleasing. We can't seem to last for more than a day without copious amounts of meat protein, so we just eat those animals till the cows come home, so to speak.'

'*What was that?*' asks a flabbergasted Andro.

'We call them *livestock* so they can then become *deadstock* at our disposal but only at the time when we say so. We tear down centuries-old rainforests that are majestic and resplendent for wood and to clear land to raise livestock on until we make them deadstock, or more specifically to clear the land to grow food on to *feed the livestock* until they become deadstock. But don't worry, Andro, we select some species and call them pets; some are even considered man's best friend.'

'*Brutal,*' says Andro.

'Yeah, it's not perfect Andro, but it's a pretty good system. I mean, we're very lucky. It's good to be made in God-the-Father's image, for you get to rule the Earth. Better than being a *savage*, hey, Andro?'

'*Hmm. And the use of crude resources results in a polluting of your atmosphere and a rise in global warming and therefore sea levels, is that correct?*'

'Yes, Andro, that sucks a bit. I mean, I'm also worried about spent nuclear fuel rods and nuclear power stations. They can be devastating. We've already found that one out, especially when you build them by the ocean. And those spent fuel rods have a radioactive half-life of like 160,000 years. We dump the radioactive waste in the ocean too,' said Seeker.

'*Why, please tell me, does man not use solar energy and mechanical energy from the great ocean? It is freely and infinitely provided. And your planet is <u>geothermic</u>, right? It releases free thermal energy, does it not?*' Andro postulated.

'Um, dunno. We use solar energy a bit, but it's just not efficient enough.'

'*I'm sorry? The sun does not provide enough energy for you all, did you say?*' asks puzzled Andro. '*Goodness!*'

Andro politely thanks friendly-Searcher for his hospitality and beverage. He feels a bit *high and wired* from the strange caffeinated drink. Furthermore, he thanks Seeker for the discussions and his frankness. With a pleasant and gracious gesture and a very peculiar sort of bow, he softly walks over to his time-spaceship.

He enters, settles his brain-waves and connects his consciousness to that of his ship's. With a simple command in thought-form, he instructs his light-craft to proceed. '*Advance toward the Boötes constellation to the star system Arcturus. Please log: Never return to the earth-planet-Terra, for indeed it is a planet of terror. Last visit 2020. Most certainly the last!*'

Are you serious?

The Perceptive-one said this:

> Sounje, you are connected by a fractalized consciousness to Sirian entities from Sirius A and Sirius B; the Fifth-density short blue-skinned-style Arcturian beings; a fourth density Artificial Intelligence from Arcturus; the Nihal from Beta-Laporis as well as others not mentioned here, and others not perceived. This spans across a timeline of approximately 170,000 years in which these entities were a portion of your Oversoul.
>
> Because you are now energetically aligned in a fourth-density vibration, it causes you to feel misaligned in your current third density existence. You are connecting to a 'future' self in a 'previous' incarnation in Ancient Egypt in approximately 4300 BC whereby you were communicating verbally to some beings and non-verbally to others from outside your planet. These entities are connecting to you in deep understanding and resonance.
>
> This incarnation is virtually the same as your present one except for various beliefs and energetic assignments your society has placed upon you—whereby you believe it is certainly difficult to meet a physical being from other worlds, but indeed, very difficult to contact specifically, your 'probable future self'.

'Hmm, I wouldn't like to share that one publicly, they'd lock me up and throw away the key,' thought Searcher wisely.

Chapter 15

The many and the one

After those out-of-body experiences as a young man, the search had well and truly begun for the Searcher. He read many books, seemingly devouring them, and avoided fiction, for books had to be relevant to his quest. Starting out with Castaneda, Lobsang and even Shirley, he ploughed through anything that would open his mind to other realities and other dimensions of thought.

Spiritual books, philosophy, new-age, religious, Eastern, Western—it didn't matter as long as they were insightful. For a Seeker is always on the look-out for *insight* to help make sense of their own experiences and the world at large. From those many books, he took what resonated with him and discarded the rest.

It was an exciting time and an expansive one, which spanned more than three decades. Searcher also noticed how others either didn't bother, or some, like his Christian acquaintances, just focussed on *one* book only: the *Book of Books*. This intrigued Seeker no end.

In fact, the *Book of Books* wasn't one book at all. It was a collection of books encompassing the Old Testament and the New Testament. Some say there are 66 books, and some say there are 73 books or otherwise still. It varies depending on the religion or sect. And some say those were chosen from many more books, possibly hundreds written by the scribes of old.

It's both widely believed and widely contested that around 330 AD, Constantine, the Ruler of the Roman Empire, went to work and collated, interpreted and altered the texts to his liking. Constantine was the first to propose a single *canon* for all Christians to agree upon, and was the one who commissioned, inspected and approved the *Book of Books*.

Either way, many students of faith focus only on that document. Sometimes Searcher thought that was wise because he himself had read *everything* and had learned *nothing*. He was envious of anyone who stayed committed to their path, their beliefs and their teachings, but he could not follow a religious path: he had to *paddle his own canoe*.

In fact, his very vision of the Messiah-Prophesised was of him paddling down the river, paddling his own canoe and being *followed* by either lovers who wanted to be *saved*, or haters who wanted to kill him for no legitimate reason.

No, Searcher could not be a Christian, but fortunately the only ones who wouldn't ever judge him for that would be the Christians. After all, the rabbi taught, *'Judge not, lest ye be judged.*[20] Christians would not judge Searcher, no way!

People often look at a religious figurehead, such as a Buddha or Christ, a Shiva or a Muhamad, as if they were sitting at the apex of a very large pyramid with all the *little ones* humbly praying for scraps like needy, hungry little dicky birds. Searcher, however, saw it in reverse as if the Immaculate One was standing arms stretched at the bottom of the pyramid, holding everyone above him. An undercurrent, you might say. Such was his love, courage and inspiration.

Sometimes, a knock at Searcher's door would occur. 'We come representing Christ. Would you hear our words, friend?' Searcher was always pleasant, never rude like some. For these people, after all, were doing what they thought was right, spreading the word of God, or so they believed. He was always bemused by how they first assumed he wasn't a Christian or of *their* own faith before he had even uttered a word. That made him laugh inside but not outwardly.

He even told one Christian group that he was a Muslim and they disappeared quite abruptly. Seeker was always wary of the door-knockers though, for the Immaculate One himself has warned, '*Beware, many will come in my name claiming to speak for me. Do not be deceived, do not follow them.*'[21] Searcher was always suspicious of anyone claiming to represent God or the Saviour as if they had their own telephone line to the Almighty.

It was the same for gurus and the so-called saints. There were many who taught so eloquently, articulately, persuasively on the great truth of truths. They could open your third eye, release you from yourself and ultimately lead you to enlightenment; but they just couldn't keep their peckers in their pants when those hot, young luscious students waited on their every word—or, worse still, the *too young*, who so engrossed the holy-paedophiles.

Preparing the way

He was an *Essene*. They were the peoples who would prepare the way for their coming master, commencing even two hundred years before his coming and subsequent ministry. The Essenes would hold the energy; hold the space. For it was to be a grand coming, like a comet coming to earth. Would he become like a rock landing in a stream, simply making a splash, scattering fish and then resting at the bottom without a purpose? Or would he make such a mighty blast that the world would be forever changed?[22]

Excitement was in the air and built and built. The Essenes prayed fervently that the light would enter the darkness and free all who were trapped. Those were the darkest of times, perhaps even darker than today. The common people were greatly oppressed and dominated.

He came! The Essenes shielded the child and fanatically so, for they knew what was to come. He didn't disappoint; in fact, he was far greater than they had conceived. He was Immaculate! As he grew up, he walked with countenance. He possessed a love and wisdom that had not been known on this planet before. He had a mission, yet never was he in a hurry.

He was *present* and was always calm and serene. Even unto his darkest hour, he was the *eye of the storm*. As anger and hatred surrounded him, he remained still—loving, composed. He did not lose his way. He did not give up. He did not feel forsaken. Others much later would claim that. For humanity alone, he took it to the end. Even his torturous death left a wonderful symbol as he hung up nailed and tied to a wooden cross, arms outstretched in *surrender*. Then, it was over. He was gone …

Their Master, their Messiah and Saviour had been taken. Some saw him again for a short time in the days that followed: his chakras blazing like mini-suns and creating a golden, auric field around him. They would later call it a *halo*. Soon after, however, he took wing unto his Father in Heaven, the inner sanctum.

His Father was Spirit, Creator, Prime Mover, First Cause, All that Is, I Am that I Am, the Alpha and Omega. The Essenes had had a purpose, a crucial one, and now it was over. They loved their teacher with all their hearts, but the pain of his departure was almost too much to bear. 'How can we go on without our master?' Each in their own way lived out the rest of their days trying to follow the *Way of Christ,* yet disillusionment and abandonment took up residence in the inner cave of their hearts.

Some were persecuted and murdered. Some went on to spread the word of He who had taught them the grandest of secrets. It was difficult. It was an arduous life. But they, the Essenes, had achieved their mission; they had prepared the way for their master. A comet that illuminated the skies!

He gathered his friends and enemies alike into his loving heart and ascended the *Stairway to Heaven,* paving the way for countless souls. And that one lifetime, that one ministry, that one message of *love and forgiveness* would remain on planet Earth for millenniums to come, burning as an eternal flame in the darkness.

Sitting on the fence

Searcher was a *try-hard*. Unfortunately, this trait was not particularly advantageous to searching and seeking. Part of the tension and strain was from an inner pull, an inner drive. Everything he attempted seemed to fail. Furthermore, he did not possess the ability to stick at things when they were not paying dividends.

The Searcher

To paraphrase the Fonz,[23] 'If you knock on a door and it opens and someone slaps you in the face, how many more times will you keep on knocking?' Now this was a great recipe for avoiding people who had wronged you, like, why go back for more? Pretty soon you wouldn't be knocking, you'd be their doormat.

Seeker-Gra applied the Fonz's little gem to rewardless efforts as well. 'Why keep trying if it's just not working out?' he thought. However, this dynamic would work against him. Being a paradox in nature, he really only got going when the going got tough.

He was a cyclist of sorts and enjoyed both cycleway and mountain biking in the bush. Seeker would cruise along a flat surface or down a hill, never in a hurry, but as soon as an uphill arrived, he would push hard. Some friends had purchased eBikes, but Gra could not afford one due to his endless stupid career decisions and subsequent unemployment from being too old and useless.

The motor on an eBike assists one's efforts greatly. Up hills sometimes five kilometres long they would ride. Searcher would push hard, dangerously hard to keep up with his eBiker mates or any road cyclists who might be climbing ahead. He just loved that push, the competitiveness, especially the delight if he should pass them.

Seeker also enjoyed jogging in the bush, mostly if it was 40°C or higher, and even better during a bushfire. He once snugged up to tree trunks whilst helicopters were flying overhead water-bombing, feeling both terrified and excited. During summer, curiously, if the temperature rose above 40°, the flies and mosquitos seemed to go away and hide and the bush walkers and die-hard cyclists were nowhere to be found; except maybe in front of their home air conditioners or sucking up the cool at the shopping centres.

That really did make Seeker laugh to himself and not in a humble way. Yes, it seemed like there was only Searcher and the brown snakes out there during heatwaves, and although he never won a race in his life, he would always win that one.

Once he was swimming in the ocean pool during a furious storm against all common sense and was subsequently picked up like a ragdoll and thrown out of the pool by the imposing swell. He was dragged extensively along the cement and lost bark off his limbs. Unbeknownst to Seeker, a 40,000-tonne bulk carrier ship had come aground and *pashed* the shore right in front of his city a few kilometres north, at exactly the same time he had been hurtled out of the pool. Yeah, the Pasha Bulker storm!

Now, you may think all these things were part of a death wish or were the result of sheer stupidity, and he wouldn't argue. But for Seeker, there were other reasons for his irresponsible behaviour.

Firstly, it was just like the time he and Brave-brother swam among the sea of blue-bottles. They didn't want to get stung—that would be absurd—but they wanted to *feel alive*. For sure he did some silly things at times to just feel alive and strong.

Secondly, upon self-reflection, he was frustrated because the world was telling him he was too old to be employable. So, he would run in heatwaves, swim in dangerous storms, beat the crap out of his boxing bag, or swing his kettle bell that was just too heavy for him. It was frustration and, in turn, a release.

However, what he came to realise was he didn't respond well without a struggle and, ultimately, that is neither healthy nor efficient. If things were *easy*, such as riding his bike on an even surface or downhill, he didn't try. If things were hard, such as uphill, he would shine. That works fine until one grows old and weary. Searcher started to see the pattern and became tired of the struggle, the strain, the effort.

He dreamed of buying an eBike to just cruise like his mates did; do it easy for once. And a twist of fate would eventually provide it. He purchased an eBike and tallied hundreds of kilometres riding in the bush in his very first week. He was obsessed. Never had he enjoyed anything so much since his childhood motorbiking days.

Following each ride, he told his mates, 'Best ride of my life, fellas. Unbelievable.' Except, he kept saying it after every ride and they were no doubt sick of hearing it. Dalefin now called him *Marty-Gra* because he had such a sore ass from riding too much.

As time rolled on, however, he noticed how he missed the effort, the struggle and the strain. He no longer ran out of breath or had to work hard on the eBike. It was all about the fun of riding recklessly through narrow, windy, up-and-down trails without any real effort. So, Marty-Gra thought long and hard about this predicament and about his life.

He also contemplated his voice, for he was most certainly not endowed with a natural singing voice. He wanted with all his will and might, above almost anything else, to be able to entertain crowds by singing as well as his guitar playing. Over the years, he practised profusely, trying to improve his voice to an acceptable level. He would play the equivalent of a full gig and more at home every day, beating away on his jazz vocal songs. But improvement was negligible.

Conversely, a mate who might never have practised singing in his life would walk in and sing like a bird. Should one, therefore, accept their limitations or should one fight against them, never giving up? Searcher was never quite sure and so, sat on the fence. Searcher-the-fence-sitter! And Searcher sang, '*It blows my mind, sitting here. To scratch my head, to wonder why? Nothing seems to make any sense. The days go by and the weeks just fly, I'm sometimes down and sometimes high. Too scared to jump off the fence.*'[24]

It was pretty much the riddle he'd been wrestling with all his life, one that might hold the key to victory—that is, effort or no effort. Unfortunately, Marty-Gra's inclinations leaned towards effort. At work, for example, he would give one hundred per cent of himself. His work ethic was admirable enough. Everyone he'd ever worked for, and with, said the same.

One mining boss said to Seeker-Gra that he was the best *fitter* he had ever had. That made Seeker emotional, and emotion is something rarely shown around the tough men of mining. The truth is, Seeker was actually the worst mechanical fitter on the planet, but the boss implied that he put in. He gave his best, got on with supervisors, worked any overtime requested, and was always punctual and hard-working. Scooter taught Seeker the value in that, for he was not much better as a fitter, but inherently understood how to work his freckle off and do the right thing.

Others were smarter, stronger, more knowledgeable and superior in every way to Seeker, but they might not get on with their colleagues, be a team player, be reliable, work hard or be respectable, and so forth. However, this Searcher-Seeker who had worked with thousands and thousands of people at the smelter, the steelworks, the coal mines, the ambulance and other industries was a good worker but a terrible slave. There is a great difference between the two; at least, that's what he believed.

Searcher had been working in a store warehouse, a big box full of boxes of things. He was closed off from the world, stuck working with just a boss, an admin lady and an engineer. From working in heavy industry, mining and the ambulance, the small family-type business was quite a shock. He persisted but felt *boxed in* with all the *boxes* inside the big *box*.

One hot summer's day his weighty owner-director boss came out of his cool air-conditioned office and from his mezzanine deck yelled out, *'Work hard, you dog.'* Seeker was working hard. He had lifted and packed 2000 kg of boxes prepared for shipping and performed other so-called urgent tasks. He had sweat pouring down his face and running off his nose. In an instant, he reflected on all the opportunities he had blown in industry, mining and the ambulance.

Here was the *fool of all fools*: the Searcher. From serving and helping others in their time of need in the ambulance, to lifting boxes and being treated like a slave. Perhaps the boss was jesting, but Searcher never talked down to anyone like that. It was a challenging period, but one that the Searcher took full responsibility for. Ultimately, he blamed no-one but himself. It was hard to do that, but at least he didn't blame anyone else for being the biggest fool who ever lived.

Intriguingly, some people can actually work in those environments quite comfortably, he noticed. The *coin* seems to override any sense of constriction. But Searcher is an eagle and an eagle must fly. In fact, over the years, strangely enough, many people said that he looked like an eagle with his penetrating eyes and gaze.

One so-called master once said Searcher lit up a room because his eyes sparkled. Nothing could be further from the truth, though.

Cyclone-Izzy is an eagle too. Actually, no—she's more like a phoenix that one.

And Searcher sang, *'So I see you'd like to turn me, into something that is nice. What do you know of an eagle, who tears across the skies? When your world is full of sadness, you've gotta see the inner game. And don't get caught up, or so messed up, or find someone else to blame!'*[25] Yes, both an eagle and a fool was Searcher-the-Seeker. A true dichotomy!

Seeking on Seek

He had applied for hundreds of jobs without reply. A few large organisations did email a *thanks but no thanks,* but generally speaking, no-one bothered. It often takes many hours of one's time to prepare a job application. Some companies in addition to the regular résumé and covering letter, requested the answering of stupefying and bewildering questions, which took thousands of words to answer. Yet still, they didn't bother responding.

Finally, he was given an hour-long interview for a very low-paying monkey job in a coal lab. He had experience in the field and was more than qualified with a range of extra skills and licences. The two interviewers were really impressed by Seeker and said they'd give him a job on a handshake if they could, but it would have to pass through human resources.

As soon as he heard the words *human resources,* Seeker said to the interviewers, 'I've been around the sun too many times, fellas; that will be the end of that.' He was right. Gone were the days of a job on a beer and a handshake; human resources had to make their money by excelling at the *cull,* and my how they excelled!

In his most arrogant and frustrating moments, he felt like saying, 'How about all the applicants gather round and do push-ups on the floor right now? Whoever lasts the longest gets the job based on ticker alone, regardless of age.' He didn't, of course. That was a ridiculous and conceited notion.

Searcher, who was once quite employable, was now on the trash heap, even though he felt fitter and stronger than ever. He became sick of seeking on Seek because seeking on Seek felt too much like seeking so he stopped seeking on Seek altogether. He only had himself to blame. Perhaps he would ask Cyclone-Izzy-daughter for her opinion, she was always full of ideas … later.

True friends

The interesting thing about true friends is that they can see your holes—your blind spots—and they know your internal lies, but they love and accept you anyway. In Australia they won't say it, especially if you happen to have an appendage between your legs because you've gotta act tough, but they bloody well feel it and it's as real as your first kiss.

'God, it's good to be an Aussie,' thought Seeker. He only ever had a handful of friends and didn't care for more. Some he hadn't seen for decades, but that didn't matter to him. 'A friend was a friend is always a friend!' You see, Seeker's friends knew he was a fool, but they were fond of him anyway because they just sensed he was also a beautiful loser—bleeding on the wall.

It would take the rarest and most precious of parents, wife, children, family and friends to accept him. Other less-fortunate souls appeared to have no-one supporting them through their life's journey, but Searcher was blessed. He had it all. He didn't always see it—if he had, he might well have reached out to them more when he was standing on the cliff face with bottled emotion, wrestling the dog—but it was there just the same.

They say, *No man is an island.*[26] Ain't that true! We each think of our own needs, wants and desires. Why not? There's nothing wrong with that, but what kind of life could we possibly live without others? It's others who make up the fabric of our existence. And would life be worth living if we were all alone in the universe?

These things and more Searcher pondered as he journeyed onward learning those things a Searcher inevitably must learn, sooner or later. For him *later*, for he was a slow learner indeed. Ultimately, the search must end, though.

He was like a fish swimming around looking for water, asking other fish, 'Have you seen the water? Where is the water? I just have to find the water.' Sometimes the answers are right in front of us, too close to find. Searcher was searching for the meaning of life, himself or happiness, all the while existing in those things.

A fool was he ...

There was a man, a fool was he.
Was given eyes but could not see
   His feet on earth, his head in sky.
     His search unearthed, a useless lie
So plain to see, for all but he.
It was a dance, no mystery
   For world is dream, a dream so real.
     Amusing play, a spinning wheel
And time so short, a call so deep.
The Searcher lost, in endless sleep
   Awaken now, no when or how.
   A step too far, will not allow
Those endless skies, or senseless cries.
Did not unveil, did not disguise
   A truth so bare, yet oh so rare.
   He could not find, not here nor there
     a fool was he ...[27]

Chapter 16

Flossie at peace

It was going to be a difficult time. Already the loved ones had endured a terrible stretch, watching Flossie fade away. They were by her side. It was not easy to witness. Searcher had some experience in medical things but was completely ignorant regarding palliative care. He assumed the medicos would quietly over-medicate a person to save them from further suffering whilst they would gently sail off into the sunset, peacefully: a compassionate, loving form of treatment. It is not like that at all.

Passing can be cruel, but so is prolonging a life when all hope is gone. In her last days before the coma, Flossie, who had wasted away to a shadow of her former self, embarrassingly expressed to Brave-son, 'I'm so old and worn out, son. How can Tippy see me like this when I go?'

Brave-son said, 'Don't you worry, dear mother. Tippy will be waiting for you, as you're all aglow in your wedding dress.'

Each of Flossie's loved ones would whisper in her ear it was okay; it was alright to let go. Searcher was the last to do that. Being both the healer and fool, he kept hope and felt loyal in so doing. He still thought he could somehow blast healing energies at his dear mother from a distance. He was deluded, desperate, or both.

Finally, when he realised Flossie could not and would not survive, he changed tactic. He made a plea with God. '*God, please give me her cancer. I beg you. She does not deserve it. It's a fair deal. She has been a beautiful woman, a fine mother, and I, a woeful son. She does not deserve to suffer. Give me her cancer that she may live. A deal is a deal. A fair fucking deal, hey? A life for a life, a mother for a son.'*

Evidently, no deal was agreed to. It is the height of all human arrogance to ask to bear the cross of another. It cannot be! It's just not the way of it and Flossie-Mother would not have allowed it, had she known. Flossie's soul-sister watched Flossie's three children gently wash her broken body. The hospital staff were wonderful and allowed them to provide the care for their beloved.

The doctor was supportive because she had become close friends with Flossie over the years and tried to hold back her tears, unsuccessfully. Flossie's sister said it felt almost reverent standing back watching the three siblings wash and dress their dear mother with dignity, grace and respect.

Drama was present in the days and weeks before Flossie passed to the great-beyond-of-no-time-and-place, and drama persisted in the following days. It is not uncommon when emotions are high.

A wonderful funeral saw her take flight. Brave-brother-son said some poignant, moving words about her life, and then sang a song he had written long before: '*Thank you, Mum, for all the things you've done. Thank you, Mum, you're my number one. I know you sometimes doubt yourself; I know you have regrets. But let me just remind you, Mum, that you're the very best. To me. Your loving son.*'[28]

Searcher-son stood strongly, arm interlocked with Brave-brother's, Pearl and Ciarán at the rear. A mini-drama was unfolding. Something was not right. The pallbearers were somehow tangled up with the trolley legs, as they held Flossie's coffin on their shoulders. The funeral staff were trying to intercede but were not verbalising the issue.

The bearers were confused and wondering, 'What the fuck is going on?' All the while looking serene in front of Flossie's admirers, while they rocked from side to side. It was actually terribly funny, except for the four bearers who were mortified. Flossie would be bursting at the seams had she been *there,* somehow. They proceeded to carry the women they all loved on their shoulders.

As they advanced along the long, long red carpet, Searcher raised and kept his right arm up, fist clenched and continued. It wasn't for show. It was in honour of the one whom he and those present had loved so much. It was to *victory in death*. A sign of bravery in suffering. She had lost the battle but won the war. Flossie was triumphant. She lived a fucking good life and all who knew her mourned that day but smiled. Now that's something!

A few months passed and some details had to be sorted. There was conjecture regarding her ashes and the inscription on Tippy's headstone, where she would finally be put to rest with her soulmate, metaphorically. Various ideas were proposed but none would satisfy everyone. Her children and the aunties would have their own opinions. It was concerning for all.

Then on one unforeseen night at 4 am and from the beyond, Flossie spoke to Searcher-son. She said these brief words, *'Hi, love. The name on the headstone must be [... ... ...]. I lived with compromises and, unfortunately, the ending requires compromise from all of you.'* Searcher was dumbfounded. Whilst it wasn't exactly what he personally wanted, he felt that from the heavens Flossie had taken a complex jigsaw puzzle and come up with the most fair, respectable, well-thought-out and decent thing to do.

However, it would come at a cost. 'What have you done to me, Flossie-Mother?' He was acutely aware that if he should pass this message or instruction onto the others, apart from thinking him deluded, they would think he was trying to manipulate them to get his own way. Besides, should one *not* believe in life beyond the physical (which everyone absolutely has the right to do), then why would they blindly accept such an instruction?

Secondly, even if Flossie did continue on in a place beyond the grave, why would she talk to Searcher and not the others?

Searcher would rather poke his own eyes out than lie about his own mother from beyond the grave. *Being-from-afar* had long ago advised him to, 'Always maintain the power of silence, least you invite the knives in your back.' Searcher had rarely heeded that advice, and his back held many invisible scars. On the other hand, he felt he should respect his mother's wishes. Seeker-Searcher did not have a telephone line to Flossie or anyone else, nor did he wish for one.

It was not the only message he received, however, as he had also received messages for others in their grief, but rarely passed them on for fear of anger, judgement and disbelief. It was a *grave* predicament—excuse the pun, Flossie! This weighed heavily on him. Should he pass on Flossie-Mum's instructions or run and hide like a coward?

As it turned out, he did pass them on. It was a very costly decision. Ultimately, though, wonder of wonders, Flossie got her way. It all ended respectfully and well may she be at peace.

Chapter 17

A dream revelation

The Searcher would have a dream that was unquestionably the most profound one of his life. Curiously, he had always lived near the coast and his various near drownings and incidents had often occurred involving large bodies of water or the ocean itself.

During the retreat where he experienced his brief awakening, he had felt the pure *waters of life* rushing through him like a cosmic waterfall. The *ocean* had witnessed him in his darkest hours at the cliff face and had soothed his soul. Now a dream set in water would map out his life, his struggle, his pain … and his potential salvation.

> Searcher was caught in a rip. He was out in rough seas and was being smashed by large waves. Over and over he would raise his head only to be smashed back down again. He tried and tried to swim towards the bank, to no avail. He kept afloat but the waves were unrelenting and punished him profusely. He refused to give up and kept swimming throughout the day. All day!
> Suddenly, his perception changed, and he became a frantic man concerned about the guy out in the water drowning in the rip. A third man was standing with arms folded, watching the commotion but refusing to assist. The second man on the beach was beseeching the third, 'Please, please help. That man will drown out there.'

The Searcher

Searcher continued his battle. It was now dusk, and the situation was dire. From nowhere, Searcher came swimming in with another person who was drowning. He saved him, plopped him on the sand, performed CPR and then quickly swam back out into the rip. The onlooker was flabbergasted. 'Why would he save another but not himself?' It didn't make sense. The third man was one of authority somehow and was unyielding. He remained with arms folded, dressed in uniform appearing hard and remorseless. He said to the panicked onlooker, 'He has to save himself. No-one can do it for him.'

It became quite dark. The struggle continued. Over and over the waves hit Searcher as he did the best he could to stay afloat. All night. All night!

Finally, morning arrived. Searcher was done. It was over! There was no more energy left, he was depleted. Beaten. Crushed. Overcome. It was time. Still in rough seas, he had to give up. He couldn't go on for another second. Searcher let go. He stretched his tired and weary arms out over his head and leaned backwards and floated to his fate. He was done. He gave up. The fight was no more. He surrendered!

The rip carried him out far as he floated, and everything became calm. The seas calmed down. The struggle was over. He felt serene. Finally, after all the years of searching, of seeking, of struggling, finally the search was over. It was 'here' all along. All he had to do was 'let go'.

You see, the drowning swimmer was Searcher. The concerned man on the beach was Searcher. The hard-arse on the beach refusing to help was also Searcher. The swimmer who was *saved* by Searcher was Searcher. They were all roles, characters. All relevant to his life.

For he had been the struggler. He had been the compassionate one. He had been the merciless one. He had been the saved one. He had been the awakened one. He had been the arsehole. He had been it all. But he had never been himself. He had never let go. He had never surrendered to life; for he only knew struggle. He had never let it be!

What next?

Life continued on for Searcher, but the truth had been shown. He could not escape from himself, his lies. Flossie, his dear mother, had long before paraphrased to him, '*To thine own self be true, son.*'[29] It had been a long road of exploring, seeking, searching and questing. Maybe he was not alone?

Perhaps everyone has a little of the Searcher inside of them, wishing to go downstream. It's only natural. All of his life he had thought he had three heads. Perhaps he didn't. Maybe it would all be worth it in the end. For who is to judge a life? 'There is no shame in seeking,' he accepted.

After all, didn't the Messiah say, '*Seek and ye shall find*'?[30]

Searcher looked up at the stars and contemplated, 'Life is a tapestry, woven together as we each play our part, friends and enemies alike. Each human life is a book. A living book. And as each moment comes and goes, another word, another sentence is added upon the corridors of time, our book. The author is us. The Creator has given each of us creative free will to write our own book, howsoever we please.'

He remembered what the Pleiadian had uttered to him long ago, '*We all live under the same roof; not separated, not isolated, not segregated, not detached, not fenced off. Yes, we all live under the same roof, and that roof is God's roof, however you perceive Him or Her to be, or not be. That roof is: the Canopy of the Stars.*'

Searcher was unsure what to do with himself. He had stopped searching. It wasn't that there was no more to search for, but the sun was setting. He had applied for countless jobs but evidently was now too old and useless. He'd sent promos of his jazz act to all the entertainment booking agencies without reply. He had relinquished the idea of being an energy-healing practitioner, since it hadn't helped Flossie in her time of need.

A diploma in counselling without a degree was as useless as tits on a bull, or so he had found out. They say, 'Every dog has its day.' Searcher felt perhaps he had already had his day. He fell into a rut. Sitting in the evenings in the garden Kiki made in honour of Flossie, with his best mate Flash, their eight-year old rabbit who was exceedingly addicted to salted peanuts, he wondered what was to come.

The dog still stalked him at times, but he put him on a diet and tried to ignore him. Regretfully, he had an accident in the bush on his eBike whereby he went flying through the air and smashed into a tree, destroying his shoulder rotator cuff. Tree trunks don't give: tree 1, Searcher 0! What next? What to do?

Searcher was discussing things with Izzy-daughter when she proposed an idea, 'Why don't you write, Fadja?'

'Um, write? What do you mean write?' asked Seeker-Fadja.

'Just write something. You could like, write a book.'

'A book? I would have nothing to write about, Izzy.'

'That's just it, Fadja, you just sit down and write and see what comes out. You just never know,' advised Cyclone-Izzy.

'Hmm. Okay, I'll try, but I really have no idea.'

A book

So, Seeker-Searcher started clanging away on the keyboard. Stuff came out. Mostly baloney and not chronologically ordered; however, Izzy told him not to worry about that. 'You just keep on typing, Fadja. Don't censor it, and don't read it as you go,' said Izzy, who was actually a part-time professional writer whilst she was studying film. He did as suggested. And more and more surfaced.

Searcher knew deep down that he was a boring kind of guy, no doubt about it, but lots of things emerged from somewhere in the deep recesses of his mind. Topics on work, music, friends, family, healing, depression, meditation, dreams, loss, and all manner of weird shit, just spewed out. It was therapeutic in a way.

Up and out the chapters churned at a frantic pace—and just as quickly stopped!

'Izzy. I've written that book.'

'What? Already? It's only been three weeks, less,' said Izzy.

'Yeah, fifteen days actually. Although it'll probably take fifteen years to fix up. Anyways, I googled things and they say you need 80,000 words for a decent-sized book. I only have about 70,000 words or so, but I have nothing more to say.'

'Word counts depend on the genre,' stated Izzy.

'Well, I don't know what genre this book fits into, but I may not have enough words. It's a shame but I really gave it my best shot, daughter, soz.'

'Eighty thousand words is for fiction novels. Yours is non-fiction.'

'Maybe. But are you sure? My life is a fiction in some ways, daughter, no-one would believe some of this stuff regardless,' Searcher replied.

'Don't play it by the rules [she's a free-spirit], just wrap it up and let me read it first before anyone else and see what happens,' Izzy continued. 'Some authors ruin their books by trying to stretch them out to a publisher's required word count and therefore make it boring reading.'

'And what happens next, daughter?'

'Well, then you have to edit it and send it off to a publisher. They'll have a read and if they like it, they will go about editing it some more—or you'll have to self-publish.'

'Edit it? What will they do, Izz?'

'They'll just throw out all the crap!' she replied.

'Um, Izzy, if they do that there will be nothing left to read,' said Seeker.

'You never know, Fadja, you just never know. So, what's it all about anyway, Glendelyn?'

'Well, Izzy, I just started writing like you told me to. I let it all flow and pretty soon I noticed a pattern therein. The more I wrote, the more I realised I had been a *searcher* for most of my life. In fact, it was blatantly obvious as I wrote, but not so obvious as I lived it.'

'Hmm. Groovy! And what will you call the book, Fadja?' asked Izzy.

'Well, I was going to call it *Paddle your own canoe,* but I thought people might think it's all about canoes or something. So, in the end, I just called it *THE SEARCHER.*'

Addendum

Ah, reader, the book is complete. No really, it's done! You have finished; good effort! You know the bit where the Searcher told his daughter Izzy what the book was about and its title? Yeah, well, that was the ending. Hmm, are you not satisfied with that ending? It wasn't quite resolved, was it? Spare a thought for poor ole Searcher; he would like things to be resolved too! Let's see. Perhaps you want something different, an alternative ending. Okay, okay. Let's see what we can do …

An alternative ending

Coppertop did start at age fifteen working at that dusty aluminium smelter affectionately called the CAN—the one where his hero-dad Tippy used to work at years before. Where they would both in their own time and space daydreamingly stare up at that giant chimney stack, which could be seen for miles and miles reaching up to the skies like the Beanstalk of *Jack and the Beanstalk* fame.

And, do you know what? He stayed there, sucking in alumina and bauxite and carbon dust for many a year, working until he dropped suddenly, just like his father had, slipping away to that great-beyond where Tippy and Flossie and all the rest of 'em went.

He didn't meet the love of his life and go on and have tin lids and the rest. He didn't venture out and play music, become a healer, experience weird stuff, work underground, care for patients, get a bit suicidal, and all the many things. No, he stayed there, sheltered, comfortable and secure. And he was a happy man. A bit of a loner, for sure, although occasionally he would still think of that one sweet

The Searcher

Leah-Lovebloom with those enormous coconuts that could fill a room. (Don't tell White-Tiger, though!)

Brave-brother-of-Coppertop, who went on to create his own philosophy, so to speak, became quite pensive. He was now an old man. He had seen some things! And he started to wonder whether there might have been any truth in what Whacky-younger-brother-now-gone had believed regarding the beyond and all that weird stuff.

You see, the Callithumpians who go *downstream* believe that when you die, you go back into the earth and return to nature. Searcher agreed with that. They also believe that when you die, you live on in the hearts of everyone you had known and had loved; thus, you do *live on*. Searcher agreed with that. But they didn't really get into any of that stuff where the so-called soul lived on in other dimensions and reincarnated and so forth. That was a bit of a stretch.

So, one day, Callithumpian-brother quite by chance found out that an old zany woman was offering psychic readings online, at a price. Lo and behold, it was the crystal-wearing-incense-loving-new-age-spiritual-woman who tried to heal Searcher's laughing heart chakra in Costa. She had now gone on to become a real-life psychic-medium and was very well known far and wide for her talents.

Callithumpian-brother decided to see if Medium-lady could reach across to the great-beyond-of-no-time-and-place, which he was not really into, and contact that Whacky-Searcher-brother of his. She did it all on Skype, for a price.

Well, she went on to tell the old-Callithumpian-sceptic how his younger brother the Searcher had indeed crossed over to the great-beyond-of-no-time-and-place. He first saw Tippy and Flossie and all the grandparents and aunties and uncles and friends and well-knowns who had gone before him, and it was a mighty celebration.

After Searcher shot through the *Tunnel of Light*, he made his way to some great big place, which wasn't really a place but what the others called a *realm*. Anyway, he really loved it there because in an instant he got to visit everyone he remembered from his time on Earth.

Searcher thanked Bach and the greats for their exquisite music and thanked many masters and teachers for their contributions. He acknowledged the artists and poets and writers. He thanked Jimmy, Stevie, Gary and the others for their incredible guitar and vocals, although he had already done so once before when he was *alive* in a dream—when he saw them on a railway line.

He thanked Bruce for his martial arts wisdom and dedication, and English-Jon for touching his heart. He even thanked Ole-Lillah for being such a badass to the young boys. She was actually preparing for a new life as a military general. He thanked four mop-top Liverpudlians for delivering the *greatest message of all time*, but mostly, and most excitedly, he thanked all those loved-up-hippies who had gone to Earth en masse to create the great revolution of the 60s.

Brother-Callithumpian listened patiently. Medium-lady then said something a bit curious. She had picked up how, when they were lads, the two brothers, it seemed, had both nearly drowned in a rip or some such in the ocean. Brave-brother confirmed this as he remembered back through all the years to that fateful day when mighty Greek-god had saved the young Coppertop from Mother Ocean and he had saved his own little brave arse.

She said Searcher wants Brave-ole-brother to forgive himself for not saving his useless younger brother, Searcher-Coppertop, from that awful rip; for it was just meant to be and not at all his fault or responsibility—that he cannot be held responsible for fate!

And then unexpectedly she said this: 'Coppertop actually stopped breathing in the ocean that day and had what some call a *near-death experience.*'

She said that for a short time, when he was underwater, he went to the Land of the Living Light where Emmanuel and Eagle and the others showed him two paths that he might take.

One was a *steady* path where he would work at a local industry. He would not make a family, nor partner and have all the things, but he would be quite content. Whilst he wouldn't stretch so much, he would nonetheless be quite settled.

On the other path he would become a searcher and experience many weird and wonderful things. He would become a *searcher-looking-for-Searcher* but would find *nothing*. That wouldn't be such a bad thing actually, because *nothing* was quite sweet. Either path, was his choice alone to make.

They told him it didn't really matter, because over the span of forever and eternity, we get to live all of it.

Psychic-medium-lady suddenly told Callithumpian-brother that her energies were waning, that she couldn't continue on unless he could pay an extra one hundred dollars for her efforts. He rolled his eyes and declined.

Finally, in closing, she said Coppertop-now-gone-ghost-spirit had thanked her for trying to patch up his heart-chakra back in Costa; but, because she was now indeed so psychic, she felt he was humouring her.

It was all a bit much for the Callithumpian, who had lived a damn good life himself. He had been a fine paramedic, just like Brother-in-law-Pearl, and a nurse as well. He had a family, wrote great songs and had created his own philosophy on how to live happily in the world. He truly did *paddle his own canoe*.

He and Brother-in-law-Pearl had become paragliders and also loved surfing in that great-big-beautiful-mother-ocean that had once tried to snatch the two young brothers up. They were both good family men.

Brave-brother decided to have a beer and let it all sink in. Taking a sip, he looked up at the glorious spread of stars above and with his two feet firmly planted on the ground, said to himself out loud, '*Ah what the heck, who knows?*' And he laughed for the longest time …

Parting words

If the Searcher could say anything to you right now, reader, he'd no doubt say, '*Enjoy your life, friend. Don't get all too serious like I did. Searching ain't finding. Life goes fast, very fast. Enjoy the ride and, for Christ's sake, lighten up before it's too late. It's over in a blink of an eye. Wink.*'

But Searcher couldn't say that. He was too busy revving up for a journey, and boy, was he excited. Evidently, Tippy and Flossie had gone back again to reignite their love for each other. This time, they would get to live out all of their days together without premature departure. *Tippy and Flossie* were now *Timothy and Florence*, better known as *Tim and Flo*, which sounded like *Time and Flow*, which was kind of how their destinies unfolded.

And Searcher-now-Finder, well, he was ready to go. Down through that tunnel of light, all the way down to his new-mummy-once-Flossie's sweet warm, safe and comfortable womb of creation. And from the *realm* he yells out, 'Come on, Beautiful-sister and Brave-brother of mine, word's out in the *realms* that Tippy and Flossie have gone back again and consummated their sweet marriage and with new names and faces, they intend to start a little family, just like before. They're wishing for *three little angels* to complete their love. Hurry up and return already, will you? This time it's *my* turn to be the older, wiser brother.'

The end, and the beginning …

Endnotes

[1] Matthew 18:3.

[2] From the Gospel of Thomas.

[3] Pope John Paul II: General Audience, Wednesday 28 July 1999.

[4] Luke 17–21.

[5] Zen Kōan.

[6] Luke 4–23.

[7] A proverb of disputed origins, perhaps first stated by John Bradford: circa 1510–55.

[8] Krishna Das: American vocalist known for Hindu devotional music called Kirtan.

[9] Ramana Maharshi: renowned and revered Indian saint, Advaita exponent.

[10] Eckhart Tolle: author of *Power of Now* and *New Earth*.

[11] Ramana Maharshi: renowned and revered Indian saint, Advaita exponent.

[12] Pamela Kribbe, *The Healers Series – Pitfalls on the Way to Becoming a Healer* (2008).

[13] Albert Einstein: 20th century theoretical physicist, 1879–1955.

[14] Lee Carroll: an American channeler, speaker and author.

[15] Dr Wayne Dyer: American self-help author and motivational speaker.

[16] Bruce Lee: famous pioneering martial artist, actor and director from Hong Kong.

[17] From *Hamlet*, Act 1, Scene V, by 16th century English poet and playwright William Shakespeare.

[18] From a poem by Linda Ellis, 'Live Your Dash'.

[19] Bob Seger wrote *Beautiful Loser* in 1975. It was also recorded by Jon English in 1982.

[20] Matthew 7:1.

[21] Luke 21:8.

[22] Pamela Kribbe: *The Lightworkers Series* (2008).

[23] The Fonz: fictional character in American sitcom *Happy Days* (1974) played by Henry Winkler.

[24] Lyrics taken from *Even If I Could* (author, 1994).

[25] More lyrics from *Even If I Could*.

[26] English poet John Donne.

[27] Author.

[28] Lyrics written by John Parker from: *Thank You, Mum* (1995).

[29] From *Hamlet*, Act 1, Scene III.

[30] Matthew 7:7.